THE TRANSFER

Stories of Missionaries
Who Gave the Last Full Measure
of Devotion

———————

VOLUME I

———————

THE TRANSFER

Stories of Missionaries
Who Gave the Last Full Measure
of Devotion

VOLUME I

Compiled and Edited by

Susan Evans Woods

With Foreword by Randy L. Bott

DIGITAL
LEGEND

First Printing August 2009

ISBN: 978-1-934537-12-1

Digital Legend Press & Publishing
585-703-8760
P.O. Box 133
Honeoye Falls, NY 14472

See all of our LDS titles at: www.latterdaylegends.com

Or the complete library at www.digitalegend.com/catalog

This book is dedicated to the memory of
PARLEY P. PRATT
one of the early missionaries and martyrs of
The Church of Jesus Christ of Latter-day Saints

and

To Those Who Qualified for the Transfer

These Stories Are Theirs

But behold, all things have been done in the wisdom of him who knoweth all things.
—Lehi to his son Jacob (2 Nephi 2:24)

CONTENTS

Key: *Injured

ACKNOWLEDGMENTS

We acknowledge the contributions of many whose names are unknown to us but who are gratefully appreciated by the families and friends of missionaries who suffer trauma or death as a result of accidents or aggression in the mission field. We acknowledge their love unfeigned, compassion, support, and encouragement in the face of loss and pain.

Our thanks to those who made the special effort to collect the information, to organize it, and to share it that others may be blessed and helped in the healing process—to parents, siblings, grandparents, children, and extended family members for their unstinting devotion to telling the rest of the story.

Sincere appreciation goes to the publishing company for making it possible to produce this volume (and others) so that the stories of those who gave all will not be forgotten and will perhaps serve to help someone else who is called to suffer the death or disability of a loved one.

Finally, we express heartfelt gratitude to Him whose life made it possible to be with those called to precede us in the great Plan of Happiness—even Our Savior, Our Redeemer, Our Lord Jesus Christ, in whom we place our trust, our hope, and our faith.

PREFACE

"And he that liveth in righteousness shall be changed in the twinkling of an eye, and the earth shall pass away so as by fire."
—Doctrine and Covenants 43:32

When Elder Bradly Savage and his three companions were killed in a fiery head-on crash in Iowa at the end of January 2000, the investigating officers determined that death was instantaneous for all. The impact was terrific and killed the individual in the other vehicle as well. Subsequent events, many too sacred to share except as inspired by the Holy Spirit, proved to the Savages that their son was not only happy to be anxiously engaged in missionary work in a new and expanded field of labor, but that there was some urgency for those of us on this side of the veil to be more diligent about finding the names of our ancestors and completing the ordinances they lack.

Following the funeral service for Elder Savage in the Lehi 17th Ward, Lehi North Stake, David Merrill Tuttle invited President Robert W. Rowley of the Iowa Des Moines Mission to participate long-distance in the first-ever Parley P. Pratt Missionary Memorial Horseback Ride in memory of missionaries like the four from his mission. The letter from Brother Tuttle read:

Dear President Rowley—

Elder Savage was a member of our ward and the Sunday prior to his funeral I was pondering how I could reach out to his father and family in a way that would honor the memory of their son. Because Pete Savage enjoys riding horses, my thought was to take a ride with him and "cry together" over the loss of his son. Then, following the funeral and its messages of hope and promise, I expanded my thoughts to include others on the ride who might have an interest in honoring and remembering all missionaries who paid the ultimate price for their faith . . . and the Parley P. Pratt Missionary Memorial Ride was born.

This effort has since taken on a life of its own—it's as though I have simply been a conduit for documenting ideas for remembering missionaries everywhere, beginning with one of the first missionaries to die in the field, Elder Pratt. The attached files describe what we have planned for the first

Saturday in June. In the process of creating a fitting tribute to the four missionaries from the Iowa Des Moines Mission, we have learned of a number of other missionaries who have died or been seriously injured in their service to the Master, and they are included in our memorial service.

I want you to know about this event and also invite you to share with us at the gathering anything you would like to say with the perspective of four months. One of my high school friends lost his son in an almost identical accident in Michigan in 1988 and his testimony now is that he would not trade all the good that has resulted from this tragedy to have his son back. That may sound a bit melodramatic, but both he and his wife have experienced a confirmation of the value of their son's sacrifice. In fact, President Monson promised the Savage family that more good would result from this than could happen in possibly any other way.

In a letter to his immediate and extended family members, Brother Tuttle shared the following thoughts concerning the funeral service for Elder Savage.

3 February 2000
Dear Ones—

We attended the funeral today of Bradly Savage, one of four LDS missionaries killed in a head-on crash 28 January in Iowa as they were returning from a mission conference. Earlier today I helped set up chairs at the chapel, including an extra 200 from the stake center for the expected crowd. The entire building was filled by persons wanting to pay their final respects to a young man "transferred" to a new assignment.

In the opening prayer, petition was made for a renewal, reconciliation and recommitment of all in attendance and that prayer was answered in the course of the speakers, songs and hymns offered.

Keri Savage, Brad's mother, gave the Life Sketch, mentioning that at age 13 Brad wanted to learn to fly and after many lessons and hard work piloted a Cessna. At age 15 he learned to dive and eventually led his Lehi High School team to state championships three years running. At 19, he gave his letterman's jacket to his mother, saying, "We've worked hard for this." He was a "perfect son"—obedient, humble and caring. He watched out for his sisters and was a pal to his younger brother. His father lost a son and a best friend.

His swimming coach spoke next, stating that Brad worked hard at being a champion in athletics and in life. He took on the difficult tasks, always exercising faith: "We can do it," he would say to his coach. He was teachable and coachable.

The bishop took a few minutes to share his experience with Brad and several other young men at Flaming Gorge on a scouting adventure. Four of the young men had scaled a cliff and were one by one jumping into the water from higher and higher ledges. Suddenly, Brad jumped off and executed a double one and a half, entering the water perfectly, but leaving the bishop with his heart in his throat! He said he had recently received a phone call in which Elder Savage said he was the happiest he had ever been—doing the work of the ministry.

Elder Neunschwander of the Seventy spoke next, indicating that peace comes in spite of the tragedy because the Spirit testifies of truth. He counseled each of us to write down our favorite memories, sayings and experiences with Brad so that we will not forget them in the months and years to come. He then bore strong testimony of the reality of the resurrection, where Brad (and all of us) will come forth clean, bright, strong and whole before the God who gave us life.

After a beautiful sextet of young women sang "Well Done Thy Good and Faithful Servant," President Thomas S. Monson was the final speaker. He recalled that as a young deacon passing out little flowers to mothers on Mother's Day, he noticed they would always cry—and it was because of the memories. "Go ahead and cry," he said; "that's how we're made." He then told of speaking at the funeral of the missionary shot and killed in Bolivia several years ago and how he spoke afterwards to that Elder's younger brother. "And what if you receive a mission call to Bolivia?" The young man answered, "I would go." Sure enough, several years later, he was called to serve in that same mission.

He shared a promise from President Hinckley, who said, "God will bless this family." He then said he thought that the deaths of these four missionaries has touched more hearts, inspired more commitments and captured greater attention than perhaps anything else could have—both at home and in the mission field where they were serving. He likened the scripture concerning the Savior to Elder Savage, quoting: "And Jesus increased in stature and wisdom and in favor with God and man." His mission president said of Brad Savage: "He was a perfect missionary."

President Monson concluded by stating that we will each feel worthwhile if "something comes alive in others because of you." And then finally, "I want everyone here to doubt not, fear not, and He will direct your paths for good."

He then read a letter from the First Presidency expressing condolences and the promise that "He will come to you with a sweet feeling of peace." His final paraphrase was of the scripture that says I have no greater joy than to hear my family walks in truth.

This was a sobering event, happening as it did almost simultaneously with the Alaska Air crash off the California coast and the death of an eighteen-year-old young woman, a Lehi High School senior, in a car accident in Provo canyon.

We are grateful for the knowledge of the gospel truths that teach us of life after life where much of our existence will be worked out for the better, provided we hold on and make choices of faith and not fear.

We moved ahead with plans for the Missionary Memorial Ride, learning in the process that the namesake for the event, Parley P. Pratt, was an excellent horseman himself. They say the "outside of a horse is good for the inside of a man" and so in the spirit of priesthood horseback rides held in the late '60s and early '70s in Pleasant Grove, we organized the first-ever Parley P. Pratt Missionary Memorial Horseback Ride to honor the memory of those whose commitment to the gospel required their lives.

Elder W. Grant Bangerter, General Authority Emeritus, and also a long-time horseman, was the keynote speaker at the commemorative service held above the community of Alpine, Utah, in the spring of 2000. Twenty-four riders joined us for the initial trail ride.

FOREWORD

I have written many books and articles. I have taught for many years and have seen the impact that missions have in the lives of missionaries and their families. When asked if I would write a foreword to this book, I reluctantly agreed—not because I didn't want to write it but because I felt I was too busy. How wrong I was. I have sat in my office hour after hour weeping at the devotion, love, testimony, and spirit that radiate from each of these priceless stories.

Missions are difficult at best. When death comes to one serving a mission, the question is often asked: "Why didn't Heavenly Father protect them as they served?" Probably my greatest fear as a mission president was that I would have to inform a family that their precious son or daughter would not be returning home alive. Thankfully that never happened during my time as a mission president. However, reading these stories reminded me that when a missionary dies, a far greater impact is made than on the family alone.

I am consoled by and convinced of the fact that those who give their lives in the Lord's service have the assurance of eternal life in the world to come.

In Doctrine and Covenants 98:12–15 the Lord states: *"For he will give unto the faithful line upon line, precept upon precept; and I will try you and prove you herewith.*

"And whoso layeth down his life in my cause, for my name's sake, shall find it again, even life eternal.

"Therefore, be not afraid of your enemies, for I have decreed in my heart, saith the Lord, that I will prove you in all things, whether you will abide in my covenant, even unto death, that you may be found worthy.

"For if ye will not abide in my covenant ye are not worthy of me."

That sounds all very academic until one is asked to make the ultimate sacrifice. But what of the families and loved ones of the missionaries who gave all? There is a faith and resolute testimony that is a common thread through each of these stories that will warm your heart. Not all of the loved ones understood the purpose behind the death, but all of them manifested hope and optimism in what their beloved missionaries are doing now and that the time will come when they will be reunited with them.

Some of the grieving loved ones were privileged to see a vision or have a visitation from their departed missionaries. Others were granted that *"peace of*

God, which passeth all understanding" (Philippians 4:7) to comfort them. Some found comfort immediately while others struggled for some time before that assurance came that *"all things have been done in the wisdom of him who knoweth all things"* (2 Nephi 2:24).

As I read each story my testimony was strengthened and my resolve to live a better life was increased. I found an even stronger desire to be numbered among those who God showed Abraham were the *"noble and great ones"* (see Abraham 3:22–23) destined to share His priceless gospel with the people of a fallen world. I found myself complaining less at the sacrifices I have been asked to make and serving more with a selfless, Christlike attitude. I discovered anew my trust in a loving Heavenly Father who knows everything and orders all things according to His plan for the salvation and exaltation of His spirit children.

I challenge you to read these accounts with your eyes but also to open your heart to the sweet testimonies recorded herein. You will never look at either missions or death in the same way again. I am convinced that no matter how strong your testimony is at present, it will be greatly enlarged as a result of your reading and pondering these wonderful testimonials of noble sons and daughters of God who make the ultimate mission Transfer.

—Randy L. Bott

INTRODUCTION

In the course of my life I have felt things that defy my ability to express in words—feelings so intense, so personal, and so comforting—that to attempt to share such feelings belittles them at best and disparages them at worst. And so I do not attempt to share certain things of the Spirit, experiences meant perhaps for my soul alone. And that is sufficient for me, for now. Similarly, I have heard of sacred events that even if I were capable of sharing with the same effect they had on my soul, I would not. They are too special, too personal, and too tender to be shared without the context of the influence of Him by whom they were granted.

So, too, are many stories not included in this volume. They were given for a particular purpose at a particular time and to meet a particular need. They have served their purpose and perhaps some of them will be shared when the individuals to whom they happened choose to divulge them, but it will only be done in the wisdom and under the influence of that Being by whom they came.

Nevertheless, my sense is that many stories will be shared because through the process of documentation, those accounts produce more light, reflect more sublime truths, and promote greater faith than if they remain untold.

Parley P. Pratt, one of the original Twelve Apostles in the latter days, was an accomplished horseman, covering literally thousands of miles on horseback and afoot in the pursuit of his apostolic calling at home and abroad. In his scholarly and well-written account of his great grandfather's assassination, originally printed in *Brigham Young University Studies* in 1975, Steven Pratt provides the background, details, and sequence of events leading up to 13 May 1857, the day Parley P. Pratt was brutally stabbed and shot and left for dead twelve miles northwest of a small Arkansas town called Van Buren.

> *Briefly, the story is one of the marriage of Eleanor Jane, the birth of children and the increasingly sinister spiral of Hector McLean's drinking problem, leading to a separation just three years after their marriage. But promising to "live soberly and righteously," Hector persuaded Eleanor to return and sometime later they moved to San Francisco to help accomplish Hector's reformation. They were accompanied by their three children.*

In San Francisco they came in contact with the Mormon church and after attending a meeting with Hector and his brother, Eleanor wanted to join the Church but was forbidden to do so by her husband, who threatened her with bodily harm if she was baptized. Seeking diligently for her husband's permission to join the Saints, Eleanor at length obtained it in writing and was baptized some two years before the Pratt family came to San Francisco, preparatory to Elder Pratt's call to preside over the Pacific Mission and to set up a place for the saints to gather in San Jose, California.

Subsequently, Eleanor and other members of the Church cared for the Pratt family because Parley's wife Elizabeth was sick most of the time, bringing food, clothing and bedding. During these visits Eleanor told Parley of her home situation and Parley did visit the McLean home several times in an attempt to reconcile their differences. The outcome was that Hector became even more bitter and after Eleanor had her two boys baptized by Parley, he charged his wife with insanity, attempting to have her committed and thus "save his family from the Mormons."

Failing this, Hector then sent the children to New Orleans to live with their grandparents, Eleanor's parents. Eleanor found means to travel to find her children but was unable to convince her parents to release them to her charge and eventually returned to Salt Lake City to work as a schoolteacher at the Pratt home. One month later she was married as a plural wife to Parley by Brigham Young in the Endowment House. She then taught Parley's children for seven months and afterwards for four months boarded and taught at Brigham Young's house.

When Parley was called to a mission in the Eastern States in 1856, Eleanor asked to accompany him, "thinking to regain her children, bring them to Utah, and raise them there."

In the meantime, Hector McLean, working with the help of apostates and enemies of the church, was able to track Parley P. Pratt in his travels in the south and enlisting the services of local law enforcement officers, set out in deadly pursuit of his quarry. Hector used the charge of larceny, for the value of the clothing the children were wearing when they were "kidnapped" by Eleanor, to eventually arrest Parley, Eleanor and George Higginson, Parley's traveling companion.

At their hearing, Hector drew his pistol and pointed it at Parley, which action caused the judge to postpone the trial until the next morning. But this was a ruse to avoid the crowd of 500 spectators who had been whipped into a frenzy by the allegations of Hector McLean. Early the next morning the judge released Parley, put him on his horse and offered him his knife and *pistol, but Parley refused saying, "Gentlemen, I do not rely on weapons of that kind; my trust is in my God. Good-bye, Gentlemen."*

Hector, who had stayed up all night, was at the hotel the next morning when a small boy ran up indicating that "Parley had escaped." Hector and several of his cohorts immediately mounted and started in pursuit. Because of a light rain that morning, Parley's tracks, although he had taken a circuitous route, were easily traceable.

After a while, some of the pursuers turned back, but Hector and two others continued to track Pratt. They finally caught up with him in front of the Winn farm about twelve miles north of Van Buren. McLean fired six shots from his pistol, but they all missed, "some going through Parley's coat and some into his saddle." McLean then rode up close to Parley and stabbed him twice in the chest. After Parley fell off his horse and lay motionless on the ground, McLean and his friends rode off. But in about ten minutes, McLean returned, "got down from his horse, placed a gun next to Parley's neck, fired, and then rode off."

Mr. Winn, the farmer, witnessed the murder and thinking Parley was dead, rode to his neighbors' home for help, which took about an hour. When the neighbors returned, they discovered that Parley was still alive, but aware of his impending death. His parting testimony of the truth still rings true today:

· *"I die a firm believer in the Gospel of Jesus Christ as revealed through the Prophet Joseph Smith, and I wish you to carry this my dying testimony. I know that the Gospel is true and that Joseph Smith was a prophet of the living God. I am dying a martyr to the faith."*

Our intent is to share these stories, like Parley P. Pratt's, as much as possible using the words of the author insofar as they communicate the pathos and the meaning of the experience. Many times, in reviewing the details of a particular story, I am struck by the comforting realization that *all things are done in the wisdom of him who knoweth all things"* and then I don't worry so much about grammar, spelling, or even vocabulary. There is something very authentic about a first-person account that cannot be replicated, even with the best editing.

But this book is more than stories of tragedy and faith, sorrow and resolution—this is a book about an idea with an agenda of its own. I have said many times that I feel like a custodian or secretary to this project. My belief is that I am simply facilitating what is becoming a project with a destiny of its own, independent of my own wishes or desires, although many of my own needs are being met through this project and what it is becoming. I think these stories need to be told because they happened for a particular purpose at a particular time and to certain people capable of learning from the experiences. My hope is that others will gain similar awareness and insights from these experiences and be moved to action because of them.

Why do we read, let alone write, the stories of others? And what do we find of value in those most personal of experiences that become most generally applicable to each of us? Finally, why do the trials of others hold special interest for us who have suffered our own, if different, tests in mortality?

We accept with some trepidation the stewardship that has come to us to guard the sanctity of personal experiences found in this volume. Notwithstanding that apprehension, we choose to share them in a spirit of hope and good will, confident that those who read them will receive a personal witness of their meaning for them.

My friend and editor of this volume, Susan Evans Woods, shared some poignant experiences from her work of gathering and compiling these stories, a volunteer effort that has so far extended over four years:

> *I have witnessed many small miracles as this work has unfolded, both in finding missionary families and as I have read the stories. I have made some "friends" for the project as well. Some who were extremely suspicious and prickly at first have become my greatest allies in the work. Some who couldn't be bothered to write down their story, thinking no one would be interested, have had their hearts softened when they learned how desperately their family wanted to read and learn the details. Some who thought nobody cared at all about their beloved missionaries are so grateful to learn that somebody truly does care. Some who scoffed, saying the project would never be completed, are now highly interested in the outcome, and every submitter has asked me to let them know as soon as I know when they can purchase a copy of the book.*
>
> *Some have said they are planning to write and publish their own books including "the rest of the story," all the details, but gave me just the basics for our project. When new stories come pouring in, as I hope they will, I'll be ready to do it all over again. It will be much easier if people are looking for us instead of me trying to find them.*

And so our hearts go out to those whose loved ones were willing to be prepared to make the ultimate sacrifice, if necessary, to publish peace and extend the opportunity to learn of the greatest truth the world has ever known. This volume is one initiative to bridge the gap between sorrow and joy, shock and understanding, acceptance and reconciliation.

—David Merrill Tuttle

MISSIONARY STORIES

Statistically speaking, the two years or 18 months spent serving the Lord in missionary work are by far the safest of any comparable two-year period as measured by recent demographics—far safer than staying home, according to those who keep records of missionaries.

Nevertheless, in the work of the Lord we must allow for the possibility that the ultimate sacrifice is sometimes required for His work to proceed on one side of the veil or the other. Of the more than one million missionaries who have served in this last dispensation, less than one-tenth of one percent have ever qualified for "the transfer," thus making it an extremely rare occurrence in the work of the Lord.

This book (the first of several volumes) is a compilation of such stories as told by loved ones. In it, you will learn of these unwelcome sacrifices which were somehow deemed necessary or even foreordained to open doors, to turn keys, and to bless thousands of lives.

Although the topic of death may seem depressing or morose, once readers learn more of the experiences and of surrounding events, they sense the guiding hand of the Lord and the tragedy turns from crisis to consolation, then to faithful resolve, and ultimately to humble gratitude.

Compiled over the span of four years, these pages include stories of missionaries who have served from the earliest days of this dispensation to those called as recently as one year ago. Included in this volume is the story of a General Authority who was taken while serving in Chile, a curious case of being "transferred" in an extraordinary manner.

Each story becomes a microcosm of the life of many missionaries—a series of events that prepared the individual to serve, premonitions on the part of the missionary or family members, the "perfect accident" that takes a life or maims a missionary for life, followed by a series of miracles and "understandings"—these and many other bittersweet stories are shared by families whose sorrows and compensating blessings make their loved one's story at once most personal and yet universal.

THOMAS JEFFERSON ADAIR

Born: 28 May 1884, Nutrioso, Apache, Arizona
Parents: Samuel Newton Adair and Helen Genette Brown Adair
Siblings: Charles Newton, Harriet Genette, Byron Abraham,
Jamima Jane, William Orin, Mary Virginia, Anna Catherine,
Sarah Edna, Josephine, and Marcus Owen
Mission: Southwestern States, labored in Arkansas
Time of service: April 1904 to July 1906
Cause of death: Typhoid, malaria fever
Date and place of death: 1 August 1906, St. Johns, Apache, Arizona
Age at time of death: 22
Place of burial: Luna, Socorro, New Mexico
Story related by: Byron Neal Chapman, great-nephew

THOMAS JEFFERSON ADAIR WAS A COWBOY on the Blue River Wilderness, south of Nutrioso, Arizona, where his father, Samuel Newton Adair, was a rancher. Samuel served a mission with Jacob Hamblin among the Hopi and Navajo Indian tribes in Southern Utah and Northern Arizona. Samuel Jefferson Adair, father of Samuel Newton Adair, founded Washington, Utah, and lived there 20 years. A monument in his honor stands in that city.

Thomas received a good education. He attended the Stake Academy at St. Johns and there took a missionary course prior to his mission for The Church of Jesus Christ of Latter-day Saints. He received his call to the Southwestern States and was set apart on 1 April 1904. He was assigned to labor in Arkansas.

Elder Adair received a letter from Mission President James G. Duffin at the headquarters of the Southwestern States Mission in Kansas City, Missouri, informing him of what he should take. "Bring no books nor extra clothing except one pair of garments. Knit garments are worn by almost all the elders. . . . We have made special arrangements with the 'Western Knitting Co.'. . . in Salt Lake City, whereby Elders can get . . . a 20% discount. . . . Also, if you want to get a Prince Albert suit in Salt Lake City, go to West's Mail Order House. . . . They have agreed to sell you a $21 suit for $14. We supply Elders here at the office with suitable grips, clothing of all kinds (except garments), books, tracts, etc. We keep on hand Bibles specially suited to our work. . . . Bring no trunks or valises: you cannot take them with you in your travels, and we have no room to store them here. May the blessings of the Lord attend you on your journey to this city and throughout your mission."

A few pages from Elder Adair's journal indicate that he and his companion spent part of their time looking for food and for places to sleep. After eating a morning meal, they were on their way, teaching as they went and seeking food and lodging each night. They used each opportunity to preach the gospel and bear their testimonies.

"Friday 5 August 1904. We arose this morning feeling able to pursue our journey, and shortly after eating our breakfast began to do so. We ate dinner with a man by the name of Moreland. After dinner we had all the muskmelons we could eat.

"Wednesday 10 August 1904. After eating our breakfast we borrowed a kettle, a tub, and some soap and went to the spring and washed our clothes. We got our washing out about noon, ate our dinner, and then wrote some letters while our clothes were drying. When they were dry, we put them in our grips and started on our journey. We walked five or six miles and found us a place to stay. The man's name was Mr. Wickersham."

There are no details to indicate when or where Elder Adair contracted typhoid malaria, but malaria generally comes from drinking impure water or is contracted from mosquitoes. He had served 28 months as a faithful missionary when he contracted the disease. He was released from his mission and started for home.

Evidently, Elder Adair's parents received word he had arrived in St. Johns, Arizona, on 23 July 1906, and was quite ill with a fever. His parents lived in Nutrioso, about 75 miles from St. Johns, and they traveled to his bedside to assist him. They found he was too ill to travel any farther; he passed away about a week later on 1 August 1906. Elder Adair's body was transported from St. Johns, Arizona, to Luna, New Mexico, where he was buried.

Elder Adair was noted for his exceptionally energetic and lively disposition. He was greatly respected by his family and siblings for faithfully serving a mission. His father desired that a good young woman be sealed to him, for he filled a good mission and was worthy of that blessing. He had also hoped and longed to hear his son preach and to see him dressed in the clothes he preached in.

The missionary spirit has prevailed in our family. A number of nephews and a niece (my mother), filled missions, partly because of Thomas Jefferson Adair's desire to serve. My wife and I have both filled two missions, 4 of our 6 daughters have filled missions, and so far, 8 of our 34 grandchildren have served or are serving missions.

According to the First Presidency, the Church does everything possible to ensure the health and safety of missionaries serving in the world. Young men and women in the mission field are safer than their peers who remain at home. I feel that because of Elder Adair's attitude he continues his work as a missionary on the other side of the veil and that he has joined other missionaries called into the eternal service of our Father in Heaven.

GOTTFRIED ALDER

Born: 20 July 1848, Schwellbrunn, Appenzell, Switzerland
Parents: Johann Ulrich Alder and Susanna Barbara Zuberbuehler Alder
Siblings: Johanna Barbara, Johannes (John) and five siblings who died
as infants—Johannes, Gottfried, Konrad, two unnamed
Spouse: Anna Regina Reusch Alder
Children: John Jacob, Emma, Charles Gottfried, Joseph, Emilie,
Anna Louise, Albert Hyrum
Mission: Germany, Switzerland
Time of service: 22 April 1898 to 18 March 1899
Cause of death: Pneumonia
Date and place of death: 18 March 1899,
Chur, Graubunden, Switzerland
Age at time of death: 50
Place of burial: Manti, Utah
Story related by: Joyce J. Alder,
wife of the late Lyle G. Alder, great-grandson

GOTTFRIED ALDER WAS THE SEVENTH OF eight children born to
Johann Ulrich Alder and Susanna Barbara Zuberbuehler, in Schwellbrunn,
Appenzell, Switzerland. Gottfried's parents were baptized members of The
Church of Jesus Christ of Latter-day Saints in 1860. Gottfried followed two
years later, baptized at the age of 14, by John Huber on 1 February 1862.

On 25 August 1869, Gottfried, at the age of 21, immigrated to the
United States with a group of 454 Saints. He traveled from Liverpool
on the ship *Minnesota*, with James Price, as captain, and Marius Ensign,
Church leader. The ship arrived in New York on 6 September 1869.

Gottfried then traveled on to Salt Lake City, and shortly after his arrival there, he married Anna Regina Reusch on 27 September 1869; Anna had immigrated in the same company as Gottfried.

They made their home in Manti, Utah, where four sons and three daughters were born to them. Gottfried was a farmer, and he labored on the construction of the Manti Temple. There were few dull moments for Gottfried and his wife as they went about their daily chores, raising a family in this new land and serving in their callings as members of the Church.

At the age of 50, Gottfried was called to serve a mission to Germany, which at that time included his native country of Switzerland. From his journal we have an accounting of his journeys and labors.

On 21 April 1898, he traveled on the Rio Grande Railroad from Manti to Salt Lake City. Upon his arrival, he was set apart by Brigham H. Roberts in the Salt Lake Temple. From Salt Lake City, Elder Alder traveled to Philadelphia, Pennsylvania, where he boarded the steamship *Macelund*. The following day, 1 May, he wrote in his journal: "Everything well and healthy. Hit a sand bar and got stuck. Three steam ships came to rescue."

Gottfried's described his journey across the ocean as "stormy." He wrote of waves as high as mountains, and he did not feel well from the swaying of the ship. Twenty-one other elders and one sister were on the same ship. His companion was Elder Conrad Keller, one of his good friends from Manti.

After resting for a night in Liverpool, they boarded the ship *Ashton*, which Elder Alder described as a "beautiful, clean ship." On 27 May 1898, Elder Alder arrived in Bern, Switzerland; he then traveled on to Zurich. However, Elder Keller was required to stay in Zurich, so Elder Alder parted company with his friend.

Elder Alder traveled to his birthplace, Schwellbrunn, where he wrote: "I saw our house and picked some flowers from my grandfather's property and took them along." The following day, 27 May 1898, he visited his sister Johanna Barbara. Although he did not record his feelings in his journal, it must have been a joy for him to see his house and once again meet with the family and friends he had left behind in 1869.

He traveled near and far handing out the pamphlet called "Eternal Truth" and shared his testimony of the truthfulness of the gospel with those who would listen. Missionaries during that time were dependent on others for meals and boarding. Elder Alder often labored in the fields, picking beans, potatoes, and apples, in exchange for food and lodging. Some sisters were willing to wash his clothes.

On 5 September 1898, Elder Alder wrote: "I received a card from President Bowman in Bern telling me that our beloved President Wilford Woodruff had died. It made me feel ill. It will be a very hard thing for the Church of Jesus Christ."

Elder Alder continued to preach as he moved from place to place and was always grateful for letters from his wife, his brother Johannes, and friends. On 24 October 1898, he wrote: "Healthy and well. I had something to eat this morning and then I went to Brother Schmidt's to help him cut some wood, and in the evening I went back home. I received a letter from my dear wife and Louisa. I received my blessing but I could not settle down and sleep as I always thought about my blessing and I felt very heavy and depressed because nothing in it was said that I would return home healthy and well. Other than that it was a very good blessing."

Elder Alder was laboring in Chur, one of the most remote parts of the German–Swiss Mission. It was in Chur that he became very ill. During his sickness he stayed in the home of a Brother Braun and family, who gave him all the kindly care he could have received if he had been with his own family. When his symptoms became worse, medical help was summoned and a letter was sent to President Bowman, who immediately wrote Elder Keller (who was in a nearby area), asking him to go see Elder Alder.

On 13 March 1899, a telegram was sent to President Bowman stating that Elder Alder's case had become critical. President Bowman left immediately, reaching the bedside of the sick man at the same time as Elder Keller arrived. The illness had developed into pneumonia, with one lung being clogged, and the other nearly so. Elder Alder suffered from a high fever, making it very difficult for him to sleep.

Elder Alder was administered to and he rallied. For some time he seemed much better, so President Bowman returned to Bern, assured that Elder Alder would recover. However, he relapsed, and on Saturday, 18 March 1899, Elder Gottfried Alder passed away. His body was placed in a hermetically sealed casket and prepared in such a way that his remains could be sent home at a later date.

President Bowman and Elder Keller wrote letters to the grieving family in Manti. The *Southern Star*, a Swiss newspaper, ran an article about Elder Gottfried Alder's death, stating: "The brethren feel as if they had passed through a very painful and sad experience, one they never wish again, and now that it is past, they, with us can only ask while bearing testimony to the zeal of a fellow laborer and beloved brother, that the spirit of consolation may rest upon the stricken household of the departed, that they, in due time of the Lord, may be able to see through this providence and acknowledge a Father's hand."

In November 1899, nine months after his death, the body of Gottfried Alder was accompanied by Brother Conrad Keller, his friend and companion, from Switzerland to his home in Manti, Utah. From the *Manti Messenger*, a local newspaper, we read: "On November 18, 1899, the body was brought from the Sanpete Valley Railway Depot to the Tabernacle where impressive services were held, and the remains were followed to the cemetery by a number of vehicles. . . . The sympathy of the community is extended to the bereaved family and the *Messenger* joins by hoping that the family realize that to some extent that the Almighty does everything for the best for his children in the earth."

Sources:
Gottfried Alder missionary journal
Southern Star, Switzerland
Manti Messenger, Manti, Utah
Latter-day Saint Biographical Encyclopedia, 1951

BRYAN KEITH ANDERSON

Born: 19 October 1958, Idaho Falls, Idaho
Parents: Keith B. Anderson and Eileen Scully Anderson
Siblings: Judy, Cora
Mission: Oklahoma Tulsa
Time of service: 13 December 1978 to 16 March 1979
Cause of death: Bicycle/auto accident
Date and place of death: 16 March 1979, Bartlesville, Oklahoma
Age at time of death: 20
Place of burial: Annis Little Butte Cemetery, Rigby, Idaho
Story related by: Keith and Eileen Anderson, parents

BRYAN KEITH ANDERSON WAS BORN 19 October 1958 in Idaho Falls, Idaho, to Keith B. and Eileen Scully Anderson. He attended public schools in Rigby, Idaho, and graduated from Rigby High School. Bryan was a member of the Idaho National Guard and was active in athletics and outdoor sports.

His mission call from President Spencer W. Kimball was to the Oklahoma Tulsa Mission, and he entered the Provo Missionary Training Center on 9 November 1978. Elder Anderson was one of the many young men in The Church of Jesus Christ of Latter-day Saints who give two years of their lives to teach the gospel.

A few days after he was transferred from Tulsa, Oklahoma, to Bartlesville, Bryan and his companion, Elder Scott Newton, dressed in their dark missionary suits, were riding their bicycles. They were riding in an area north of the town of Bartlesville about 7:45 p.m. along Virginia Avenue when a van hit Elder Anderson's bicycle and knocked him 125 feet into a ditch. The driver reported he did not see the riders. Elder Newton was also struck by the auto, but he was not seriously injured, and he refused treatment at a Bartlesville Hospital. Elder Anderson died of his injuries.

From the *Tulsa World* newspaper article dated Sunday, 22 April 1979, the story continues:

"His mission was accomplished. Indirectly, the way the lad met his death was the final impetus that led to the largest family baptism of record in the history of the Tulsa and East Tulsa Stakes, according to Dr. William H. Day, Talequah, East Tulsa stake president.

"Twelve members of the interrelated Williams, Woodruff, McCulloch, and Golden families were baptized Friday night . . . by Bishop Clyde Jensen. The thirteenth family member, Linda Williams, age 7, will be baptized in October when she will become 8—the youngest age permitted for baptism under LDS church laws.

"The mother and sister of Doug Williams had joined the LDS church years before. Williams affiliated with another denomination. The remainder of those baptized Friday had made the decision earlier to join the LDS.

"The Williamses had suffered years of personal loss. One young son nearly died of meningitis. Physicians had done all they could for him, but his recovery was attributed to prayers of his family and concerned friends. They later lost an infant daughter, Laura, to pneumonia. When another daughter, Linda, was stricken with the same disease, 'her treatment turned the hearts of the Williams family toward better nutrition for the health of the whole family,' Day related. 'The knowledge gained was in perfect agreement with the teachings of the Word of Wisdom doctrine of the Mormon faith.'

"With Linda again well, Doug Williams kept a promise he made to his wife's father, that Patty would complete her education goal. The entire Williams family entered into the project of helping Patty to become a doctor.

"In the fall of 1978, as she was preparing to enter the Osteopathic College of Medicine, a drinking driver struck and killed the Williamses' teenage son, Randy, as he was riding his bicycle.

"Another family council determined Mrs. Williams should not let this deter her from completing her education. At the college, she met Jensen, a faculty member.

"As Jensen learned more about the tragedy-starred family, discussions followed; then lessons from missionaries, family home evenings, and a family council meeting. Each member of the group arrived individually at a decision to be baptized.

9

"But it was the death of the young missionary [Elder Brian K. Anderson]—so like that of Randy—that impelled the group to select Good Friday evening as the time they would be baptized and join the church together."

Elder Anderson was to have served as a missionary for a two-year period. Services were held in the Rigby LDS Stake Center. Bishop Keith Madsen of the Rigby 5th LDS Ward officiated. Elder Derek A. Cuthbert of the First Quorum of the Seventy of The Church of Jesus Christ of Latter-day Saints spoke words of comfort and hope.

Bryan was given military rites at the graveside by Company A 116th English Battalion of the Idaho National Guard, Glen W. Bennett as bugler.

Interment was in the Annis Little Butte Cemetery in Rigby under the direction of Eckersell Memorial Chapel of Rigby.

Dallas Nielsen Archibald

Born: 24 July 1938, Logan, Utah
Parents: Ezra W. Archibald and Marguerite Nielsen Archibald
Siblings: Gayland, Lennis
Spouse: Linda R. Archibald
Children: Teresa Dawn
Missions: First Mission: Uruguay, 1958 to 1961
Second Mission: Spain Seville Mission President, 1979 to 1982
Time of service: 1992 to 1998, General Authority
Cause of death: Drowning
Date and place of death: 14 December 1998, Santa Barbara, Chile
Age at time of death: 60
Place of burial: Larkin Sunset Lawn, Salt Lake City, Utah
Story related by: Linda, wife

DALLAS NIELSEN ARCHIBALD WAS BORN in Logan, Utah, on 24 July 1938, to Ezra Wilson and Marguerite Nielsen Archibald. He graduated from Ben Lomond High School in Ogden, Utah, and served a mission to Uruguay from 1958 to 1961. Upon returning to the United States, he served four years in the U.S. Coast Guard. After his marriage to Linda Ritchie, he received a Bachelor of Arts Degree in Spanish from Weber State University in Ogden, and a Masters of International Management from Thunderbird Graduate School in Glendale, Arizona.

A career in international business took Dallas to live in many states of the United States and to countries around the world, including Japan, the

11

Philippines, Canada, Puerto Rico, South Africa, Mexico, Spain, Venezuela, Brazil, and Chile. He served as mission president of the Spain Seville Mission (now Malaga) from 1979 to 1982. He and his wife and daughter, Teresa, were living in São Paulo, Brazil, in 1992 when he was called to be a General Authority. He served in the Brazil Area Presidency for five years and then, in 1997, was called to be the Area President in Santiago, Chile.

Elder Dallas N. Archibald of the First Quorum of the Seventy and president of the Chile Area for The Church of Jesus Christ of Latter-day Saints was just a fisherman at heart. He identified with the fishermen of the New Testament: Cast your nets . . . Cast your rods . . . Cast your words. He fished for fish, and in the semantics of the gospel, he fished for men. His love of mountain streams and trout took root during his childhood and youth. His love of fishing for men blossomed while he served as a young missionary in Uruguay. He was a teacher of renown and a powerful motivator; he changed people's lives.

On Monday morning, 14 December 1998, at the Bio Bio River in Santa Barbara, Chile, Elder Archibald took a well-deserved break from church duties after a long weekend of meetings and stake conference sessions, to fish with President David K. Broadbent of the Chile Concepcion Mission. Elder Archibald and President Broadbent were both expert fishermen. Mission presidents also need breaks from the intense responsibilities of church duties and are allowed P-Days to enjoy a recreation of preference, such as fishing, with family and friends. For Elder Archibald, Preparation Day meant relax, wind down, forget about the clock and the schedule. Whenever possible, he found a lake or a river. Southern Chile was a paradise for fishermen, and the Bio Bio River was one of the most spectacular places in the world for such an outing. After packing the gear in the car, they drove alongside the river through pristine mountain scenery sharing thoughts about the days of work and the days of rest.

The Bio Bio can be rough when at its peak, but after two years of drought in Chile, the river, though deep, had been reduced to a calm and rather ordinary flow, meandering lazily through a spectacular wilderness of flatlands and canyons. The two men felt comfortable with the river and the surroundings. Once upstream, they parked, walked to the river's edge, and slipped into float tubes. From there they journeyed leisurely to a box canyon where the deep water was still and silent as a lake, and where there were fish in abundance.

Elder Archibald floated a few yards ahead as they moved on slowly. They were grateful the morning was bright and sunny. Had it rained, as it did the day before, they would not have been enjoying the peace and wonder of the river.

Suddenly they saw a small area of turbulence where a tributary merged and had, over time, carried a few rocks into the Bio Bio. Elder Archibald motioned to President Broadbent, indicating that they should shift their trajectory slightly. In response, both float tubes rotated, and President Broadbent turned his back to Elder Archibald.

President Broadbent navigated the area successfully in a matter of seconds. He looked around and was startled to see Elder Archibald swimming, no longer in his fishing float tube. Because a float tube is almost like wearing a piece of clothing and is extremely difficult to remove, he assumed that the float tube must have had some defect. As Elder Archibald angled toward the shoreline, he waved, apparently communicating that the two should meet on the riverbank around the approaching bend. Then Elder Archibald, an expert swimmer, swam around the bend and out of sight.

President Broadbent rounded the bend a few seconds later expecting to see Elder Archibald waiting for him on the bank, but he was not there. Because so little time had elapsed, he assumed that he had passed Elder Archibald somewhere. He climbed out and walked back around the bend. Nothing. He walked up and down the banks of the river calling Elder Archibald's name, expecting him to step out of the brush at any time. Still nothing. Twenty minutes later, unable to quell the anxiety churning within him, he walked to the nearest road, flagged down a trucker, and called the national police and the area office of the Church in Santiago.

By nightfall, despite a massive search effort, Elder Archibald was still missing. His float tube had been recovered intact, with no defect. The police in Chile issued an all-points missing persons' bulletin which was picked up by the wire services and sent around the world on the Internet. By the next morning, the extensive search for the leader of The Church of Jesus Christ of Latter-day Saints in Chile was a major news story.

Throughout that week, the press in Chile and Utah covered the story. Feeling a need to be with her daughter and the rest of the family who were in Utah, Sister Archibald flew from Santiago to Salt Lake City on 18 December. Word came by phone to the family on 20 December that the search was over. Hope of finding him alive was gone. Elder Archibald's body was later found floating on the blue-green surface of the river in a narrow, golden canyon not far from where he was last seen. He was the first General Authority to die in an accident in 60 years.

Elder Jerald Taylor, first counselor in the Area Presidency, with help from the area office in Santiago, handled the multitude of details and arrangements in Chile. The casket containing Elder Archibald's body arrived in Salt Lake City on Christmas Eve 1998. Memorial services were held in Chile and also in Brazil, where he had lived and served for almost 15 years. In both of those countries and at the funeral in Salt Lake City, throngs gathered to bid him farewell. Everywhere there was a sense of disbelief that his charisma and enthusiasm had been stilled. As his daughter commented in brief remarks at the funeral: "He always had a knack for turning everything into an absolutely wonderful, beautiful thing."

The funeral in Salt Lake City was under the direction of the First Presidency and was held at the Ensign Stake Center on 28 December. Members of the First Presidency spoke, as well as Elder Richard G. Scott of the Quorum of Twelve and Elder Harold G. Hillam of the Seventy, both personal friends and associates in church service.

Elder Hillam said: "Elder Archibald loved people, he loved nature, and he loved life, but he didn't love any of them as much as he loved his Heavenly Father and his Savior, Jesus Christ."

Elder Scott said: "I speak for the thousands of individuals around the world who loved Dallas, loved his service, appreciated his devotion. . . . He's been a lot of fun and a great person to be with. He's also been very caring and tender."

President James E. Faust said: "Dallas Archibald was both righteous and favored. We are all shocked by his sudden passing. Of course we grieve. Of course we mourn. But I should like to look on the positive side of his life. He's done so many things, brought to pass so much righteousness, particularly among the Latin people who love him and whom he loved so very much."

President Thomas S. Monson said: "Dallas Archibald was a man with no chink in his armor, no guile in his soul, no flaw in his character. There wasn't room, because love was so dominant in his heart."

President Gordon B. Hinckley said: "He was a remarkable man, there's no question about it. . . . His capacity to teach the gospel will be magnified in the area to which he has gone."

And his wife, Linda, confirmed: "He is now on (an) extended tour of duty. But I know that in the perspective of eternity, it won't be long until we are together again."

In the midst of all the publicity, there were some personal experiences that were held close to the heart by the family: In 1997 his daughter had a dream wherein her bishop came to her door and told her that her father was missing. That dream came to pass on the night of 14 December 1998.

Sister Archibald had an experience in the Santiago Temple two weeks before the events at the Bio Bio that left a profound sense of peace and a distinct feeling that everything was going to be okay, although she did not understand at the time the reason for such a powerful confirmation.

The night before the fishing trip, Elder Archibald confided to President Broadbent: "I don't feel like I'm ready to leave Chile yet, but I have the strongest impression that I'm going to receive a change of assignment."

And, six months following his death, in May 1999, he was seen in the Santiago Temple at the sealing of a family he had been influential in reactivating.

Truly, at the Bio Bio River on the morning of 14 December 1998, Elder Dallas N. Archibald received a change of assignment, a transfer to a new area of responsibility, where he continues to be a fisher of men.

Source: Originally part of the book *Things a Baked Alaska Taught Me— and Other Uncommon Lessons from the Life of Elder Dallas N. Archibald*, by Linda R. Archibald (Orem, Utah: Granite Publishing and Distribution, 2001).

Constance Ethel Green Bennion

Born: 19 April 1932, Baltimore, Maryland
Parents: Clyde Constantine Green
and Roxie Mae Creighton Green
Siblings: Edna, Clyde Creighton, Donald Allison
Spouse: Jerald H. Bennion
Children: Craig, Lorill , Jeffrey G., Wendy, Curtis
Mission: Dominican Republic East
Time of service: September 1997 to September 1998
Cause of death: Cardiac arrest
Date and place of death: 24 September 1998,
Santo Domingo, Dominican Republic
Age at time of death: 66
Place of burial: Wasatch Lawn Memorial Park, Salt Lake City, Utah
Story related by: Jerald H. Bennion, husband

CONSTANCE (CONNIE) GREEN BENNION converted to The Church of Jesus Christ of Latter-day Saints at the age of 22 after reading the Book of Mormon. The Spirit inspired her that the book was true. She had no missionary teaching or association with the Church until after she had read the Book of Mormon. Connie went to the public library to read all she could find, both pro and con, about the Church. She located the Church in Baltimore, Maryland, on her own and attended a meeting in September 1954. The ward missionary couple taught her each week for two and a half months.

She was baptized in November, the only member of the Church in her family.

During very difficult years as a young woman, Connie was raised by her widowed mother, sisters and brothers, and aunts and uncles. After graduation from high school she worked as a secretary and a fashion model. While investigating the Church, she met Jerald H. Bennion, a medical student at the University of Maryland.

Within a few weeks of her baptism, Connie was assigned to produce the ward roadshow. She knew nothing about roadshows, but soon learned, and the show was a success. She held many church positions during her lifetime; the last was as a missionary in the Dominican Republic.

Connie married Jerald Bennion in 1955 in Baltimore, Maryland. Ten days later they were sealed for time and all eternity in the Logan, Utah, LDS Temple. They were lifelong sweethearts and had a wonderful life in Salt Lake City, Utah. Connie had a close relationship with her 4 children and 17 grandchildren, who all lived nearby. She had a loving touch as a mother and grandmother, with sparkling eyes and a kind heart.

Connie served as a teacher in the Primary, Relief Society, and Young Women's organizations. She was an officer and president of the Salt Lake County Medical Auxiliary and an officer in the Utah State Medical Auxiliary. She helped develop and run a countywide child abuse prevention program as well as taught and supported those in a teenage crisis shelter.

A year after my retirement, Connie and I decided to serve a mission. We both greatly desired and planned to be missionaries. Neither of us had medical problems, and we were not being treated with medications. We had a wonderful relationship with other couple missionaries in the Provo Senior Missionary Training Center. Although it was difficult to leave family and friends, we made some great new friends, which made our service a little easier.

Our mission assignment was to care for the physical and emotional problems of missionaries in the various missions on the island of the Dominican Republic. There were 600 missionaries, and we saw many each day that needed our help. Connie developed a good relationship with them, and some even stayed at times in our apartment, frequently for dinner.

One day we stopped at a bakery to purchase rolls to feed the missionaries who were coming that night to eat with us. The rolls were warm and would taste good for our lunch. As we drove home, Connie laid her head on my shoulder and slipped peacefully away from mortality. Everything possible was done to restore her heart and lungs, but she died. No one knows why she died; she had no previous disease, but her death certificate reads "cardiac arrest."

It has been over eight years since she passed away, and everyone misses her. Our family feels she is teaching her parents and forebears the principles of the gospel, and perhaps this is the reason she was taken from the earth. We have done temple work for many of her family members. As her children and grandchildren have met together in the temple to perform ordinances for Connie's family, we have felt her spirit there.

I have maintained good contact with the mission presidents in the Dominican Republic with whom we served and have received books and notes from the missionaries there. Connie's name was placed on a member's house that she knew in Santo Domingo.

Connie's life and mission will have an eternal effect on all her family and friends. Four of her grandsons have completed successful missions and many more are preparing to go. She believed one of the best things a person can do is to fulfill a mission.

Joshua Vaughn Berrett

Born: 16 June 1974, Salt Lake City, Utah
Parents: Vaughn Kimball Berrett and Hallie Virginia Hawkins Berrett
Siblings: Jason Paul, Caroline Jean
Mission: Arizona Tempe
Time of service: 1993 to 30 May 1995
Cause of death: Automobile accident
Date and place of death: 30 May 1995
Age at time of death: 20
Place of burial: Salt Lake City, Utah
Story related by: Hallie Berrett, mother

JOSHUA VAUGHN BERRETT WAS AN EXPECTED and wonderful joy, born on Father's Day, less than one year after a stillborn sister, Esther Lynn. Three years later, Jason brought happiness when he joined our family, and our hearts and home were filled with joy when Caroline was born.

Josh loved basketball—he loved playing the game with his friends, and, like his dad, he became a walking encyclopedia about basketball and football. He was friendly and kind to everyone; he truly loved life and had a great love of the gospel of Jesus Christ. His seminary teachers enjoyed his frequent visits to discuss the scriptures.

There was never a question if Josh would serve a mission for The Church of Jesus Christ of Latter-day Saints, but when. Three months before his 19th birthday, Josh sent in his mission application papers. He was made an elder in April of his senior year of high school and turned 19 within a month after graduating. Most of those who signed his yearbook mentioned his upcoming mission. When the call came, Josh was surprised to be called to the Arizona Tempe Mission, but he went forward, willing to touch the lives of those he served.

Josh was never apprehensive to leave his family. He admitted he would miss us, but he knew that he wanted to serve the Lord. He chose a favorite scripture for a plaque that would hang in the ward building until his return: D&C 112:28: *"But purify your hearts before me; and then go ye into all the world, and preach my gospel unto every creature who has not received it."*

Everyone in the mission loved and looked up to Elder Berrett. He had a wonderful, warm smile; served obediently; and refused to break mission rules. His regular weekly letters were filled with his happiness at seeing people's lives change when they accepted and lived gospel principles. Josh had a unique sense of humor, and at the end of each letter he wrote: "I'm through writing, so I hope you're through reading, goodbye."

Josh expressed apprehension about coming home at the completion of his mission. His father had passed away while Josh was serving, and Josh expressed sadness that he had left home with two parents and was coming home to only one.

On the day of the accident, Josh and his companion, Elder Rogers, were driving on a country road at Higley and Queen Creek. As his companion turned left, a truck hit into the passenger side, killing Josh instantly, only three weeks prior to his scheduled mission release. Mission President Steve Allen stated that the car was so badly demolished, it was a miracle Elder Rogers survived, suffering only a few broken bones.

Our stake president, LeGrand Curtis, and his counselor, Denny Berrett (a cousin to my deceased husband), came to tell me about Josh's death. President Berrett had been our bishop and knew I had been through a difficult time with my husband's death. President Berrett told me he had been working in his garden when he felt my husband's spirit, and a little later felt Josh's spirit. Soon after that he received the phone call about Josh's death. His words comforted me, and I knew Josh was meant to be with his dad. He loved us all, but he adored his dad.

Many of us received spiritual comfort and help before Josh's death. His sister Caroline dreamed about her father dying, which I believe was a gift from her Heavenly Father. After her father passed away, Caroline said she felt that I was going to die. I told her about the uneasy feelings my husband experienced during my pregnancy with our stillborn daughter. I told

Caroline that it could be someone else who might die. Josh's friend Shawn Bekkmellom was set apart for his mission the night Josh died and said he envisioned Josh holding the Savior's hand.

President Allen sent a two-page letter telling us some wonderful stories about Josh. President and Sister Allen held a missionary farewell for Josh and sent us a videotape of the beautiful service.

President Gordon B. Hinckley, President Thomas S. Monson, and President James E. Faust sent a letter full of comfort and shared the insight that Josh has gone on to a higher realm and is still preaching the gospel. The Missionary Department of the Church sent a consoling letter signed by L. Aldin Porter, Rulon G. Craven, and Earl S. Tingey. Elder David B. Haight came to the viewing and gave us his loving concern. Elder J. Ballard Washburn sent a letter telling us Josh is a special young man, how he felt the Spirit and recognized everyone's excellent attitude. I also received a letter of condolence from Utah Senator and Mrs. Orrin Hatch. People in Josh's mission sent loving letters and cards expressing their love. The bishop from Queen Creek, where Josh served at the end, wrote that he and his ward members loved and appreciated Josh, and he shared some spiritual experiences.

Elder J. Ballard Washburn presided over Josh's funeral. My father spoke, noting that Josh's grandmothers and I were able to comfort everyone else. Family and ward members shared love with us.

When our second son, Jason, began to plan for his mission, people said, "How can you let Jason go, when you lost your first son?" I replied, "Jason struggled a lot more than Josh, then turned his life around, and now he wants to serve the Lord. Why wouldn't I be happy about that?"

Through this whole experience, I know the Lord is very mindful of each of us and He is there to guide and comfort us if we will just call on Him for His help. I also learned from the scriptures that Heavenly Father will not give me more than I can handle. I know I picked this bag of problems, and I don't want anyone else's problems.

My dear sister, Stacy, called me a few weeks ago and said that if it had not been for me and my strength, she wouldn't have become active in the Church or been endowed in the temple. Recently her son, Dustin Godnick, was in an alcohol-related auto accident and was left a quadriplegic. Stacy said she could bear it all because of how I handled my personal tragedies with strength and bravery. I feel she is the braver one, because I don't think I could handle what she does. So, you see we all help one another as we share our lives and struggles. Dustin has since been endowed and married in the temple. He has made great changes in his life. He was a torchbearer for the

2002 Olympic Games in Utah and speaks at youth firesides warning that drinking causes serious problems.

Josh's companion, Elder Stephen Rogers, who was driving when Josh died, asked President Allen to phone and see if I held any feelings of blame toward him. I said, "No, Josh is where he is supposed to be, with his dad in heaven, and I hold no ill feelings." Elder Rogers came to see me after he completed his mission, and we have kept in touch.

The man who drove the vehicle that killed my son has never contacted us, but if he does, I will tell him that the accident was Josh's steppingstone back to his Heavenly Father. His is a plan of love, and I know of no greater love than our Heavenly Father's love for each of us. If we exercise our faith and help others, we will find our way to God.

After Josh's death, I became depressed, lying in bed all day. I realized I needed to think of others and began looking for someone to help. I started taking my handicapped niece, Karalee, to dinner and the movies. We had lots of fun, and her parents had some free time. I know Karalee is very close to heaven; she sometimes tells me she sees Vaughn, Josh, and Grandpa. I am grateful she has helped me miss Josh and his father, Vaughn, a lot less.

Two years after Josh's death, I visited with my cousin at a family reunion. He told me of an experience when he couldn't find his young daughter and feared she had drowned. While he shared this story, I felt a pain in my heart for Josh so intense I thought my heart would burst, and I realized I hadn't properly mourned his death. It dawned on me what Heavenly Father may have experienced at the death of his son, Jesus Christ. My son died in a car wreck; His son was whipped, mocked, and spit upon, then crucified by his own people. I felt so sad for our Heavenly Father; and then my tears began to flow.

Jason and his fiancée Adrienne were married 11 November 1998. Thanksgiving Eve, a few weeks later, my daughter Caroline was away. That night Josh came to me in a dream telling that as my kids left home, I would be much lonelier, but that he and my husband would watch over me. Now I am a grandmother and have told my grandchildren about their Uncle Josh who died while serving the Lord.

Enos 1:27 reminds me of my husband, Vaughn, and my son Josh, who are in heaven, sharing the gospel with others. *"And I soon go to the place of my rest, which is with my Redeemer; for I know that in him I shall rest. And I rejoice in the day when my mortal shall put on immortality, and shall stand before him; then shall I see his face with pleasure, and he will say unto me: Come unto me, ye blessed, there is a place prepared for you in the mansions of my Father. Amen.*"

I love my Heavenly Father and Jesus Christ, and am grateful for the wonderful gospel plan we have and how we view death as a new beginning toward eternity. I thank my Heavenly Father and Jesus Christ for being there for me and my family.

Norman Black

Born: 5 March 1927, Kirtland, San Juan, New Mexico
Parents: John Martin Black and Sylvia Evans Black
Siblings: John Owen, William Morley, Loren, Marion, Harold Chester,
Thomas Leroy, Carl Evans, Ethel, Sylvia Ruth, Nellie
Mission: Central Atlantic States
Time of service: 5 May 1948 to 23 May 1949
Cause of death: Drowning
Date and place of death: 23 May 1949, near Cherokee, North Carolina
Age at time of death: 22
Place of burial: Kirtland Fruitland Cemetery,
Kirtland, San Juan, New Mexico
Story related by: Jay Black, nephew; Francis Black, nephew;
Elaine Ferguson, niece; and Dale Jolley, mission companion

NORMAN BLACK WAS THE YOUNGEST OF 11 children born to John
Martin and Sylvia Evans Black. John's mother was born in Wales and
emigrated with her family after they joined The Church of Jesus Christ of
Latter-day Saints. Sylvia's father, Thomas Evans, was a coal miner, enduring
the dangerous and difficult circumstances in the mines. He and his wife were
grateful for the opportunity to flee the religious persecutions and the coal
mines for the freedom they hoped to find in America. Sylvia was raised in
the Four Corners area of New Mexico, where she met and married John
Martin Black.

Norman loved motorcycles as a young man and had plenty of wide-open space to ride in the deserts in the northern New Mexico area. He later served some years in the U.S. Army and was stationed at a base in Fukuoka, Japan.

Several of his older brothers served missions, and he followed their examples, receiving his call to serve in the Central Atlantic States, Robert J. Price as mission president. Norman traveled to Salt Lake City to spend some time in the mission home and then went on to his mission, which at that time took in all of North Carolina, Virginia, and West Virginia. He sent a picture home on 1 May 1948 of the countryside in Roxbury, North Carolina, with this written on the back: "This is what a little bit of North Carolina looks like. Pretty nice, huh?"

Norman was serving in Cherokee, North Carolina, with his companion, Elder Dale Jolley. Elder Jolley kept a journal and corresponded with the Black family, relating the following:

"We had a great time as we served in Cherokee, N.C. Norman had been in the mission field longer than I when he came to Cherokee. I think he only had about six months left on his mission. We got along good as companions; we were almost the same size. I'm about 6'2" and Norman was just a little shorter. You can be proud of Elder Black, he was a good missionary."

Elder Jolley also wrote: "It was 2:00 p.m. on a Monday over P-Day. We had been working on Elder Black's car, putting new brake shoes on. The cabin we were living in had no running water, so Elder Black said, 'I'm going down to the river to clean up.' He put on his basketball trunk, and I told him I'd go with him, and we went down together. We had no place to bathe at that time, except at the home of a sister whose husband was not a member, and had two young girls and little privacy."

Elder Jolley was careful to say that he and Elder Black were not breaking mission rules, saying that Elder Black was a fine elder and would never disobey the rules. They lived in an area with very poor living conditions, and they had permission from the mission president to bathe in the lake formed by a dam.

Elder Jolley continues: "There had been some trouble in Cherokee with a local minister. Talk was going around that the missionaries were out there to try to get young ladies to go to Salt Lake and live in the Salt Lake Temple.

"The water at the river was cold, so we cleaned off as fast as we could. There was a small dam down stream that backed the water up so it was quite deep. We had cleaned up and I started up the bank ahead of him. I'd only gotten part way up when he called for help. I turned and saw him in the middle of the river. At that place it was about 30 feet wide, but it was deep. I got to him, he grabbed me and we both went down. I got him up and almost to the bank when I lost my grip and he went under again. I got him up again, and he started to struggle, and we both went under and I lost him. Elder Black had to hold me; he was not a good swimmer.

"A young man about 18 years old and his younger brother were on the far side of the river and with a small row boat. I yelled for them to bring the boat, and they came to help. They had on their street clothes. The young man dove for him and got Elder Black almost into the boat when they lost him again. Norman was a big man, and he had no strength to lift himself into the boat, and I could not lift him up. By the time they found him the next time, he had been in 45 minutes. We held onto Norman's clothes and pulled him to shore. I tried giving him respiration until the ambulance came. There was a doctor with the ambulance, he said he [Norman] had been under too long." A death certificate was issued in North Carolina, and Elder Black's body was shipped home to Kirtland, New Mexico, by rail on 25 May 1949.

George Albert Smith was president of the Church at that time, and he and his counselors, J. Reuben Clark, Jr., and David O. McKay, sent a letter of condolence to the Black family, writing: "We join in [President Price's] expressions of sympathy and his feeling that your son, Norman, has been called to a more important mission. The dispositions of the Lord are not easily understandable, but we know that nothing happens to any of us which is contrary to the great economy of life and living which He had laid down for all of us, and we are sure that Norman has gone where he can continue his great work in the salvation of souls."

The letter continues: "May the Lord's peace and comfort rest upon you, and may you indeed be the beneficiaries of that great promise which He made to His disciples in the Passover chamber the night before His crucifixion, in which He gave to them a message that came not only to them but [to] all who have since lived, and who will live in the future: '*Peace I leave with you, my peace I give unto you: not as the world giveth, give I unto you. Let not your heart be troubled, neither let it be afraid*' (John 14:27)."

Letters of condolence were sent to the family of Elder Black. Poems were written in his honor, including one titled "His Real Mission Just Begun," written by a family friend, Lucy S. Burnham. Sarah Walker Evans, sister-in-law to Norman's mother, Sylvia Evans Black, recorded the following in her journal about Norman's death: "Funeral service today at Farmington chapel, then went to Kirtland, N.M. Cemetery to bury him near other loved ones. All his brothers and sisters from Blanding, Utah, were here, parents holding up fine."

Elder Jolley reported that missionary work opened up in Cherokee after Elder Black's passing and that there was no more trouble with a local minister. Elder Jolley's new companion was an Elder Baker, and they went to the home of Sister Thompson and her daughter. They were not members of the Church at that time, but Elder Jolley and Elder Black had met with them several times. Elder Jolley wrote: "We always sang a song before giving the lesson. After he [Elder Black] passed away, it was two weeks before I went back with a new companion. He and I sang the same song, and Sister Thompson and her daughter started to cry. After the meeting, she said, 'Elder Jolley, I guess you would like to know why we cried.' She said, 'Elder Black was standing by you as you sang the song, and he was dressed in white clothing. I felt you needed to hear this from me.' Sister Thompson and her daughter were later baptized."

Fifty years after Elder Jolley returned from his mission, he and his wife returned to where he and Elder Black had lived and served. In a letter dated 10 February 2005, he related: "The little house we stayed in was still there, and the river has changed. The dam . . . has been taken out, but the place looked the same." Elder Jolley again reiterated that they were not swimming and were not breaking rules. He wanted to set the record straight and clear Norman's name, saying, "He was an Elder that listened and obeyed and was a good man. I loved him dearly and wish I could have done more."

Francis Black, Elder Norman Black's nephew, was called to the Central Atlantic States Mission, going there in November 1949, just six months after the death of his uncle. He served in the same area as his uncle and knew some of the same people, including Ma Tahquitte and her family, as well as Sister Thompson and her daughter Cathy. Francis related that the work picked up after Norman's death. Francis also knew Elder Jolley, Norman's companion, but never served with him. Francis had one of Norman's mission suits altered to fit and wore it during his mission.

David Richard Boivie

Born: 9 April 1969, Calgary, Alberta, Canada
Parents: Richard Lynn Boivie and Lorraine Carol Salt Boivie
Siblings: Douglas, Greg, Garret, Steven, Krista, Scott
Mission: Japan Fukuoka
Time of service: June 1988 to 14 August 1989
Cause of death: Head injuries from a bicycle–automobile accident
Date and place of death: 14 August 1989, Sasebo, Japan
Age at time of death: 20
Place of burial: Cardston, Alberta, Canada Cemetery
Story related by: Carol Boivie, mother

DAVID RICHARD BOIVIE'S HEIGHT OF 6'9" made for a very interesting life for him. When he was in second grade, he was taller than his teacher. He grew so fast in grade eight that he spent a lot of time on crutches, as the muscles would tear from his bones. He was not naturally gifted with athletic abilities, but he had the gift and desire to work constantly to improve his coordination and skill. He was a mentally tough competitor and became a star basketball player, competing with two provincial all-star teams. He was scouted to play at the college level and chose to play at Ricks College (now BYU–Idaho), in Rexburg, Idaho.

David had always planned to serve a mission for The Church of Jesus Christ of Latter-day Saints and was our first missionary. He received the call to the Japan Fukuoka Mission while he was away at school and phoned to read his call with us. He was very excited to be going to Japan.

My daughter and I drove David to the Provo Missionary Training Center. He kissed us good-bye and never looked back. David was never one to look back; he was always looking forward and anxious to be on his way. On his mission cards, he had the following words printed: "The road to success is always under construction."

He wrote home each week, asking us to keep his letters, as they would become his mission journal. We have over 150 typewritten pages that are filled with his struggles, spiritual experiences, and funny things. He was very visible in Japan and wrote of his experiences as a "giant trying to live in a culture where people are small," which included showering while on his knees and not being able to shut a bathroom door.

After two months as a new and struggling missionary, David attended a zone meeting and was interviewed by the zone leaders. One of them bore testimony about David, saying that Boivie Choro (Elder Boivie) would be one of the greatest missionaries that area would ever know. When David wrote home about that occasion, he said that it had been such an overwhelming spiritual experience for him, he knew it would be true. He was more successful than most missionaries in that area, as the average number of baptisms was low. I think he was noticed by everyone because of his stature, and his love for the people and for the Lord added to his success.

David and his newly arrived missionary companion, Elder Poche, were riding their bikes down a windy mountain road when a car came around the corner on the wrong side of the road. David pedaled to avoid the car, but the front corner caught his bike and threw him into the air. The back of his head hit the car; he somersaulted over the car, hit the back of his head on the back of the car, slid to the ground, and again hit the back of his head. He was pronounced dead at the hospital. I feel sure that when he realized where he was after the accident, he was anxious to be on to this new venture.

When the stake president and two bishopric counselors knock on your door at 11:30 p.m., you know they aren't delivering good news. They told us the sad news and gave us priesthood blessings. David's mission president phoned and spoke to us—then we were left alone, weeping, and waiting out the night so we could get on with all that we had to do the next day. We told our children and others in the morning that David had died and then began making the first of many difficult decisions.

The American military base in Sasebo located a coffin that would accommodate David's height. He died on a Sunday, which was Monday in

Japan, and his body was not returned home until the following Saturday in Canada. The funeral was scheduled for Saturday. During that week as we waited for his body, our home was filled with people, including parents of missionary sons. One mother said, "I feel guilty saying this, but I'm glad it was not my son." I answered that I am glad it was not her son, because I would not wish this on anyone.

The Japanese culture does not allow a body to be alone, and the Japanese Saints were very concerned because David's mother and family were so far away at this very important time. A missionary accompanied David's body home; his father met him and drove him to Canada to attend the funeral. He brought David's final papers and a note from the driver of the car that had caused the fatal accident. We don't blame anyone; we felt that David would have survived if it had been the Lord's plan.

My husband and I went to the funeral home at 7:00 a.m. and spent some time with him. Then the children came to say their farewells to their brother. We were contacted by Elder David B. Haight, of the Quorum of the Twelve, who told us that great blessings would come from David's passing. We also received a letter from Elder M. Russell Ballard, of the Twelve. We did receive great blessings, but we learned that joy is not the absence of pain. We trusted in the Lord, even though we didn't understand.

There were other letters from members of the Missionary Department, and we spoke with David's mission president. Elder Jacob de Jager of the First Quorum of the Seventy, spoke at the funeral, and we buried David in the Cardston Alberta Cemetery, next to the Salt plots, his mother's family plot. We received letters from all over the world, many from other young missionaries who had chosen to serve because of David's example. He was a well-known athlete, and we were made aware of how many lives he had influenced.

In April of 1991, we received a letter from Elder Peter L. Jackson, who was serving in the Kobe Japan Mission, serving the Japanese people as David had done. Elder Jackson told us that before his mission, he was visiting the city of Nagasaki and met David. He wrote: "Although he was busy, he took a few minutes to talk to me. . . . He gave me a phone number and left. When it was time for me to leave, I called the number, but found that your son was not there and that other missionaries would meet me. The next morning before going to meet the other missionaries, I was told of a Church missionary [who was] killed on his bike. . . . I found it was your son that I had met a few days before. I was so shocked. The whole day I was in disbelief. But I tell you this story to tell you that I was never going to serve a mission;

I never wanted to think of the sacrifice. But upon my return home, I thought about your son's ultimate sacrifice for the Lord and His service. I thought about your son serving and giving his life. I thought how I was not even willing to work. From your son's example, I prayed and decided to serve a mission. But what makes this more special is, I am serving in Kobe Japan where I always wanted to serve, in Japan. And I am serving the Japanese people where your son was teaching. I didn't know your son but for five minutes, but his influence was great. I hope this letter doesn't bring any hard feelings to you. It was my intent to let you know a way of your son's influence on a person."

We sent four of our other children as missionaries, and each one of them thought about the possibility that they might not survive but had the faith to go. Some people have questioned how we could send other missionaries from our family, but we never even thought about it. Because of some events that occurred, we feel that David knew he would die—it was something that was between David and the Lord that had been revealed in David's patriarchal blessing. We had some very sacred experiences, and we have come to understand that the Lord's hand and David's choice were evident in this event.

We asked all of David's returning missionary friends to report home to us if they could. We had a number come visit with us, and one who served in Japan who has since left the Church said that his mission was so difficult that he envied the fact that David had died. We visited with another family whose missionary died. We know of some families who doubt the truth of the gospel when difficult trials come to them.

Life is always a treasure, and we cannot be afraid to live it, because we know we all must die. The real challenge is to live in such a way that we know we can return to our Heavenly Father. Someone once told me they thought I had lived a tragic life. I don't feel that way. I think our lives have been filled with many blessings, and in spite of the fact that we have had trials, we know that this life is the test. As far as we are concerned, the Lord's ways are not ours, and that is fine. We know He blessed us with comfort, and we know He is in charge.

Joseph Israel Bookstaber

Born: 14 November 1977, Boston, Massachusetts
Parents: Richard M. Bookstaber and Pamela Flynn Bookstaber
Siblings: David, Daniel, Paul, Erica, Stephen
Mission: Thailand Bangkok
Time of service: 9 July 1997 to 8 November 1997
Cause of death: Bicycle–automobile hit-and-run accident
Date and place of death: 8 November 1997, Chiang Rai, Thailand
Age at time of death: 19
Place of burial: Fair Mount Cemetery, Chatham, New Jersey
Story related by: Pamela Flynn Bookstaber, mother

FROM EARLY CHILDHOOD ON, Joseph Israel Bookstaber was a gifted young man with a passion for classical music, math, and science. He excelled academically and hoped to make a career as a professor of math and physics. He had a cheerful disposition, loved to laugh and make others laugh, and had an insatiable curiosity for the world around him. He was obedient to the commandments and had a testimony of the gospel. Joseph was one of three members of The Church of Jesus Christ of Latter-day Saints in his high school of 1,200 students in Millburn, New Jersey. He graduated with numerous academic and music honors and awards; he was co-valedictorian of his graduating class in 1996. Joseph was also an Eagle Scout.

Dr. Davida Brautman, Joseph's high school French teacher, wrote of him in a letter of recommendation: "He is one of the brightest, most enthusiastic, sweetest, gentlest, finest young men it has been my privilege to meet and to teach. He is mild-mannered and even-tempered, thoughtful and simply lovely to be around . . . the most gracious young man I know."

During his senior year of high school, Joseph received his patriarchal blessing from his grandfather, Dennis E. Flynn. The blessing mentioned Joseph's many talents and priesthood responsibilities. He was told he would serve a valiant mission, which would bring him great joy. After the blessing elaborated on his mission, it ended. There were no promises about Joseph's future after his mission. I wondered what that meant and asked my father, the patriarch. He simply stated, "That's all there was; there wasn't any more." I asked Joseph if he wondered about his future after his mission, but he was happy with the blessing and didn't feel anything was unusual about it.

Joseph attended Yale University, majoring in math and physics. His friend, Seth Harris, a fellow student at Yale, wrote that Joseph gave him hope in humanity because of his love of everyone and everything, and that he desired only to follow the guidelines of his religion and to raise a family. "Family always came first with Joe, and I like to think Joe considered all the people he lived with last year to be brothers rather than classmates."

In April 1997, Joseph received his mission call to the Thailand Bangkok Mission. He was excited to go there and happy to accept the challenge to learn the language and work with the Thai people. In his farewell address, he stated that faith in Christ means nothing unless we put His teachings into practice, adding, "To be active in the Church requires us to attend our meetings, read the Book of Mormon and other scriptures, including the *Ensign*, and to pray every day. . . . We can't reap the blessings of righteousness unless we first labor to sow the seeds of good works through obeying the commandments and trying to live as Jesus taught."

Joseph glowed with excitement as he prepared to enter the Provo Missionary Training Center (MTC). He knew that Heavenly Father was mindful of his life and that He had a plan in mind specifically for him.

Joseph's letters home were happy and hopeful. He enjoyed the difficult challenge of learning the language and described his classes, teachers, and speakers at the MTC as "excellent." He was there during the Pioneer Sesquicentennial Celebration on 24 July 1997 and participated with the other MTC missionaries for the grand finale at BYU Stadium. He wrote: "We got our cue, and the latter-day Army of Helaman flooded into the perimeter of the field from all angles. We sang, 'Called to Serve,' and the live Tabernacle Choir backed us up. The audience of 60,000 went crazy; they all jumped to their feet, clapping and cheering as we waved at them. Some of the people started crying as we stood on the field and sang."

Joseph arrived in Thailand on 11 September 1997. He wrote that his calling to Thailand was "awesome—I can't think of any place I'd rather be." Joseph was serving in Chiang Rai with his companion, Elder Joshua Levi Jones, for two months before his death.

On the evening of 7 November 1997 at 7:30 p.m., Joseph and Elder Jones were riding their bicycles to an investigator's house. Both wore helmets and stopped at a red light. When the light turned green, Joseph was hit from behind by a car, and the driver sped on. Joseph was thrown 15 meters. Unconscious, he was taken by police rescue to the hospital. He never regained consciousness and died five hours later, at approximately 12:45 a.m. on 8 November 1997.

News of Joseph's death brought an outpouring of sympathy from friends and strangers from all over the country. Several of the apostles wrote personal letters. Elder Marlin K. Jensen of the Quorum of the Seventy visited our home. The hundreds of cards and letters were surprisingly comforting; it truly helped to feel the whole Church mourned with us.

A memorial service was held in the Thailand Bangkok Mission on 11 November, attended by more than two hundred missionaries. A memorial service was held at the LDS Student Branch at Yale University, on 17 November, presided over by President Dennis Strobel. The funeral was held 13 November in the Short Hills Ward, Scotch Plains, New Jersey Stake. Elder Donald L. Staheli, Second Quorum of the Seventy, represented the Church. He read a letter from the First Presidency, expressing their sympathy and love. Elder Staheli also read some journal excerpts shared with him by Elder Joshua Jones, Joseph's companion:

"During these two months, I came to the realization that Elder Bookstaber was an incredible and talented person in academic pursuits, and he had all the possibilities of being the greatest friend I have ever had. We talked a lot about life and how we ought to live, and we discussed the doctrine of the Church in incredibly fine detail. I told Elder Bookstaber that the situation we were born into was because of our faithfulness in the premortal existence. He was pleased by that information. . . . He is a very stable motivation in helping me to love the members and to be wise in spending our time in seeking out investigators.

"Throughout the last two months, we saw numerous Thai funerals, and Elder Bookstaber was boggled that people should grieve so much, and he expressed that he was not afraid to die . . . if he worked hard and followed the mission rules; he had done the Lord's will and it was well with him. . . . His head softly rested on his pillow every night with the Lord."

Shortly after Joseph's death, I realized the Lord had prepared and strengthened me to be able to endure this traumatic event. My scripture study had lengthened and intensified. The scriptures came alive so vividly. I realized after learning of Joseph's death that I felt calm and at peace, knowing that the Lord was in charge. I felt the presence of the Comforter from the moment the stake president and bishop came to inform me of Joseph's death. I was surprised at how constant and real the spirit of the Comforter was. That spiritual strength stayed with me for about a year and a half, then gradually faded away.

I knew almost immediately in a very clear and sure way that the Lord had taken Joseph for His own purpose and that He expected me to make this sacrifice and give Joseph freely. I understood at the time that this sure knowledge was a gift to me from the Lord. I worried that Joseph would not be happy in the spirit world, but I was given the words in my mind, "Joseph is living a rich and fulfilling life." My fear and anxiety left.

Some time later, I was in the celestial room of the temple, thinking about Joseph. I felt him say, "I am just on the other side of the mirror." I could not see him, but I felt his close presence for several minutes, and I sensed his happiness and love for us. Another time when I accompanied our ward youth to the temple to perform baptisms, I felt Joseph's presence with us at the font. I felt his joy at the baptisms that were being performed.

One of my grown children who has left the Church called to tell me he felt Joseph come to him and give him a big, long hug. He sat alone, crying for some time and told me he had felt "pure love."

How generous the Lord has been with the Comforter. Because of His tender mercy, my faith has increased, I have no fear of death, and I wait eagerly, with a mixture of sadness and joy, for the day when we shall see Joseph again.

Mark W. Brand

Born: 30 December 1957, Pasadena, California
Parents: Dean O. Brand and Betty Davis Brand
Siblings: Bruce, Vance, Ryan
Mission: Florida Tallahassee
Time of service: 21 January 1977 to 6 January 1979
Cause of death: Automobile–bicycle hit-and-run accident
Date and place of death: 6 January 1979,
between Hernando and Inverness, Florida
Age at time of death: 21
Date and place of burial: 10 January 1979, Kaysville, Utah
Story related by: Betty Brand, mother

MARK W. BRAND HAD A LOT OF FRIENDS, was on the high school debate team and football team, and competed in both speech and drama competitions. He competed at the state level in humorous readings for which he received a superior rating. He was a Sterling Scholar at Davis High School and competed for that award at the state level.

Mark was anxious to serve a mission for The Church of Jesus Christ of Latter-day Saints. We kidded that he would go somewhere he had already visited, which turned out to be true. Mark had won a state Vocational Industrial Clubs of America (VICA) contest award and attended the National VICA finals in Florida. Six months later he was called to serve in the Florida Tallahassee Mission.

A few days before his missionary farewell, Mark received his patriarchal blessing, which contained a comforting passage. He was promised that he would be protected during his mission and that he need never fear for his safety or well-being. He would be given special capacities and responsibilities beyond those of other missionaries, for which the Lord would magnify him. Later that night, Mark told me that he was very relieved by that passage, as he was afraid something would happen to him on his mission, and he had prayed prior to his blessing for an answer for his fears.

My husband, Dean, had been baptized a member of the Church just two weeks before our marriage, and I don't think he truly understood the commitment it took to be an active member. He slipped into inactivity a few years later and remained so up until the last few months of Mark's mission. Due to the powerful faith and commitment Mark demonstrated on his mission, my husband decided to take a temple preparation class with me and prepare to go to the temple so we could be endowed, sealed, and have our children sealed to us.

Mark loved his mission and treasured every day. He had been an outstanding missionary and had been a zone leader and district leader for more than 14 months. His mission president wrote that he was in the top two percent of the missionaries in that mission, and when a certain part of the mission wasn't having conversions, he sent Mark, and the conversions rose. When Mark was killed, just three weeks before he was to be released, we were stunned beyond belief. My thoughts immediately went to his patriarchal blessing and I remembered the reassurance he had received.

A few weeks before his death, Mark sent us a letter as his Christmas gift, written 14 December 1978:

"Dear family,

"This is a very special time of year and a very special time to be a representative of our Savior. I would . . . briefly tell you what Jesus Christ means to me. The testimony of Jesus Christ that I have gained on my mission is something for which I am very grateful. I know there are very few people in the world with this opportunity.

"Christ . . . has become a friend, someone who is real, and like you, someone I admire and would like to be with. Also, I have come to know Christ as a father and a creator. . . . I have also come to know Christ as a brother, and that we were with Him in the premortal existence when he stood forth with His plan for earth life for us and volunteered to atone for our sins. This has helped me to understand the supreme atonement of our Savior; for without this Atonement, the whole plan connected with the creation of man would have been dissolved. I know that the Atonement gives us an opportunity to be freed from sin and to overcome the natural man and become like our Father in Heaven . . . as our brother, Christ set the perfect example for us to follow: how to live, how to be happy, how to endure. . . . Probably the greatest example Christ gave us was love, and He commanded us to love Him and told us the way to love Him (John 14:15). So, I'm very thankful for being able to . . . serve the Lord and I thank you for your support and training . . . How about reading Luke, Chapter 2 [on] Christmas Eve? Ya'll be good and have a Merry Christmas."

Elder Brand and his companion were riding their bikes home after a day of teaching and tracting on Saturday night at 6:30 p.m. They were hit by a drunk driver who was later caught. Mark's companion survived.

Mark's death truly upset his father. He could not see how a young man so dedicated to the Lord could be killed after he had been promised he would be safe. Dean's older brothers who are not of our faith didn't understand why we couldn't send money for Mark to buy a car, and perhaps his life would have been spared. These questions and pressure made my husband feel terribly guilty, that he had not been a good father, or protected his family.

I asked ward and stake leaders for an answer as to how Mark could have been killed after receiving that blessing. The best answer came from our stake patriarch who said that Mark would receive all the blessings he would have received had he stayed on earth, as he is now a missionary on the other side of the veil.

A few days after Mark's funeral on 13 January 1979, I awakened at 4:30 in the morning with a strong impression that I needed to write a letter to Mark's mission president. I went to the computer and typed the words as they came to me, feeling as though they flowed from Mark through me to the 11 missionaries he had served with and traveled with from Utah to the mission field. Those missionaries were to be released to return home the next day. The mission president phoned me after reading my letter, saying that there were words and slogans in the letter that were unique to the Florida Tallahassee Mission. At the final gathering of the 11 missionaries, this letter from Mark was read to them. I still have the original copy with the notes and impressions I received, and several of the missionaries who were there when the letter was read told me of the experience. The letter follows:

"To my brethren: Tonight as we gather together I feel very close to you. During the two years since we left the mission home and made that flight together to Tallahassee, our paths have crossed and re-crossed many times.

"Some of us found our testimonies here in the field and others brought them with them. But whichever way it was with you, we are not the same as when we arrived. I testify to you that all the things we are teaching are true. I know that Jesus is the Christ, the Redeemer of this earth. I am joyous in my new calling.

"According to the patterns of returned missionaries, some of you gathered here tonight will become inactive even to the point of losing your testimonies. Just as in the mission field, this comes not from big things but from breaking the rules. Little rules such as skipping meetings, questioning those in authority, not being full tithe payers, and not going to the temple of our Lord, and these little rules then become bigger until you find yourselves in darkness. The way back is hard. I challenge you to keep the rules—every one. Pray often and stay close to our Lord. Let's keep our group and not lose a single elder. Let's be a 'no-leak' group.

"Don't let your mission end. Preach the gospel the rest of your lives both by words and action. Teach by the Spirit. Keep in touch with each other and help each other be strong. Do it. When during your lives you travel through Utah, visit my family and comfort them and encourage them. When you feel prompted by the Spirit to contact my family, DO IT.

"I leave my testimony and my love for you to take with you back to your homes. We will be together again soon. When we have that reunion, I don't want you to have to apologize for anything you have done with your lives. Choose your companions prayerfully. I loved my association with all of you. It was the greatest.

"Love, Elder Brand"

We had planned to meet Mark in Florida at the conclusion of his mission and to have the opportunity to meet some of the people he had worked with. He could hardly wait for us to meet these people he loved so much. Several weeks after Mark's funeral, Dean and I had the privilege of visiting Mark's mission and meeting the people he had loved and served. We treasured each day and had a great experience.

A few months after Mark's death, Dean and I completed the temple preparation class and were sealed with our children on 12 July 1979. The next day, 13 July, our second son, Bruce, left to enter the Missionary Training Center to serve a mission. Our third son, Vance, also served a mission in 1985. Our fourth son, Ryan, suffered cancer at the age of 19 and was unable to serve a mission but has since fully recovered, married, and is the father of three children.

Dean again drifted into inactivity for the next 20 years. Then, he was called to teach our ward high priest group. And, as a result of attending Missionary Memorial firesides and horseback rides sponsored by Brother David Tuttle and the Parley P. Pratt Missionary Memorial project, Dean was activated. We were able to return to the temple where he participated in sealing all of his extended family members. Dean remained fully active in the Church until his death, 29 April 2008, of Alzheimer's disease.

I have felt comforted about Mark's death. I received a confirmation from Mark that he is fine and very free and that we shouldn't worry about him. On his Preparation Day, the day before he was killed, Mark sent individual letters to each of us, including his grandparents, which was most unusual. The letters arrived following his death.

A few years ago, the missionary who was with Mark when he was killed came to see us. He said that for a few days prior to his death, Mark had talked as though he wouldn't be going home, but would serve an extended mission, which turned out to be true.

James L. Burnham

Born: 25 December 1797, Brookfield, Orange, Vermont
Parents: Elijah Burnham and Abia Bowen Burnham
Siblings: Abiah, Polly, Elijah, Betsy, Ariel, Joshua,
Abigail, Luther Sylvester, Jacob, Sarah
Spouse: Fanny Hibbard Burnham
Children: James Lewis, Fanny Flavilla, Luther Sylvester,
Edwin Perry, Harriet Florilla, Julius Caesar,
Sarah Henrietta, Rhoda, Emily, Alonzo Freeman
Missions: First mission: Wales
Second mission: Eastern States
Time of service: October 1840 to 1842
Some time in 1843 to 22 March 1843
Cause of death: Tuberculosis
Date and place of death: 22 March 1843, Richmond, Berkshire, Massachusetts
Age at time of death: 45
Place of burial: 23 March 1843, West Stockbridge, Massachusetts
Story related by: Evva Burnham, great-great-great-granddaughter
(family records; church records; Nauvoo records; state records)

JAMES L. BURHAM'S FAMILY MEMBERS WERE probably farmers, but
it appears from family histories that he was an itinerant preacher, an occu-
pation which his son James Lewis also embraced. The area where James
raised his family in Vermont was often served by itinerant preachers from
different denominations that began to surface. James bought a pew in the

first Methodist Church that was built in Waitsfield, Vermont, which suggests he may have been a member of that church.

At an unknown time, James and Fanny became members of The Church of Jesus Christ of Latter-day Saints and moved to Illinois about 1837. Why they left Vermont is open to question, but it could have had something to do with their joining the "Mormons." Five of their 10 children accompanied them to Illinois: Luther Sylvester, Harriet Florilla, Julius Caesar, Sarah Henrietta, and Emily. James L. Burnham was ordained a seventy in 1839 at Far West, Missouri.

In 1840, James purchased 40 acres of land at $1.25 per acre for a total cost of $50 in the Richmond Township, McHenry County of Illinois, from the government and was the first owner after the Indians gave up their rights.

James departed for a mission to Great Britain on 7 October 1840. He wrote a letter from Overton, Flintshire, North Wales, on 10 February 1841: "I have organized two branches, with about 150 members, and we are continually baptizing, whether it be cold or hot. There is great opposition."

Elder Burnham spent his mission in the country of Wales at the same time Dan Jones, a well-known Welshman, served there as a missionary. At the conclusion of his mission in 1842, he was listed as company leader for the ship *Hope*, a U.S. ship that sailed from Liverpool on 5 February 1842 with 270 Latter-day Saint passengers, arriving in New Orleans on 1 April 1842, after 55 days at sea. The Prophet Joseph often greeted passengers coming up the Mississippi from New Orleans as they disembarked, but it is not known if he was present when this group of converts arrived.

A monument honoring the missionary work of Elder James Burnham was erected in 1969 by the Daughters of Utah Pioneers organization, in Merthyr Tydfil, Wales, near the LDS ward chapel. The marker reads:

> The Welsh Mission
> Oct. 1840, James Burnham, First Missionary From Zion for the Church of Jesus Christ of Latter-day Saints, arrived in Wales, and the first branch was organized at Overton Flintshire with 32 members, Merthyr Tydfil Conference, organized 1844, contained 6 branches. Numerous Welsh publications by Dan Jones earned him the title of "Father of the Welsh Mission." In 1849 a company of 250 Welsh Saints came to Salt Lake Valley. In 1852, there were over 5,000 converts in the mission.

Soon after James's return from Wales, he received a call to serve in the Eastern States, where many of his family members lived, to complete more missionary work. His brother Luther Sylvester lived in Northfield, Vermont, and his son Edwin Perry lived in Roxbury, Vermont. James's enthusiasm to teach the gospel outdid his energy, and he succumbed to illness as recorded in the following reports. The tuberculosis that took his life also killed his son James Lewis two years later.

Elder Edwin D. Woolley wrote from the New York, New York South Mission on 22 March 1843: "He had baptized 20 persons and organized a branch of the church in the Little Rock Village, Massachusetts. On this date also James Burnham, a missionary, died at Richmond, Massachusetts from excessive labor and exposure." From the *History of the Church*, 5:309–10 we learn: "Elder James Burnham died in Richmond, Massachusetts, aged 46. He had been on a mission to England and Wales about two years, and was then on a mission in the Eastern States, and, through excessive labor and exposure, brought on quick consumption. He left a wife and several children to lament his loss."

From the *Times and Seasons* 4 (no. 12): 187–88, by Benjamin Andrews, we read: "I am requested by Sister Burnham to inform you that her husband, Elder Burnham, is dead; and as you are acquainted with his history, she desires you would notice his death in your paper. I have this moment returned from a visit to see her, and found that deep affliction is her present lot. She gave me a letter from Brother Phineas Richards (I think he is a brother to Dr. Richards of Nauvoo) which states that Elder Burnham after leaving Illinois, visited his mother in the east part of the State of New York; thence traveling east, he visited some branches of the church, and built up new ones in Massachusetts, where his labors were very abundant which brought on indisposition that terminated in a quick consumption. He died after being confined six weeks and five days, without a struggle or a groan . . . in the 46th year of his age. The next day, he was removed to West Stockbridge in the same state, where he was interred. . . . Brother Burnham had his right mind to the moment of his death, excepting a short time, about four days before, he was a little wandering; in which time, he clearly manifested what was foremost in his mind, for he was constantly preaching, and praying, or in some kind of devotion. He was perfectly resigned, during his illness, and longed for the time, (as he knew it must shortly be) when he should be present with the Lord."

The editor of the *Times and Seasons* made the following response to the above letter: "We know that he shrunk not from toil, but hardly expected that he would have renewed his labors so soon; his form, however could not sustain so great labor, and he has sunk under the burden; he has died in the cause of God; and dying proclaimed the truth of the gospel, which he preached while living. He has left a faithful wife, and several amiable children to mourn his loss with whom we deeply sympathize. In this afflictive dispensation we must submit to the wise behest of Jehovah, and in taking leave of him until the resurrection morn, as a tribute or respect we must say, he slumbers with the dead, 'peace be to his ashes.'"

James's death was recorded in the Vital Records of Richmond, Berkshire, Massachusetts, p. 89, as follows: Burnham, James, Illinois, Mar. 22, 1843, a. 45.

Little is known about James's wife, Fanny Hibbard Burnham, following his death. Although no death date for Fanny has been verified, it is believed she died in McHenry County, Illinois, presumably in a home on the property James purchased in 1843.

Keith Wynder Burt

Born: 19 September 1908, Cardston, Alberta, Canada
Parents: William Willden Burt and Edith Wynder Burt
Siblings: Vernon, Beryl, Nedra, Nina, Bruce, Beth,
William, Elinor, Kent
Mission: South America
Time of service: 29 October 1928 to 13 November 1928
Cause of death: Drowning
Date and place of death: 13 or 14 November 1928,
off the coast of the State of Virginia
Age at time of death: 20
Place of burial: Lost at sea
Story related by: Susan E. Woods, niece,
from her biography of the life of Elder Burt

KEITH WYNDER BURT WAS THE SECOND of nine children, all born at home. He and his siblings enjoyed their growing up years in Cardston, in the shadow of the Alberta Temple. They spent many happy hours hunting squirrels, helping with the town herd of cows, and playing with each other and their cousins in the close-knit community. Keith's father owned and operated Burt's Grocery Store on Main Street in Cardston, next to the dry goods store owned by his uncle Charles Burt. In 1924, William Burt was called to serve a two-year mission for The Church of Jesus Christ of Latter-day Saits in England, leaving his family to care for themselves. Members of the Burt family faithfully served in whatever capacity they were called.

In 1928, Keith was called to serve a two-year mission in the newly opened South American Mission. He and his family made preparations, purchasing clothing, scriptures, and cruise ship tickets to South America. Keith was to sail to South America aboard the American Cruise Ship *Vestris*, bound for Rio de Janiero, Brazil.

Keith's father drove him to Salt Lake City by car, where Elder Burt met his companion, Elder David Huish. The two took the train to New York, where the ship was docked. From a letter mailed 15 November 1928 from Brooklyn, New York, Elder Huish related to the family that he and Elder Burt had an exciting time sightseeing in New York before boarding the ship. He reported that the ship was beautifully decorated, with every luxury imaginable for two young men to see and experience.

What was to be a remarkable adventure turned tragic, and Elder Huish records what happened on 12 November. The ship, carrying 328 passengers and crew members, sank just 240 miles off the coast of the State of Virginia. None of the 29 children on board the *Vestris* were rescued, and 111 people were known to be dead or missing. Elder Burt was one of the missing. The news made headlines all over the world, as numerous rescues were made and search ships went out repeatedly every morning, eventually conducting recovery searches.

Elder Huish lived to tell the tale of the sinking ship and how the lifeboat they were sitting in was still tied to the ship. Elder Huish wrote: "We saw all this and were forced to take to the water. . . . Keith . . . said to me as he jumped out of the life boat, 'We'll have to take our chance.'"

Elder Huish spent weeks following the disaster searching the beach that was lined with bodies of those recovered in the exhaustive rescue attempts. The final word that Elder Burt's body had not been recovered came from President W. H. Steed, president of the mission in New York City, dated 19 November 1928. Elder Burt and 114 others lost their lives, including the captain, William J. Carey, who went down with the ship. The ship was not seaworthy and was not equipped with a radio or means to call for help. Elder Burt's body was never found.

Keith's mother, Edith Burt, saved all the newspaper clippings, letters of condolence, and insurance papers connected with the loss of the *Vestris* and her son, in a small black box. People from all over the world, members of the Church as well as people from other faiths, sent letters of compassion and condolence to the family, as they all mourned the loss of the "Mormon" missionary. They shared loving words and faith-promoting stories, wrote poems of sympathy, and fasted and prayed for the suffering family. The number of united prayers offered for the missionary and his family was countless. The family freely attested that they derived strength from these prayers. Letters were also received from Elders Melvin J. Ballard and James E. Talmage, of the Quorum of the Twelve; and the president of the Church, Heber J. Grant. Loving words of sympathy and comfort came from Elder Rey L. Pratt of the Quorum of the Seventy, Zina Young Card, and others. President Heber J. Grant informed the family that Elder Burt was the first missionary in the history of the Church to that point to lose his life while on the way to his field of labor. Notices from the shipping lines detailed the lost possessions of Elder Burt, including his violin on which he was proficient.

The story of Elder Burt has been handed down through the ages in our family. Because of the significant spiritual appearance of Elder Burt to his father in the Alberta Temple, accounts of that visitation were recorded in several LDS church publications. The autobiography of Elder Melvin J. Ballard, *Crusader for Righteousness*, includes a version of the appearance, as does *Gospel in Action* by Thomas Romney. Duane S. Crowther's book *Life Everlasting* gives the story, as does Melvin S. Tagg in the book *The Life of Edward James Wood*. Articles have appeared in numerous other publications.

Elder Burt appeared to his father, William Burt, in the Alberta Temple, where Brother Burt served as an ordinance worker. Brother Burt grieved terribly over the loss of his son and became physically ill and suffered extreme mental anguish, praying and fasting to know why this had happened and why he could not have a body to lay to rest. Elder Burt told his father not to grieve for him, that he was fine and doing missionary work on the other side of the veil. Confirmation was made to Brother Burt that his son had actually appeared to him, through the words of the then temple president, Edward J. Wood.

Elder James E. Talmage wrote a letter of comfort to his former missionary companion, William W. Burt, Keith's father, on 4 December 1928 from Salt Lake City:

"I know that in such bereavement as you are enduring, mere words mean little; but I feel assured that your knowledge and enduring testimony of the gospel of Jesus Christ will sustain you and yours even under this great trial. Someday you will understand better than is now possible the reason why such sorrow should be permitted to come upon you. You may rest in the comforting assurance that all is well with your boy, and that, moreover, he is working as a missionary though in a different field, and we may say in a different world, from that to which he had been first assigned.

"If the Lord had given us an absolute guaranty that missionaries traveling to or from their fields of labor, or while engaged therein, should always be exempt from the possibilities of accident or illness, there would be a lesser degree of the spirit of sacrifice in the going forth of our missionaries than is now manifest in the fact that they go to meet conditions such as they are, and to be subject to risk of limb, health, and life. . . . May the Lord be mindful of you and give you a goodly measure of the peace and comfort such as He alone can give."

In a letter from Elder Melvin J. Ballard, dated 7 December 1928 to the Burt family, we read: "He [meaning Elder Burt] could have done no missionary work anywhere in the Church to have obtained the distinction that has come to him. He has fallen as a martyr to the cause. . . . That he is still a missionary, there is no doubt. The Lord has simply transferred him to another field. Why he should have to sacrifice his life we cannot tell. I have had a feeling that it is the beginning of a series of disasters upon the waters. The devil rides as a destroyer upon the waters. He was surely there; and yet in the death of your son there was no triumph, for he goes innocently and purely to his Father's realm where he will continue his labors."

Elder Huish was reassigned to serve in the British Mission in December 1928 and stayed in touch with the Burt family until his death in 1995. The family received $4,000 in insurance money, which was adequate to build a home in Cardston. They moved into the home in the fall of 1929 and into the Cardston First Ward.

In 1987, a headstone was purchased to place on the graves of William and Edith Burt. Under their names is the inscription: "In Memoriam, Keith Wynder Burt, Missionary to South America—Lost at Sea; Sept. 1908 to Nov. 1928."

The story did not die with Keith's immediate family when they ended their mortal lives. Children from succeeding generations are being told the story, and all have been blessed with the knowledge that their loved one determined to serve the Lord in spite of the dangers all missionaries face.

Most of Elder Burt's siblings served missions, and many from the second, third, and fourth generations are preparing to serve. Keith's death has not deterred family members from serving the Lord and His children, and many have said they felt that Keith served his mission through them. We all view heaven as a friendlier place with Keith and other loved ones serving on the other side of the veil. In spite of the sadness, much good has come from the incident as we have pondered Elder Burt's transfer from South America to teaching the gospel to those who have passed on.

Lewis Jacob Bushman

Born: 16 July 1872, Lehi, Utah
Parents: Martin Benjamin Bushman and
Lucinda Ladellia Goodwin Bushman
Siblings: Mary, Martin, Laura, Nancy, Sarah,
Edith, Esther, Rhoda Emerette
Spouse: Martha Spencer Bushman
Child: Martha Ruth
Mission: Southern States, Kentucky
Time of service: May 1897 to October 1897
Cause of death: Typhoid fever
Date and place of death: 31 October 1897, Kentucky
Age at time of death: 25
Place of burial: Lehi, Utah, 5 November 1897
Story related by: Lewis L. Griffin, grandson; Jean Griffin

LEWIS JACOB BUSHMAN WAS BORN 16 July 1872 in Lehi, Utah, to Martin Benjamin and Lucinda Ladellia Goodwin Bushman. Lucinda was one of the passengers on the ship *Brooklyn* that sailed around the cape to San Francisco in 1846. Her mother died on the trip.

Lewis graduated from Lehi High School and Brigham Young University. He was sent by Karl G. Maeser to be a seminary teacher in Escalante, Utah, a small community near Bryce Canyon, Utah. He met his future wife, Martha Spencer, in his seminary class.

Lewis and his fiancée traveled by horseback to Salina, Utah, then by train to Salt Lake City, Utah, to be there for the dedication of the Salt Lake Temple in 1893. Lewis and Martha married in the Salt Lake Temple on 2 November 1895.

The rest of the winter of 1895 and the summer of 1896, Lewis worked in the co-op store in Lehi. Wages were very low, so he went back to teaching school. On 5 January 1897, a daughter was born to Lewis and Martha, named Martha Ruth Bushman.

During the latter part of February, a "Box B" letter came from the authorities of The Church of Jesus Christ of Latter-day Saints, asking Lewis to fill a mission sometime later in the spring. It was a hard decision for Lewis to make. The baby was only three months old, but they dared not turn down the call.

Lewis left for Salt Lake City after school was out. From Salt Lake he traveled first to Chattanooga, Tennessee, then was transferred to Kentucky (he was in a swampy district), where he labored for six months. He wrote in his letters home that he attended many meetings and he wrote about the length of his talks.

His wife, Martha, wrote the following account of Lewis's illness and death: "I received a letter from my husband telling me he wasn't very well, but he thought it was only a bad cold, and he would soon be out again. However, the next two days brought a letter from a brother Martinue telling me he would write me in a few days. Right then I began to worry because I knew Lewis was sick if he could not write to me himself. I worried so much about him, fasted and prayed, that he may soon be well and back to his work."

Brother Wakefield was Lewis's mission president, and he was with Lewis about an hour before he died of typhoid fever, on 31 October 1897. Lewis's body was shipped home by train. A brother-in-law purchased a ticket for the body and accompanied it to make sure it was kept on the train. They arrived in Lehi on 5 November, and the hearse had to take the body to the cemetery at once for burial, as the body was in bad condition.

His wife, Martha, had not been told he had died when she arrived in Lehi that same day on the train from Salina. When she was told that he had been buried for five hours, she nearly fainted, writing, "The shock almost killed me."

Lewis had been sick only four days. He was desirous of filling a good mission, and even though he was ill, he had stayed up and worked too long. He worked two weeks while he was sick, until he could not stay up.

Martha lived for 55 years after his death. She said she went to the Salt Lake Temple, and when her name was called to come up to the veil, President Joseph F. Smith came and sat down by her and said, "Are you the young woman that lost your husband in the mission field?" "I told him I was, and I had to shed a few tears. He gave me some very consoling words. I told him that Lewis had to be buried without his temple clothes—only a suit put on in the casket. He said, 'Don't let that bother you for one minute, for he will have them on when you meet him.' He said, 'What are people doing for temple suits that you are working for today? They are just as busy up there getting suits ready for the ones getting their endowments as they are here now.'"

Anson Vasco Call, Sr.

Born: 9 July 1834, Madison, Lake County, Ohio
Parents: Anson Call and Mary Flint Call
Siblings: Mary Vashtia, Cyril Moroni, Chester and Christopher (twins), Ruth (adopted), Dan, Hyrum
Spouse: Charlotte Holbrook Call
Children: Charlotte Vienne, Anson Vasco Call II, Joseph Holbrook, Mary Vashtia, Ira, Hannah, Lamoni
Spouse: Elize Kathrine Kent Call
Children: Chester Vinson, Sidney Banagor, Ida
Mission: England
Time of service: 1864 to 4 August 1867
Cause of death: Illness
Date and place of death: 4 August 1867, Laramie Plains, near Rock Creek, Wyoming
Age at time of death: 33
Place of burial: Bountiful, Utah
Story related by: Lois J. Nelson, great-great-granddaughter
Sherryln Ida Call Acosta, great-granddaughter, (from diaries and letters in their possession)

ANSON VASCO CALL WAS THE FIRST CHILD of Anson and Mary Flint Call. His parents had recently embraced the LDS faith and were soon at the forefront of Church affairs, encountering all the hardships faced by other Saints. Anson Vasco dates the earliest recollections of his life to the persecutions of the Saints in Adam-ondi-Ahman. As the Saints were driven from place to place by mobs, he often suffered from cold and exposure. He was baptized into The Church of Jesus Christ of Latter-day Saints in Nauvoo, Illinois, 1842, at the age of 8 years. When he as 10, he and his parents viewed the bodies of the martyred Prophet, Joseph Smith, and his brother Hyrum, patriarch.

He came to Utah with his parents in 1848, crossing the plains as a teenager at the age of 14. He was a diligent and ardent student, learning the fundamentals from his educated mother and her sister, teacher Hannah Flint Holbrook. He had superior business ability, which caused him to be chosen for various responsibilities and positions of trust in the community in which he lived.

With his wife, Charlotte Holbrook, his first home was at Willard, Utah. Charlotte and her family were closely associated with the Call family as they crossed the plains to Utah. Charlotte was talented and hardworking. She spun, wove, knit, and sewed the clothing for her family, as well as fulfilling the other responsibilities of a mother of seven children.

Anson and Charlotte's permanent home was in Bountiful, Davis County, Utah, where they settled in 1853. Anson was called to serve a mission for the Church in 1857 to the Sandwich Islands. He reached San Francisco, when he was summoned back by the news of the coming of Johnston's Army to Utah, and he returned home, serving duty as a scout in the region of Green River, Wyoming.

On 10 November 1856, he married Elize Kathrine Kent. Her children were Chester Vinson, Sidney Banagor, and Ida.

After the danger of Johnston's Army subsided, Anson Vasco and his families returned to their homes in Bountiful. In 1864 he was called to serve a mission in England. He labored faithfully in New Castle and in Bristol. Anson Vasco kept a meticulous diary, writing in Pittman shorthand, which was popular in the 1800s (the diary was later transcribed by Dorothy Bryson). He kept detailed records of his service in England.

In an entry made Sunday, 24 June 1864, he wrote of a dream he had written about before: "During the night I dreamed the following dream. I saw my wife, Charlotte, had left my house and gone back to her father. I entreated her to return. All the powers of personal persuasion I was master of, all in vain. Her father and mother did the same but she could not be persuaded to come back. On awakening from my sleep I found myself much exhausted and troubled in mind and remained so for a number of weeks."

Charlotte wrote to her husband in November 1864, telling him that she was pleased to receive his letter and happy that he was enjoying himself. She stated that her health was not very good that summer, although she had enjoyed her time with the children. She wrote: "Vienne and Anson have not been to school much since you left, but they are well clothed, have shoes for the winter and started school November first. . . . Vasco, give yourself no trouble about things here. They will be taken care of now. Your father will start south in a few days and leaves Chester to take care of things here. . . . The children talk of father every day and think it is a long time since they saw him. Tell me if you have a comfortable place to stay and as good a living as you had here. . . . Vasco, write often and let me know how you get along. You must excuse my writing, for I am much more used to turning the spinning wheel than I am to writing. . . . Your affectionate wife, Charlotte Holbrook Call."

Anson Vasco was a branch president at Sheffield when he learned that Charlotte had died on 9 July 1866. The transportation of mail was slow at that time, and Anson Vasco did not receive the news of Charlotte's death for some time. He recorded in his journal that he now knew why he had dreamed about her; "I felt that she was then dying which was all too true, for I soon learned that she had died on the 9th of July, the day I was 32 years old." He was informed that relatives had taken the children to rear as their own, and he knew he could not have made better arrangements had he been there. He felt his missionary duties required him to remain in England. When his health became precarious, he was released to return home.

He did not live to reach his loved ones at home in Utah. He died 4 August 1867 on the Laramie Plains, near Rock Creek, Wyoming, just three days' journey from Salt Lake City. His friends and brethren, Heber P. Kimball and Guernsey Brown, cared for him in his last sickness and his burial. His body was later exhumed and carried to Utah the following spring. He was finally laid to rest at the side of his wife Charlotte in the Bountiful Cemetery.

When his father, Anson Call, learned of his son's death, he wrote in his journal that it was "sad intelligence . . . and a great blow to my household, and if ever we needed Divine assistance, it is now." He continued that he had anticipated his son's death after he had not heard from him for some time and that he had had "serious reflections by dreams . . . and peculiar feelings and state of mind for some time past, all of which seemed to foretell his dissolution."

The news of his death came in a telegram from President Brigham Young, but the particulars of his death were not known. On 6 August 1867, Anson Call received the following letter about his son's death from Samuel Carlisle, who wrote: "[Your son] died on the night of Aug. 4th at 12 o'clock without a pain or groan. A few minutes before his death he asked me if I did not think that the Lord would spare his life just 21 days, the time we had allotted for traveling to Fort Bridger, where he thought he would see you or some of the family. But God ordained otherwise.

"He was strong and resolute to the last, and never gave up till about one hour before his departure. His cry was, 'Lord, spare me until I get home.' As he lay in the wagon, I sitting at the bottom of the bed watching him, he never took his eyes off me. Just before he died he said, 'Mr. Carlisle, I think I am going. Come and lay your hands upon me,' which I did and prayed in my feeble way for the Lord our God to bless him, when at the close of the prayer he gave a very loud, 'Amen,' as if his soul was full of anguish, and said, 'If it is the Lord's will that I should go, I am ready.' The burthen of his soul was, 'Oh my people.' Anson V. was a man of few words, hence the hidden trouble that none but God and himself knew. . . . I washed him clean from head to foot. He was very thin, and where the pain affected him on the left side, the flesh was a little black. We dressed him in a new suit of white garments, white stockings, and put a white linen cloth about the face and a white cambric handkerchief over the face. We went some distance to buy some lumber to make a coffin, the size of which was 6 feet 2 by 1 foot 6 inches. We buried him about 30 feet from a telegraph pole . . . one mile from Rock Creek, about 50 feet or so from the main road." Mr. Carlisle continued saying that they carefully placed his body into his blue blanket and lay his head on a feather pillow in the coffin. He placed a headboard at his grave, scribed an inscription, and painted it black. On the telegraph pole he wrote: "He fought and battled long in the weary house of clay, the die was cast, his time had come, and so he's gone away. Respect his ashes."

Anson Vasco Call died in the prime of manhood but had been actively involved in the early days of the settlement of Utah and in spreading the gospel in the British Isles.

William Osborn Chipping

Born: 1 September 1910, St. Albans, Hertfordshire, England
Parents: Harry Chipping and Ada Chipping
Siblings: Stanley, William, Frank
Spouse: Constance L. Chipping
Children: Delia, Andrew, Christopher, Cathryn
Missions: First mission: Birmingham District, England
Second mission: England Bristol
Time of service: 1949 to nine months later in 1949
March 1978 to 6 August 1978
Cause of death: Massive heart attack
Date and place of death: 6 August 1978, Milford,
South Wales, United Kingdom
Age at time of death: 67
Place of burial: Salt Lake City, Utah
Story related by: Constance L. Chipping, wife

MY HUSBAND WILLIAM OSBORN CHIPPING and I decided to leave our home in St. Albans, Hertfordshire, England, for America, so our children could associate with other children and members of The Church of Jesus Christ of Latter-day Saints. We also wanted to be sealed together as a family in the Salt Lake Temple, as there was no temple in England until 1958. My husband's parents were active members, but mine were not at all interested.

During the war years, my husband performed maintenance on airplanes, mainly the "Handly Page" engines, and serviced radios in military tanks.

He was president of the Sunday School Board in the British Mission and later was called to be counselor in the British Mission, serving with President Hugh B. Brown, Selvoy J. Boyer, and Stephen L Richards, and he served with Elder Melvin J. Ballard in the presidency. During that time, my husband decided he would like to serve a mission before leaving England, and he was called to serve in the Birmingham Mission for nine months. The war was almost over, and he faithfully worked to teach the gospel and collect names of all inactive members throughout the district. My husband had a very strong testimony of the truthfulness of the gospel and faithfully bore his testimony every fast day and on every other opportunity. He served in two bishoprics.

We left St. Albans in April 1950, much to the distress and sadness of our parents, as ours were their only grandchildren. It was hard to say goodbye since we did not know if we would see them again. Delia was 8 years old and Andrew was 5. We sailed on the *Queen Elizabeth* and docked in New York. From there we traveled three days on the train, arriving in Salt Lake City the end of April.

After many weeks of unemployment, my husband passed an exam to become a journeyman electrician. He created his own contracting business like the one he had in England. We settled down after 12 months, making friends with ward members, and our children were quite happy. We became busy in the Richards Ward and later the Bryan Ward of the Sugarhouse Stake. My husband served twice as a high councilor in that stake. After 14 years in the Sugarhouse Stake, we moved to the Canyon Rim Stake.

Our children grew up and married; our two sons served missions in England. We, too, decided we would like to serve a mission together, and we were called to return to serve in the England Bristol Mission, leaving Salt Lake in March 1978. We planned to serve for 18 months. Our youngest son, Christopher, his wife, and twin boys moved into our home in Salt Lake.

We worked very hard, walked many miles, tracting and meeting with members and encouraging the inactive to return to the fold. We were asked by the president to buy a car. My husband had to take driving lessons to learn how to drive on the left side of the street. One day we found ourselves driving up a hill in Milford Haven, Wales, on a one-way street with all the traffic coming down to the intersection. Fortunately we hadn't gone very far, and my husband was able to back all the way down to the intersection and turn on the right road. He was very shaken up over this as he didn't like driving, but it was certainly better than walking long distances to where we had to go.

A few weeks later, Bill complained of pains in his chest and arms. A member of our ward was a doctor, and I wanted Bill to see him. As we were out one day, we passed the doctor's office, and I begged Bill to make an appointment, but no, he would not do that. I was beginning to worry about him. We continued on our way and taught and visited until it was time to return home. Days later, Bill complained of pain again, although he continued to do his work. I could see he was pushing himself, but he never made a fuss. He wouldn't take any aspirin or other pain relievers. He stayed in bed one day and slept a lot that night. I woke and heard him breathing very rapidly although he was asleep.

On Sunday, 6 August 1978, he was determined to go to Church and went to warm up the car. We lived above a grocery store and had to climb stairs to our apartment. I could tell he was struggling to climb the stairs. We had our morning prayer together, and then he went to the bathroom to get ready for priesthood meeting. I heard a noise and a thump from the bathroom. I called to him but he did not answer, and I found him bunched up in the corner of the bathroom. I rushed to the elders and told them my husband had fallen.

As we rushed in to help Bill, I could see his face was very red. We laid him down and administered CPR and called the doctor. Bill's face became pale, and he had no pulse. Everything happened so quickly; I was in shock and felt as if I was in a dream. The police and paramedics came, followed by the doctor, who told me that Bill had passed away. I stayed in the apartment until the next day. My son Andrew called to tell me he would come and bring me home. It was a long day. Two dear Relief Society leaders came to wait with me, showing their concern for me. President and Sister Wonnacott came to express their love and sympathy, which was very comforting.

I had no opportunity to say goodbye to anyone since I had to leave Milford Haven in such a hurry. Coming home was very sad, even though everyone was at the airport to meet me. I gave my report to the stake president but was not asked to speak in Church. I have been so very grateful to President Gordon B. Hinckley for attending and speaking at my husband's funeral; he spoke so highly of Bill.

I have learned through my husband's faith in the gospel to know my Heavenly Father more and to try to be more patient and loving through our Savior, Jesus Christ. My faith is strong, the gospel is true, and my Heavenly Father answers my prayers. I am grateful for the many blessings I have received since my husband's passing and have been given extra strength through the love of my four children, two sons and two daughters. I have felt the blessings of being active in the Church and from attending the temple once a week for many years with true friends and family. Genealogy has also been an important part of my life. In 1990, I had the privilege of serving for 18 months in the Washington Spokane Mission.

I know my dear husband will receive many blessings for his faithfulness in the gospel and the great example he has set for me and my family and loved ones. We will be able to rejoice together in the eternities, where we will live the gospel and teach it to others, especially to my parents, brother, and sisters. I am so proud of my family who are all active in the Church, following in their father's footsteps.

Barry Grant Clement

Born: 25 August 1945, Salt Lake City, Utah
Parents: Grant L. Clement and Val Stewart Clement
Adopted Siblings: James Atene, Carol Ludlow, Laura
Foster Siblings: Kearney Barney, Glenn Walters, Kelvin McKinney,
Gary Clark, Antonio Merino
Mission: Stake Family History Center, Springville, Utah
Cause of Injury: 4 May 1964, diving accident resulting in a broken neck
Age at time of injury: 18
Date and place of death: 18 January 2003,
Utah Valley Hospital, Provo, Utah
Place of burial: Fairview City Cemetery, Fairview, Sanpete County, Utah
Story Related by: Val S. Clement, mother

ON 4 MAY 1964, OUR SON Barry Grant Clement came into our bedroom about 3:00 a.m. and said, "I feel sick. I'll call the 'Y' [Brigham Young University, BYU] and tell them I won't be in this morning to work. If I get feeling better, I will go over for my classes." This was unusual, since he never missed work or school. He had graduated from high school with honors the year before and received a scholarship to BYU and started college immediately, not taking a break for summer. He hoped that if he studied German, he might be called to serve a mission in Germany for The Church of Jesus Christ of Latter-day Saints. He would soon be ordained an elder, he and worked as a custodial helper from 4:00–8:00 a.m., saving money for a mission.

Barry did get feeling somewhat better and danced tiny one-year-old Stephanie, whom I was tending, around the room, enjoying her laughter. He played his trumpet and the piano, but shortly after 3:30 that afternoon, that part of his life was over forever.

A crying woman came into the backyard, shouting, "My little boy is in the creek!" Seeing that our backyard was fenced, she frantically ran to the next yard where the creek widened and turned. I called to Barry, told him about the woman, and asked for his help. Immediately he was upstairs, running across the backyard to where he could dive into the creek, but he didn't know the level of the water was down. As he ran across the backyard, I was shown what was to happen and shouted, "No Barry, don't!" Then softly I said, "Oh, Heavenly Father, you are not ready for him yet, are you?"

Hearing the splash, I ran to the neighbor's backyard and saw Barry floating face down. The woman was in the water, beating the bushes and crying, "Please help me find my little boy!" I answered, "I will as soon as I get my son out of the water." When I got Barry's head up he said, "Be careful, Mother, my neck is broken." He never lost consciousness. Some men came to help, and I raced home to call for a doctor and learned that one was already on the way. Barry was carried home and placed on the family room floor. The doctor examined him and said he was paralyzed from the neck down. Barry said, "Kneel down close, I want to tell you something." I knelt and he said, "Now, Mother, when you pray, don't ask for anything special; you just thank Him that I'm alive."

Later that night at Holy Cross Hospital in Salt Lake City, he asked me and his father if the child had been found. We answered, "No, but they were still looking." Then Barry said, "I don't think there was a child in the creek, but I have known for quite some time that something was going to happen to me. I didn't tell you, because I didn't want you to worry. At least now it is here, and I can start facing it instead of worrying about it." Forty-eight hours earlier he had told a friend that something awful was going to happen.

Elder Harold B. Lee and Sister Lee came to the hospital that night, and Elder Lee gave Barry a blessing. On a subsequent visit they presented Barry with a copy of *Teachings of the Prophet Joseph Smith* with a personal note written on the fly leaf. Cards, letters, phone calls, and visits to our home in Springville continued through the years. We felt humble to have a prophet in our home and feel his love and concern.

Ward members fasted, prayed, and brought cards, food, and money, as did our extended family and friends. Newspaper articles appeared, and we were overwhelmed with the outpouring of love! Barry's words, "Don't ask for anything special; just thank Him that I'm alive," became an anchor. If Barry could accept the Lord's will, we could do the same. A month later, our bishopric came to the hospital and ordained him an elder.

About five months later, when I entered his hospital room, I could see he was very depressed, really broken-hearted. An electric typewriter and an electric wheelchair were to be delivered that day; the doctor wanted him to learn to use both before returning home. I thought perhaps the chair was the reason for his sadness and said, "Please don't feel badly about the chair." He quickly replied, "Oh, Mother, it isn't the chair, but do you realize how many months I could have been in the mission field for the price of that chair?"

By the middle of November, Barry was home, but his life was very painful and difficult. He tried so hard not to complain and didn't want to make things harder for us. He only mentioned two sorrows: "Now I'll never get my mission" and "I'll never feel a child in my arms again."

When his friends had received their patriarchal blessings, Barry didn't want one. As years went by, he still didn't want one. "I just don't feel that it is the right time." Not long after the accident, he said, "Now I can have my blessing and not read into it something that is not there." On 3 January, the stake patriarch came to our home and gave Barry a blessing. He was told that he had accepted, by covenant, the terms of his mortality and that his life had been preserved for a wise purpose.

As a quadriplegic, with braces on his arms and a strap around his chest to hold him in the wheelchair, he returned to BYU. While there, he belonged to several honor societies. He took every LDS-related religion class offered and never missed an opportunity to engage in a gospel conversation, particularly with members of other faiths. He learned to write with an extended pen in his mouth and control his electric typewriter with a pointer attached to his arm brace. He was very grateful when the computer came along. Other students were very kind, sharing their notes and opening books for him. He graduated in April 1979, with three independent bachelor degrees: German, Russian, and history. After graduation, he still spent most of his time on campus, seeking more education, until deteriorating health made it impossible to continue.

At home, he labored diligently at his computer, fully immersed in data entry for the Family History program. Pain and muscle spasms were his constant companions although he managed to get some relief with self-hypnosis. With towels on his head and shoulders to absorb the perspiration, he labored countless hours with the film reader and computer.

Utilizing a speaker-phone, computer, and the postal service, he maintained gospel contact with friends in Utah, California, Texas, New Jersey, Massachusetts, Hong Kong, and Japan, and he sent copies of the Book of Mormon to most of them.

Through the years he accepted various church callings, including teaching a Sunday School class, faithfully serving as a home teacher, phoning ward members on their birthdays, and scheduling events for the stake center. He also spent many hours tutoring Spanish speakers in English.

The last seven and a half weeks of his life were spent in the hospital. When he knew he was near the end he said, "I feel so bad. I don't want to go not having done anything for the Lord."

He asked to have his temple recommend renewed. The bishop and a counselor in the stake presidency came to the hospital on separate days to interview Barry. Each of them reminded him of what he had done and how many lives he had blessed through his faith and courage. They each gave him a blessing and promised him he would go peacefully.

Barry died Saturday, 18 January 2003, having spent nearly 39 years as a quadriplegic. In sacrament meeting the next morning, the bishop announced Barry's passing and when the funeral would be held. After the meeting, a friend said to us, "Did you notice the bishop didn't say his last name? All he said was, 'Barry died last night,' and everyone knew who he was talking about. What an honor!"

Letters, cards, and communications of every type came to us. We were astonished at the number of people we never knew who told us the effect Barry had on their lives. We had never realized the extent of his influence.

A few months after Barry's death, the bishop asked if we had ever thought of serving a mission. We said, "Of course, lots of time through the years, but we are too old now. They don't take people in their 80s." But they did! So, at ages 83 and 81, we began our 18-month mission microfilming for the Family History and Church Records program in the Alabama Birmingham Mission. Our mission was just another phase of the work to which Barry had so diligently dedicated the final years of his life.

We, his parents, feel blessed beyond measure to have been chosen mortal guardians of this special spirit. We feel certain that Barry is now the missionary he wanted to be. Throughout the entire experience and to the present day, we have felt the hand of the Lord in our lives. Without a doubt we know that Heavenly Father and Jesus Christ live and the Holy Ghost gives comfort and guidance.

Laura May Emery Crowther

Born: 6 March 1931, Athens, Maine
Parents: Leland Emery and Bertha Hinkley Emery
Siblings: Shirley Rollins
Spouse: J. Wesley Crowther
Children: James (Jim) W., Diane, Randal (Randy), Carol Ann
Mission: Missouri Independence
Time of service: October 1999 to September 2000
Cause of death: Heart failure
Date and place of death: 21 September 2000, Independence, Missouri
Age at time of death: 69
Place of burial: Malad City, Idaho
Story related by: J. Wesley Crowther, husband

LAURA MAY EMERY CROWTHER was born 6 March 1931 in Athens, Maine, the older of two daughters born to Bertha Hinkley and Leland Emery. She spent her childhood in the woods of Maine and was surrounded by a loving family. Laura had a loving temperament she displayed throughout her life. She was close to her younger sister, Shirley; they seldom quarreled or became angry with one another. They both loved to cook; Shirley made the main dishes while Laura made the desserts. Laura especially liked to bake cakes and treat friends and family to new dishes from recipes she found in magazines, which became a tradition she continued all her life.

After graduating from Coney High School in Augusta, Maine, Laura began a professional career, working as secretary to the administrator of Augusta General Hospital. After several years in this position, Laura wanted to broaden her horizons and secured a position as personal secretary to the administrator of the U.S. Information Agency in Washington D.C. At the time, Wesley Crowther was a law student attending George Washington University. The two met and later married.

Laura and her roommates had been contacted by the missionaries of The Church of Jesus Christ of Latter-day Saints and were invited to attend a young adult meeting of the Mutual Improvement Association (MIA). The Washington Ward of the Church had a large population of students who attended one of the several universities or worked for the government.

Wesley was serving as president of the Young Men's MIA, and from his vantage point near the pulpit, he quickly spotted Laura, a lovely new visitor. He made it his personal business to welcome and involve her in the MIA activities. She was soon occupied, working with Wesley, in preparing the 1955 New Year's Eve party for the young adults. She and Wesley ended up washing and drying dishes until 3:00 o'clock New Year's morning and began a partnership that continued for the next 45 years.

Laura continued to study with the missionaries and soon asked Wesley to baptize her a member of the Church. She had planned to take an overseas assignment for the U.S. Information Agency, but with some urging from Wesley, she agreed to marry him instead and accompany him west, after his graduation from law school that spring, to fulfill his commitment for two years of service in the United States Air Force. Because Laura had been a member of the Church for only a few weeks, they were not eligible for a temple wedding. They opted for the next-best alternative and returned to Laura's former hometown, Windsor, Maine, where, on 11 June 1955, they were married in a Methodist church by a Baptist minister and were serenaded to the strains of "Ave Maria." The couple honeymooned their way across the United States to Malad City, Idaho, where they spent a few weeks with Wesley's parents before continuing on to Mather Air Force Base, near Sacramento, California, to begin Wesley's tour of duty. Laura, never one to shirk, found employment as a secretary for a local civil engineering firm. At Mather AFB, on 3 June 1956, she gave birth to James (Jim), the first of her four children.

The first Christmas away from Maine was difficult for Laura; she had never had one without snow or been away from home. One day after bemoaning her homesickness to Wesley, they jumped in the car and drove nearly a hundred miles up the mountain toward Lake Tahoe. At the first substantial snow bank, they got out of the car and had a ferocious snowball fight. After a couple of hits, Laura declared she was satisfied, and they returned to Sacramento.

In 1957, after Wesley's Air Force commitment, the little family returned to Malad City, where Wesley established his law practice. Laura enjoyed her new life as a mother and homemaker and continued to increase her faith in the gospel. On 14 June 1957, she and Wesley took their son Jim to be sealed in the Salt Lake Temple. Over the next several years, three more children joined the family: Diane, Randall (Randy), and Carol Ann. Laura continued to teach her children to love the Lord, and they all learned to exercise their faith and served in various church assignments. The two boys served missions in the British Isles, and all four children were subsequently married in the temple. As the children grew older, Laura took on the duties of Wesley's legal secretary.

Laura loved to travel and to return to her home in Maine, where she treated her children to visits to the seashore and woods that had given her such pleasure in her childhood. She insisted that her children become acquainted with quality entertainment and culture, frequently taking them to productions such as the *Nutcracker*, *Brigadoon*, the *Mikado*, and later to *Phantom of the Opera*, and *Lord of the Dance*.

In her later years she visited her children and 15 grandchildren, celebrating their birthdays by taking each one shopping and going to dinner. Unfortunately, her five great-grandchildren came too late to know her.

In 1985, Wesley closed the law office. Laura soon became bored and found employment with the FBI Regional Office in Pocatello, Idaho, transcribing records. In 1997, she and Wesley both gave in to a long-held desire to serve a mission for the Church, retired from their respective positions, and applied for a mission call.

They were originally called to serve as directors of the Mormon Battalion Memorial Visitors Center in San Diego, California. Laura was excited and in short order read several books and brochures on the Mormon Battalion. They were to begin service in February 1999, but in the fall of 1998, Wesley was diagnosed with lymphoma. By the time Laura had helped nurse Wesley back to health, it was too late to meet the call date, and they had to ask for a deferment. In the fall of 1999, they were called to work in the Missouri Independence Mission Office, with Laura serving as secretary to the mission president. In that position she got to know all the young elders and sisters and gained their love and respect.

One evening in September 2000, after a regular after-dinner walk around the shopping mall, Laura complained that she did not feel well and was experiencing strange pains in her chest. Wesley rushed her to the Independence Regional Hospital nearby, where she was diagnosed with a blockage in a vein near her heart. Doctors were unable to treat the problem through usual mechanical methods and elected to treat with medications, which seemed to work well. After a few days in the hospital she was released and agreed to take off a few more days to completely recover. By Wednesday evening she felt well enough to go back to the mall for a short walk.

Wesley was to make a presentation Thursday morning at a zone meeting in nearby Kansas City. Laura planned to go with him and return for a few hours of work at the mission office in the afternoon. When they went to bed Wednesday evening, she was feeling well. The next morning when the alarm rang, Wesley noticed that Laura was lying on her side of the bed with her back turned toward him. She did not immediately rouse up, and he naively assumed she was merely catching a few more minutes of sleep. He quietly slipped out of bed and readied for the day, but when he returned to the bedroom, she was still in the same position. Time was slipping by, and he spoke to her to see if she still wished to go with him to the meeting. When she did not respond, he became concerned, went to the side of the bed, and tried to wake her. When his efforts failed, he phoned 911. The EMT's were there in minutes but were unable to get a response, so transported her to the hospital where she was pronounced dead. The entire mission was shocked in disbelief.

Laura was returned to Malad City, where, at her funeral, she was eulogized by her bishop, Richard Cornia, her stake president, Brent Evanson, her first mission president, V. Daniel Rogers, and Area Authority Glen O. Jenson. Her children also paid tribute to her. Her son Jim recalled the words of Elder Bruce R. McConkie in an address given at the University of Utah, 10 January 1982, which gave the family great reassurance:

"We don't need to get a complex or get a feeling that you have to be perfect to be saved. You don't. There's only been one perfect person, and that's the Lord Jesus, but in order to be saved in the Kingdom of God, and in order to pass the test of mortality, what you have to do is get on the straight and narrow path . . . [and] pass out of this life in full fellowship. . . . You get on the path that's named the 'straight and narrow'. . . by entering the gate of repentance and baptism. . . . If you're on that path and pressing forward, and you die, you never get off the path. . . . What you have to do is stay in the mainstream of the Church and live as upright and decent people live . . . keeping the commandments, paying your tithing, serving in the organizations of the Church, loving the Lord, staying on the straight and narrow path . . . and for all practical purposes, your calling and election is made sure."

Laura was on that "straight and narrow path." She lived her life striving to serve the Lord and her fellow man. When the end came, she was in the right place, at the right time, doing the right thing. Would that we all have the strength to follow her example.

Hal David Dewey

Born: 11 May 1959, Logan, Cache, Utah
Parents: Wade G. Dewey and Lorna Nyman Dewey
Siblings: Steven, Neal, Cheryl
Mission: Chile Santiago North
Time of service: June 1978 to February 1980
Cause of death: Died during heart surgery
Date and place of death: 29 February 1980, Mayo Clinic,
Rochester, Minnesota
Age at time of death: 20
Place of burial: Logan, Utah
Story related by: Wade G. Dewey, father

HAL DAVID DEWEY WAS BORN with a congenital heart condition called a "truncus" in which the aorta and pulmonary arteries are fused for several inches as they leave the heart, resulting in the serious disruption of the normal circulatory patterns, which in turn leads to a considerably shortened life expectancy. At that time (1959) doctors recognized the nature of the problem, but medical technology had not advanced to the point where they dared risk its correction. They told us to "take him home and love him," and if and when corrective procedures were developed, they would let us know.

Hal was smaller for his age and ran out of breath quicker than most other kids, but he was able to do most of the things he wanted to do. When he was 14, his heart specialist informed us that the Mayo Clinic had started experimenting with this type of surgery and asked if we would be interested in pursuing the possibility. Hal (and we) jumped at the chance and applied for and was accepted to Mayo. The surgery involved separating the fused arteries, replacing one artery with a Teflon substitute thus re-routing the blood in the right directions. The positive effects were immediate. For the first time in his life, Hal's fingers and toes were pink, rather than pale purple, and his stamina was much improved.

As Hal approached his 19th birthday and prepared his missionary application papers, he was a little apprehensive about whether or not he would be accepted, and if so, where he might be sent. He had his heart set on a foreign mission, since both of his older brothers had served foreign missions, one to Venezuela and one to Sweden. He would have been happy to go wherever he was sent, even close to home, but he was elated when his call came to Chile! Hal loved Chile and the Chilean people. He picked up the language easily, and according to his mission president, spoke it like a native Chilean.

The first year of his mission for The Church of Jesus Christ of Latter-day Saints went very well; baptism rates were high, he had great companions, and he developed many close and lasting friendships among the families with whom he worked. From his letters we had no indication that his health was worsening as he approached the latter part of his mission. Everything in his letters, and the phone call on Mother's Day, was upbeat and positive. As we later found out, a Teflon artery doesn't grow as the rest of the body increases in size. To make matters worse, it also tends to accumulate calcium and other deposits over time, further restricting blood flow.

Hal desperately wanted to complete his mission and apparently did everything he could to keep his mission president as uninformed as possible regarding his deteriorating health. In spite of Hal's best cover-up efforts, at about the 16-month point of his mission, the president brought Hal into the mission office as secretary so he and his wife could keep a closer eye on him. They wanted to "fatten him up a little" since he was very thin, and they gave him the same care and concern they did for their own family members.

With all this special care and attention, things went reasonably well for Hal, until Elders Bruce R. McConkie, of the Quorum of the Twelve, and Robert E. Wells, of the Quorum of the Seventy, toured the mission. Hal had been out about 19 months at that time. As they interviewed each member of the office staff, they immediately saw that Hal was not well and told him, "Elder, you're heading back to the States tomorrow." Hal realized that while he might have considered "reasoning" with the mission president on the matter, he didn't dare try to dissuade these Brethren! So he started packing.

The mission president phoned to inform us of the situation and suggested that rather than send Hal to the Mayo Clinic for surgery, that the operation be performed in Santiago. He pointed out that there was an excellent hospital there with very competent heart surgeons. Hal's mother, however, was adamant that he be cared for at the Mayo Clinic, saying, as diplomatically as she could, that we preferred that U.S. doctors perform what would no doubt be very delicate surgery. So, Hal was sent home for a few days while the Church Missionary Department made necessary arrangements.

On arriving home, Hal received a letter from Elder Carlos E. Asay, executive director of the Missionary Department, which said in part: "Dear Elder Dewey, We are sorry it was necessary for you to interrupt your mission and return home for medical reasons. We hope your doctors will be able to correct your problem so that you may soon return to the mission field. While you are at home on a medical leave of absence, please remember that you are still a missionary and that you are expected to maintain missionary conduct." This posed no problem for Hal.

Words can't adequately express how grateful we are for the kindness, concern, and the efficiency of the Church, and particularly the Missionary Committee for their help and arrangements in this stressful situation. They were especially considerate of our personal feelings as a family and were in contact with us almost on a daily basis.

Hal was in surgery for a little over seven hours, attended by a team of some of the best heart surgeons in the world, one of whom was Dr. Puga, a Chilean. Doctors discovered that Hal's heart had developed more problems than anticipated. The old Teflon artery was partially blocked and had to be replaced with a larger one, but two of his natural valves were malfunctioning, and a hole had developed between two of the heart chambers. His heart was also greatly enlarged. But, as the head surgeon later reported to us, all the repair work seemed to have gone well. Then, as they were finishing up what they all considered to have been a very successful series of corrective procedures, Hal just quietly slipped away.

The surgeon told us, "It surprised us all; it just seemed like Hal had some place he needed to go." The doctor expressed his personal regrets and deepest sympathy, commenting on what a fine young man Hal seemed to be.

Although deeply saddened by Hal's passing, we are grateful to have had him for as long as we did on earth and to have him as a permanent part of our eternal family. He was a faithful missionary to the end. He gave copies of the Book of Mormon to several of his nurses and was looking forward to his recovery and returning to Chile to finish his remaining five months. His mission president had promised that upon his return he could finish his mission in Arica in extreme northern Chile, Hal's first and favorite area.

The Church's concern for Hal and us didn't end with his death. Arrangements were made for his mother's return from the Mayo Clinic and for the return of his body. Elder John H. Groberg of the Quorum of the Seventy represented the Church at the funeral and spoke at Hal's services. We received letters of condolence from President Spencer W. Kimball, N. Eldon Tanner, and Marion G. Romney of the First Presidency. Elders Carlos E. Asay, Vaughn J. Featherstone, and Jack H. Goaslind, Jr., of the Church Missionary Department sent letters of condolence. We also received heartfelt letters from Hal's mission president and members of his family.

All in all it has been a bittersweet experience from which our entire family has grown spiritually. We are profoundly grateful for our membership in the Church and for the kind, considerate help we received in this time of trial. We're especially thankful for our knowledge and testimony of the gospel and the Plan of Salvation. It is great to know where Hal is, of his well-being, and that we will again get to enjoy his association—each of us doing so with a new heart! His mother has recently joined him, and what a tender reunion that must have been.

Twenty years after Hal's death, another Hal Dewey received a mission call to Chile: Elder Chad Hal Dewey, our grandson and a nephew of the original Hal. This latter Elder Dewey was born a year after our son Hal died and was named for him. Chad Hal had of course heard a lot about his uncle and even carried his missionary picture in his wallet. When Chad Hal Dewey learned of his own call to serve a mission in Chile, one of his hopes, unlikely as it seemed, was to run into someone who may have known his uncle, who served there some 20 years earlier. During his first year in Chile, he didn't find anyone who knew his uncle and had given up asking.

One day he was asked to go on a "split" arrangement to a section of Santiago where he hadn't been before. After learning his name, a Sister Cuevas said she was converted by an Elder Dewey over 20 years earlier and that he had died during heart surgery in the U.S. A wide-eyed Elder Dewey pulled out his uncle's picture and showed it to her. Tears and hugs followed as Sister Cuevas told Chad that she knew that one day she would know about Elder Dewey, although she didn't know how, adding, "Now he, in a sense, has arrived at my home for a second time." Before they parted, Sister Cuevas got our address from our grandson and later sent a beautiful letter to my wife and me, telling us about our son Hal and her conversion. She included a tape recording of her singing "Called to Serve," with her daughter, in Spanish. That was a very special experience for the two Elders Dewey, for the Cuevas Family, and for us.

Royce Harold Durrant

Date and place of birth: 27 April 1971, St. George, Utah
Parents: Harold Leon Durrant and Bonita Terry Durrant
Siblings: Paul Terry, Loraine
Mission: Argentina Trelew
Time of service: June 1990 to 9 May 1991
Cause of death: Asphyxiated by natural gas
Date and place of death: 9 May 1991, Rawson, Argentina
Age at time of death: 20
Place of burial: St. George City Cemetery
Story related by: Bonita Terry Durrant, mother

ROYCE HAROLD DURRANT WAS BORN in St. George, Utah, on 27 April 1971, the oldest child of Harold and Bonita Durrant and the first grandchild of Merrill and Leola Terry of Enterprise, Utah. Royce was born into a family that showered him with love and attention. Three of his uncles adored Royce, playing with him as if he were a toy! Even though they later married and had children of their own, Royce continued to capture a place in his uncles' hearts. Eventually, a brother, Paul, and a sister, Loraine, joined Royce in our family.

Royce's dad is a great sports fan, and we spent many Monday nights at the park learning to bat and catch the baseball. When it was time for Little League, Royce and Paul were favored players, and Royce became the main pitcher on his team. Though he knew there were nine other players responsible for the wins and losses, Royce often felt persecuted, saying, "When they win, they praise the pitcher, but when they lose, it's his fault!"

Later in the season, Royce emerged as the quarterback of his Little League Football team, and he faced the same problem: Every win or loss was blamed on the quarterback, but despite that, Royce's team won the tournament. Brandon and Riley Snow were brothers from the Shivwit Band of the Piute Indian Tribe, and they were friends of Royce who played on the line in front of Royce. They protected him and provided a hole so he could slip through the line for many touchdowns. It was the talk of the town that Royce would be a great high school quarterback, but he never played football or baseball in high school, preferring to join the golf club.

He had a great personality and was a friend to all. He was active in his priesthood quorums and achieved the rank of Eagle Scout. He and his brothers grew up with the knowledge that when they turned 19 years of age, they would serve missions for The Church of Jesus Christ of Latter-day Saints. Royce's high school years went by quickly. He was 18 when he graduated, so he planned a year at Dixie College before his mission.

Royce's only rebellion was his hair. He talked to his dad and me and asked that he be allowed to let his hair grow for the next year. Reluctantly we agreed, realizing that hair length would not destroy his testimony. In May, I mentioned to Royce that it was time to fill out his mission papers. He didn't say much, but left on his bicycle a while later. He came home, looking handsome with a missionary hair cut.

Royce never expressed a desire to request a certain mission, but since he had taken a Spanish class in high school, he felt he would be called to a Spanish-speaking mission. When his call came to the Argentina Trelew Mission, he was excited. This was a new mission and included the southern half of Argentina. I kiddingly told Royce not to be surprised if his first assignment was to Tierra del Fuego—just 500 miles from the Antarctica.

We soon had everything ready to go, and he picked out a couple of hymns he wanted sung in the sacrament meeting where he said "farewell"— "I Believe in Christ" and "Lord, I Would Follow Thee." These hymns were both relatively new at the time, and the words were appropriate for the mission he served.

Royce's first letter home came from his house in Tierra del Fuego, a cold and windy place for most of the six months he served there. I couldn't help but smile. He later sent a picture of himself standing at the airport with his mission president. The wind was blowing so hard that Royce's hair was standing straight up.

His first companion was Elder John Hall III. Elder Hall stopped by at the conclusion of his mission and shared an experience he had with Royce. He and Royce were teaching a family, but after a period of time, the father dropped out of the discussions. After the family was baptized, the father died. Elder Hall said; "Boy, he's going to be surprised when Royce shows up on his doorstep in heaven and asks him if he wants to know more." We were grateful to have Elder Hall help us identify the Argentine people in the pictures that had arrived home with Royce's belongings.

Royce's first transfer came just before his first Christmas in Argentina. His new companion was Elder Ronnie Ayala from Santa Ana, California, and they were sent to Rawson, a city near the mission home in Trelew.

A very sweet Sister Garcé wrote us a long and detailed letter about these two elders as they served in Rawson. She said they were called the Sunshine Elders because when they arrived in the city, the rain stopped and the sun shone as brightly as their smiles. She said that everyone, not just Church members, knew who they were because they had big smiles for everyone. Her letter also contained the details of their deaths.

The rainy night of 9 May 1991, they came in late from tracting and hung their wet clothes around the apartment to dry before going to bed. The previous Monday they had family home evening at sister Garcé's home. Elder Ayala told her about a dream he and Elder Durrant had the previous Friday. Elder Ayala said he dreamed he was walking along a path in some sand and that someone was walking beside him. He looked up into the loving eyes of Christ and also saw Royce walking alongside the Savior. He woke with a start, sat up in bed, and stared at his companion, who was sitting up too. They had both had the same dream. Sister Garcé said she knew that the night they died, they had dreamed that same dream, but when they woke, the dream had come true. They were both asphyxiated during the night from natural gas fumes. We believe that these elders received another transfer from Christ, and we call Royce our "Eternal Missionary."

Bishop Snow and President Howard Putnam, a member of the stake presidency, came to our house at 11:00 p.m. When I saw them at the door, I knew something terrible had happened to somebody, and I thought of everyone in our family but Royce. When we sent him out, I felt that God would watch over him. We were numb with shock when we learned that Royce and his companion were dead. God had watched over our son, just not in the way we had expected.

After learning of Royce's death, many of his friends told us that Royce was a true friend. He recognized them with a friendly smile and an enthusiastic "Hi!" He always had friends at the house playing basketball in the backyard or board games in the house.

Looking back after his death, I remembered several occurrences that indicated to me that Royce knew before he left that he would not come home. Royce began to cry when his father ordained him an elder. After the blessing, Royce put his arms around his father and sobbed and sobbed for several minutes. He never said anything about this to anyone, but I felt, after his death, he must have had some premonition during the blessing that he wouldn't come home.

Royce died on 9 May 1991, the Thursday before Mother's Day. His body didn't arrive home until Friday, 17 May, and we scheduled the funeral for Monday, 20 May 1991. Elder L. Tom Perry of the Quorum of the Twelve was assigned to speak.

After the funeral, Elder Perry came down from the stand, put his arm around our son Paul's shoulders, and together they walked out to the waiting cars. He asked Paul if Royce's death would make a difference in his decision to serve a mission. Paul told him that it would not; he had made the decision long ago to serve. He planned to serve a mission and would do so with two purposes in mind: one in honor of his brother who had been called home early, and the other to fulfill his commitment to the Lord.

Royce is buried in the St. George City Cemetery.

Benjamin Robert Ellsworth

Born: 22 June 1986, Dayton, Ohio
Parents: Cory Paul Ellsworth and Amy Lynn Bowden Ellsworth
Siblings: Ethan, Atley, Emily, Cade, Colby
Mission: Argentina Rosario
Time of Service: 22 June 2005 to 2 December 2005
Cause of death: Train accident
Date and place of Death: 2 December 2005,
suburb of the city of Rosario, Argentina
Age at time of death: 19
Place of burial: Mountain View Memorial Gardens, Mesa, Arizona
Story related by: Cory Ellsworth, father

BENJAMIN ROBERT ELLSWORTH WAS BORN 22 June 1986, the second child born to Cory and Amy Ellsworth. Ben was born in Dayton, Ohio, joining his elder brother, Ethan, and was followed by sisters Atley and Emily, and later twin boys, Cade and Colby.

Ben was a good sibling, loving the girls and the twins as they came into the family. He loved sports and made friends easily. His family moved around a lot, and Ben got to see the world. When he was four, the family moved to Toronto, Canada, for two and a half years, where Ben went to kindergarten and first grade. The family then moved to Hong Kong, where Ben excelled in sports, academics, and the hand-bell choir. Once, after a hand-bell choir practice in the third grade, and when Ben was the wise old age of eight, Ben's parents had forgotten to pick him up. He casually hailed a cab and calmly instructed the cab driver, in Cantonese, how to get home. He enjoyed the ride and showed up at the apartment door to ask his mom if she had 30 Hong Kong dollars to pay the driver.

In 1996 when the family moved to London for three years, Ben was 10 and growing fast. He was a great and serious Scouter in London, earning badges and honors quickly. With the Scouts, he stood on the shores of Normandy, camped in the rain in Germany, hiked the trails of rural England, and cooked award-winning cobbler. He was a fine student in school and played sports, including rugby, which suited his taste for mud and physical contact. Ben enjoyed several trips to continental Europe, including a ski trip to the Alps with Dad. Ben made dear friends in those formative years. Even then, he was known to have a big heart and a love of laughter, but at the same time he had a very serious side, thought deeply, and often held his feelings to himself.

The family moved to Virginia in 1999 when Ben was 13. Once again, he made friends quickly, loved his ward, played sports, and was a fine young man. He cheered the birth of twin brothers.

In 2001 the family moved to Mesa, Arizona, his ancestral home. While there, he and his family learned that his twin brothers had the same awful, life-shortening disease as his older brother. Ben took the news hard and thereafter felt a guardianship over the twins and Ethan. He was the only healthy boy in the family and felt a desire to succeed, both for himself and for his brothers, whom he called "my boys."

With graduation from high school, he entered Marine Basic Training, knowing that following the training he would be released to serve a two-year mission for The Church of Jesus Christ of Latter-day Saints. He was under constant emotional duress during the 13 weeks of terribly hard work, which was by far the hardest work he had ever done. When he graduated, he had a greater love and appreciation for his family, and he was proud of the accomplishment but would not wish the experience on anyone. After that difficult time, he knew he could do anything.

Ben was now a mature, strong, confident, loving, and outgoing young man who was ready to serve a mission. He had rounded his character, remained true to the standards of the gospel, and had earned the required funds for a mission. Everyone around him was thrilled when he received his call to serve in the Argentina Rosario Mission, where he would preach the gospel of Jesus Christ. He reported to the Missionary Training Center (MTC) on 22 June 2005, confident, happy, and determined. He loved his time there and was eager to jump into the work in Argentina.

He arrived in Rosario in August and learned the language quickly. He loved his companions and the people. According to his mission president, Ben "had a bright light in his eyes. He was happy and had an infectious smile. His companion and fellow missionaries loved him deeply. He made people feel good."

Early in his mission, Ben was affected by and loved the poem "Footprints," which tells the story of Christ carrying us when we are unable to do it ourselves. Ben lost his life in a terrible train accident on 2 December 2005, knowing that the Savior of the world loved him and sacrificed His life so that we all might live again.

We have been moved by the support and love from so many people in the ward, stake, mission, and throughout the Church. We received such love and care from so many. We were touched at the sweet way in which we were informed of Ben's death, as President Turk and President Lecheminant sat with us in our living room and cried with us and blessed us. Bishop Skousen and President Turk were pillars of comfort and strength as they arranged for Ben's body to come home, and for all other funeral arrangements.

We told everyone that Ben had been transferred to the "Paradise North Mission." We believe that with all our hearts. If an angel appeared to Amy and me and said, "I've got good and bad news. The bad news is that we're going to take your boy at a young age. The good news is that you get to define the circumstances under which we take him." If that had happened, we would have put Ben EXACTLY where he was on the day he was taken from this earth. He was serving the Lord and inviting people to come to Christ. He was endowed and temple-worthy and clean. He was happy, and he was blessing the lives of all those around him. But of course, we didn't want Ben to go now.

Sweet memories of Ben often flood over me. He learned to play and performed for me, Pachelbel's Canon, simply because I said I loved the music. He carried my pack out of the Grand Canyon. He was the cuddliest, tender, soft-skinned boy, and he loved and protected his little brothers.

Ben's mission president, President Hutchison, has given us letters he received from missionaries who worked with Ben in the MTC and in Rosario. These letters are priceless and holy to us as they describe Ben during his mission as being happy, loving, driven to know the scriptures and the language. He was a shoulder to lean on. He was very proud of his family.

Elder Millett, Ben's dear companion when he passed, wrote: "Elder Ellsworth was an amazing friend. He was a wonderful example for me. I learned many things from him in our short time together, and

I appreciate the companionship and more importantly the friendship we had. He loved his family, he loved the work, and he had a rock-solid testimony of this work and of the Savior. He spoke like a champ and taught like one too, although he was the last to admit it. He had no problem stopping the hardest-looking contact and giving a pure, strong testimony of the Restoration of the true gospel of Christ. I have absolute confidence that he is already settled into his next pench (apartment), with his new, better-looking companion, teaching like mad this same gospel of good news to his ancestors. I know that his body, while lost now, will one day reunite [with his spirit], whole, perfect, without blemish or spot through Christ's infinite Atonement. He passed away in the Lord's vineyard, and as such he was taken into the Lord's house to do an equally important work. I pray for his parents, that they can know that he is well. That I know; he is well."

An Argentine elder said, "He pulled smiles out of people with just looking at them. He transmitted happiness like energy coming from all of his body."

An MTC companion wrote of Ben: "I met a man who had it all. He had that little twinkle in his eye that made him a friend to everyone. He had a voice of authority that would pierce you to the very soul. He was a man that was willing to sacrifice his life for his family, his freedom, and ultimately his God. A man of faith, a man of virtue, a man of honor."

Amy and I would probably not have described Ben in that way; we would have said he was a very good boy who was trying hard to be a good missionary. The only regret he took to the mission field was that he played too many video games and quarreled with his siblings. He came so far and just kept getting better and better. We love our Ben.

We miss Ben a great deal, but we also know that nothing is really wrong here. No foundations have been rocked at the Ellsworth house—far from it. God is in His heaven; we are all in His hands. While the reasons for an untimely death may escape us, we also know from an apostle that true disciples are "portable." Ben was portable. We are happy to leave it at that for now, knowing that this separation is temporary, that we'll see him again, that he is happy and busy, and that he is pure and clean.

The gospel gives great comfort. This is not an idle hope or wish, but is based on sacred spiritual experiences we have had. All men can have that confirmation and a knowledge of the truth of these things through the unmistakable and undeniable whisperings of the Holy Spirit.

So, we go forward with some sadness but also great joy and hope, glad that we had Ben and that he brightened our lives.

Edgar Cox Esplin

Born: 8 March 1887, Orderville, Kane, Utah
Parents: Henry Webster Esplin and Philena Cox Esplin
Siblings: Orville John, Effie, Henry, Mary, William,
Arletta, Alma, Eleanor Philena, Cora, Owen Joseph, Thomas
Spouse: Malinda Elizabeth Spencer
Children: Edgar, Cleone, Velna, Garda, Ines
Missions: First mission—Southern States
Second mission—Eastern States
Time of service: 12 January 1915 to 1 March 1917
25 November 1925 to 8 December 1925
Cause of death: Pneumonia as a result of contracting the black flu
Date and place of death: 8 December 1925, Charleston, West Virginia
Age at time of death: 38
Place of burial: Orderville, Utah
Story related by: Nayna J. Christensen, granddaughter

In 1915, LEAVING A WIFE and a six-month-old son, Elder Edgar (Edd) Cox Esplin was called by The Church of Jesus Christ of Latter-day Saints to the Southern States Mission. He spent 27 months in the mission field and loved the people very much, but he was glad to return to his family. After his return, he and his wife, Malinda (Linda) had five more children, all girls, Cleone, Velna, Hilda (stillborn), Garda, and Ines.

The Church asked for volunteers to serve short-term missions. Edd felt his family had been very blessed and had more than most in the small town of Orderville, Utah. Edd and Linda discussed this, and he decided to volunteer. He was approved to go on a six-month mission to the Eastern States Mission. He sent in all the required papers and readied his family for his absence. His oldest daughter, Cleone, writes what she remembers of that time:

"I remember Daddy doing all he could around the home and garden to have everything ready. He was a blacksmith by trade and he put all his supplies and tools in the barn. The day Daddy left, I remember a lot of friends and family gathered outside our home. They were there to wish him well and tell him good-bye. Momma and Daddy went inside, and I was sitting on the porch railing. I was crying and watching them and listening to them. I remember Momma saying to Daddy, "Edd, if you never come home, I will never regret this. 'We then had a family prayer, and Daddy left. A friend who had a car took Daddy to Marysvale (about 100 miles), where Daddy got on the train for Salt Lake City."

The missionaries congregated in Salt Lake City for a couple of weeks of missionary training, and Edd was assigned a companion, Elder S. R. Godfrey. They arrived in Chicago and then went on to Buffalo, New York. They then went on to West Virginia. They rode the train to their destination. That was a bad time for the black flu, and Edd contracted the dreaded disease on the train ride.

The two men went to the Mission Office in Charleston, West Virginia, and were told to come back the next day to receive their assignment. They were put up in a hotel that night. The next morning Elder Esplin was so ill he couldn't get up to go to the Mission Home. He was taken to the hospital in Charleston. His death certificate states that he died from pneumonia at 38 years of age, on 8 December 1925.

His body was returned to Salt Lake City, but it is unclear whether it was sent by airline or train. His faithful companion, Elder Godfrey, accompanied the body. After the arrival in Salt Lake City, Elder David O. McKay, who was an apostle at that time (and later President and prophet of the Church), and Elder Godfrey took the body by train to Marysvale. A call came from Orderville, and friends, LeGrande and William Heaton, who had a truck, went to Marysvale to pick up Elder McKay, Elder Godfrey, and the body.

A telegram had been sent from the mission home in West Virginia to inform the family of Elder Esplin's illness, but it was lost and never arrived. The family never knew he was ill until the phone call came for them to pick up his body in Marysvale, which news was very difficult for them.

Daughter Cleone wrote: "Momma and all the kids but me, because I would always get car sick, went in someone's car to Marysvale along with the truck. President McKay was so very loving and kind to all of us kids. We were living across the street from the church, and both men stayed in our home. It was a few days before the funeral, and Daddy's body was in the parlor. Men from town, along with Elder Godfrey, stayed with Daddy all night, maybe to keep ice on the body."

The funeral was held in the Orderville Ward House, where President McKay and Elder Godfrey both spoke. Elder Godfrey did not leave his companion until after the burial.

"All of Daddy's belongings and papers came home in a trunk," wrote Cleone, "including all of his tracting materials. Everything was so precious to Momma that we kids could only look at the papers and belongings if Momma was there with us."

Letters of condolence came from several people in the Southern States Mission and from many friends. One special package came from President Heber J. Grant. He sent a letter to the family and a book to each child and to mother. The book was entitled *Up from the Hill*, written by N. C. Hanks.

In a later conference report, President McKay related the incident and mentioned the bravery of Sister Esplin, which was recorded in the *Improvement Era*.

Elder Esplin's parents, Henry and Philena Esplin, had lost another son, William, when he was in the mission field in California. He left behind a wife and a son. William died just 10 years before Edd passed away.

Linda stayed strong in the gospel and never remarried. She died just eight years after her husband's death, on 16 December 1935.

The family has the following original papers in their possession:
Missionary Report, signed by Harold B. Reynolds
Application for Western Clergy Fare Certificate
Instruction to Missionaries of The Church of Jesus Christ of Latter-day Saints,
    signed by Rudger Clawson;
Originals of letters and certificates belonging to Elder Esplin.

Edward Richard Gibbons

Born: 14 May 1894, St. Johns, Arizona
Parents: Richard Gibbons and Clarissa Wilhelm Gibbons
Siblings: Mabel Clair, Wilhelm Smith, Howard Haight,
Amy Rizpah, Lydia Augusta, Francis Clive
Mission: Mexican
Time of service: 14 November 1916 to 3 November 1918
Cause of death: Influenza epidemic in 1917–1918
Date and place of death: Sunday, 3 November 1918,
Manassa, Colorado
Age at time of death: 24
Place of burial: Mesa, Arizona
Story related by: JoAnn Wilcox, great-niece

EDWARD RICHARD GIBBONS WAS BORN on 14 May 1894, in St. Johns, Arizona. He was the first child born to Richard and Clarissa Gibbons and throughout his life proved to be obedient and honorable.

He spent his boyhood in St. Johns and Concho, Arizona, helping his parents with the responsibilities involved in operating a ranch. When he was about seven years old, his father was called to serve in the Southern States Mission. This left Edward to fill his father's shoes and help his mother with the family as much as possible. He was a great comfort to her and carried out his responsibilities as best he could. His brothers and sisters admired him very much and remember him as being very kind.

Edward was baptized 7 August 1904, into The Church of Jesus Christ of Latter-day Saints and grew to love the gospel and bore a strong testimony. At the age of 22, he was called to serve in the Mexican Mission.

Edward was given a blessing before he left on his mission that he would return home safely at the completion of his mission.

Edward was noted for his noble character, and his mission president, Rey L. Pratt, said he was one of the best missionaries in the field. He had mastered the Spanish language better than any other missionary in the Mexican Mission.

His father, Richard, visited with Edward during a stopover in Albuquerque, New Mexico, while traveling back to the East Coast. He did not know this would be the last time he would see his son alive. The following account of this meeting is recorded in Richard's journal:

"Thursday, 19 April, 1917. I hurried and got a bite of dinner and then called at Edward's rooming house on the phone. The landlady answered the phone and said that the boys were out, but she told me the directions to get there. I found the place all right. Her name is Mrs. Frigit and seems to be very kind and devoted to the Elders. She said they would return soon.

"Friday, 20 April 1917. As I was very tired, I went to bed thinking that when the boys returned, they would wake me . . . but when I woke in the morning they had not returned yet. I saw two men (Edward and his companion) step into the boys' room. I supposed that they had just been out for a walk, but instead, they had been up all night with a sick girl, the daughter of Mrs. Smith, a lady friend of theirs. Mrs. Frigit sent her boys up to take the Elders' place so they could come home and visit with me.

"Saturday; 21 April 1917. I visited with the boys and had a good time with Edward. . . . At night, I heard the boys conduct a meeting on the street. Edward led out about the government being of divine origin. The boys went down and staid with the little Smith girl again, and I took their bed and rested very good.

"Sunday, 22 April 1917. The boys reported the little girl to be greatly improved. Edward told of his experiences and how instructive they had been to him. . . . He expressed how he appreciated his home. I took the train at 2 p.m."

Edward continued to labor in the mission field for the next year until the end of October 1918. It was at that time that Spanish influenza was rampant throughout the Southwest, and Edward was a victim. In fact, there were several other elders suffering with the same illness as well as President Pratt's own family.

Although everything was done for Edward that was medically possible at the time, and he was administered to by the bishop, stake president, and other brethren, Edward passed away on Sunday, 3 November 1918.

The following entry was made in his father's journal:

"Sunday 3 November 1918 . . . about 5 p.m. we received a telegram saying that Edward was dead. Mama and I were in the garden when it came, and she was completely overcome. The family all gathered around, dismayed at the startling news.

"Monday, 4 November 1918. I sent a letter to President Pratt telling him to send Edward's body home as we wanted to bury him here at Mesa. . . . We spent the evening talking over Edward's life and thinking of the many things that call up a lot of sweet remembrances."

From a letter President Pratt sent to President Joseph F. Smith, dated 8 November 1918, we learn that Elder Gibbons had died about 8:45 a.m., after being ill for five days. He noted that Edward appeared to have a light case the first two days, "but after that it seemed as though he was stricken with death. . . . He grew worse until the end came."

President Pratt continued: "The body has been embalmed and is prepared for shipment home. We expected his father would come, but I have received word that owing to sickness at home he is not able to come, so I shall accompany the body home just as soon as I feel justified in leaving Elders Call, Hancock, and Barnes, who have been sick with the same sickness for the past week. Also my little son, who for the past four days has been very sick. . . . Elder Gibbons came into the mission house the morning he took sick, and died here. . . . Physically he seemed to be almost perfect, and of all of the elders in the field it would have seemed that he was the best prepared to resist sickness and death."

President Pratt wrote a letter to Richard Gibbons on 8 November 1918, in which he recounted the following: "I have made every plan to start tomorrow morning for Mesa with the body of your son, and had hoped that the four sick ones we have in the house . . . would be sufficiently well to permit my going . . . but this evening my son again has a temperature and one of the elders is not so well, so I do not feel justified in leaving them, with the care wholly upon my wife, and she is not fully recovered. . . . I think I can fully realize how keenly you are looking forward to the arrival of your son's remains, but I trust under the circumstances you will bear with me, and I assure you that just as soon as I can with safety leave . . . I will hasten to bring his remains to you.

". . . Everything possible that could have been done for your son was done. Sister Pratt had secured the services of the best Dr. in this part of the country, who came from a town 28 miles away. . . . The President of the Stake was with him when he died. . . . Sister Pratt had the body prepared for shipping, embalmed and placed in a hermetically sealed casket. . . . The sisters of the Relief Society made the clothes and he is dressed in his temple clothes, and no pains have been spared to make everything just as nice as possible. The body is in splendid condition and will keep so indefinitely. . . .

"I well know that to no one in the world can a son be so dear, and no one in the world will so miss him when he is gone as his parents, and our hearts go out in love and sympathy to yourself and Sister Gibbons in this sad hour of your lives. But may I venture to say that outside of his parents, there perhaps is no one by whom your son was better known, and who held him in greater esteem and love, than by Sister Pratt and myself, and next to you we feel his loss perhaps the most. We come to look upon the young men who labor with us in the mission field very much as our own boys, and particularly in the case of Edward, it has seemed from the very first day that he came into our home, there has been a freeness and a feeling very akin to family relationship, and so we mourn him almost as though he was our very own, and I wish to assure you that had he been so, nothing more could have been done for him in his sickness or in his laying away."

My grandfather, Wilhelm Smith Gibbons, brother to Edward, and other family members believed that Edward's patriarchal blessing had promised he would return safely to his earthly home and were shattered when he died. As a result, most of the family have become inactive or are not members of the Church, seemingly because of Edward's death. My grandfather was never active in the Church and was very bitter.

My mother, Wilhelm's daughter, was never active, but for an unknown reason, my three sisters and I were baptized when we became eight years of age. Three of us are active in the Church today.

Edward's death was a personal tragedy for Richard and Clarissa and their family, but perhaps for Richard it was a special blessing for a greater calling. He was said to have commented to one of his missionary companions, "Wouldn't it be wonderful if we could preach the gospel to the souls in the spirit world." Edward was buried on 14 November 1918, exactly two years to the day he had departed on his mission.

Eldon Tyler Harding

Born: 24 February 1984, Provo, Utah
Parents: Susan Harding and Eldon Harding
Siblings: Randall, Josh, Susannah
Mission: Brazil João Pessoa
Time of service: July 2003 to May 2005
Nature of injury: Gunshot wound to the head
Date and place of injury: 9 April 2005, Joao Pessoa. Brazil
Age at time of injury: 21
Story related by: Susan Harding, mother

ELDON TYLER HARDING FAITHFULLY SERVED in the João Pessoa, Brazil mission for almost two years. Although his blonde hair, blue eyes, and glasses set him apart from the Brazilians he taught, he loved them and the chance to share the gospel with them.

Elder Harding is a hard working, dedicated person who commits himself to whatever task he is given. Even before leaving to serve a mission for The Church of Jesus Christ of Latter-day Saints, he dedicated himself to the Lord in order to do His will. Elder Harding's dedication, service, and the prayers of so many faithful Church members saved his life in the darkest hour.

Just two months before the close of his mission, Elder Harding and his companion, Elder Peixoto, were finishing a long day of missionary work by accompanying a helpful ward member to his home. It was already dark, but there was still plenty of time to walk Paulo through a dangerous neighborhood before missionary curfew.

As they crossed a highway, they heard a voice yelling at them from behind. They turned around to see a young man, about 18 years old, high on drugs, carrying a gun and demanding money. The boy was desperate because he had killed a man the day before and was now running from the police.

Elder Harding was the only one of the three men who carried any money and immediately gave it all to the boy. Seeing that it was only about 20 dollars' worth of Brazilian currency, he angrily demanded they open their backpacks. Of course, missionaries don't carry things of worldly worth; rather they have scriptures and pass-along cards.

The enraged boy pointed the gun at Elder Harding, who stood closest, and shot him point-blank. The bullet entered the middle of his forehead while the largest piece exited just behind his right ear. The impact knocked Elder Harding to the ground, but he remained conscious and got back on his feet.

Petrified, Elder Peixoto fell to the ground in shock as he watched the boy smash Elder Harding's head multiple times into the dirt. Paulo was pistol whipped by the young man as he wrestled him off. By this time, people were coming out of their houses to see the cause of the deafening gunshot. The shooter fled the scene, mumbling that he only had one shot left in his .38 caliber pistol.

Immediately, the members of a family who lived in the area recognized Elder Harding and began to help. The father ran to the nearest fire station to get an ambulance while the mother took off Elder Harding's shirt and tied it around the head wound that poured blood. With the help of this family, Elder Harding was able to arrive at a hospital within 30 minutes.

To his good fortune, and the mercy of God, a skilled brain surgeon happened to be at the hospital when Elder Harding arrived. The surgeon runs a chain of UniMed hospitals with many other doctors in Brazil and visits this specific hospital only a few times a month. It was truly a miracle that Elder Harding received immediate brain surgery with one of Brazil's respected brain surgeons. Elder Harding remained conscious from the time he was shot until the operation began, which is ideal when head trauma occurs.

Elder Harding's family received news of his injury that night through Church authorities. The final word of the night was that he was in surgery, and it was unknown if he would survive. His family was in turmoil and unable to sleep. Their ward bishop and stake president started a phone tree to members of the stake, reporting that a beloved missionary was shot and asking if every member would fast and pray the next day for his recovery. The word traveled quickly, and soon every member of our ward was informed, and so on, including families and friends in many other stakes. Before the night was over, thousands of members of our Church were praying and fasting for Elder Harding.

In the morning, the family received word that the surgery was successful. Elder Harding was awake and had spoken to the mission president's wife, in Portuguese! Within three days, arrangements were made for his parents to receive visas and plane fare to Brazil to help Elder Harding through his painful recovery. When his parents finally walked into the hospital room, Elder Harding looked up and said, "Hi Mom. Hi Dad." From that moment, his parents knew things would work out and the Lord would bless His missionary.

Elder Harding's head was bandaged, so the huge, gaping cut and the Frankenstein stitches could not be seen. The left side of his mouth drooped and his smile was crooked. He was confused at why his parents were there to see him before his mission was complete, and there were other residual problems. It seemed as if he had suffered a stroke and his brain was not totally functioning. He had some weakness on his right side, but that and his drooping mouth improved and returned to normal within a couple of weeks as he exercised and talked. His healing was a miracle. Most gunshot victims do not live; if they do, they are usually paralyzed or handicapped. His neurosurgeon from Arizona saw the x-rays and stated, "I've seen lots of these accidents, but most of the patients are organ donors."

Since he was still a missionary, he could not be left alone, so his parents spent all day with him and slept in his room at night. Additional surgery was required after he healed and improved, and a metal plate was inserted to replace the piece of missing skull.

The days passed quickly, and Elder Harding had visitors every day. His mission president came by on evenings when he was in town, to check on Elder Harding's progress. Friends and members of the Church stopped by to express their love and support. One family told us that everyone in their ward was fasting and praying for "the missionary that had been shot." They said, "The nonmember neighbors are praying for him, and even the dogs in the town are praying." It seemed that everyone in João Pessoa was praying for Elder Harding, even if they did not know him. Members and nonmembers felt sadness for a young man who was harmed so violently while preaching the word of God.

Elder Harding has miraculously recovered with no permanent damage to any part of his body or brain. The prayers of thousands of faithful people and the mercy of Jesus Christ saved the life of this dedicated missionary. He was given an honorable release in April 2005. One month after his injury, thousand of miles away in Phoenix, Arizona, Elder Harding walked off the airplane with a bandaged head, a great story, and a grateful heart.

Two weeks later, he developed an infection and had to have the patch removed from his skull. Six months later, during Christmas vacation, he had his fourth and final brain surgery to have a synthetic mold fitted over the missing section of skull. During that time he returned to college at Arizona State University on academic scholarship. He maintained a 3.5 GPA, which allowed him to retain his scholarship. He worked first with a window washing company, then as a bank teller.

Tyler will graduate from ASU with a bachelor's degree in accounting in 2009, and he plans on earning an MBA degree. He is active in his singles ward and has been the ward financial clerk. He has spent every day of his life since the accident serving and helping others. He knows the Lord spared his life, and he is working hard to show his gratitude to the Lord for the blessing of life.

Our family hopes Elder Tyler Harding's story will be an inspiration to others. The Lord has blessed us immensely and we have been part of an amazing miracle. The Lord has truly raised him from the dead.

Mark William Hendrickson

Born: 13 September 1957, La Grande, Union County, Oregon
Parents: John L. Hendrickson and Afton R. Hendrickson
Siblings: John E.
Mission: Utah Salt Lake City
Time of service: 6 November 1976 to 21 June 1978
Cause of death: Brain Tumor
Date and place of death: 21 June 1978, La Grande, Oregon
Age at time of death: 20
Place of burial: La Grande, Oregon
Story related by: Afton R. Hendrickson, mother

MARK WILLIAM HENDRICKSON WAS friendly and outgoing, with a sweet disposition. He loved football, basketball, and baseball. He was the starting center on the La Grande High School football team in 1974 when they won the state championship. He was the starting catcher on the varsity high school baseball team and played some varsity basketball.

Mark was taught from the time he was able to understand that he should serve a mission for The Church of Jesus Christ of Latter-day Saints, and his friends were taught the same principle. He had cousins and other relatives who had served.

Mark didn't realize there was a mission in Salt Lake City and was thrilled with his call. However, he was willing and eager to go wherever he was sent. He had positive feelings about his call and wasn't disappointed that his call was so close to home. Some of his favorite scriptures were the following:

•Doctrine and Covenants (D&C) Section 1-2: *"Now behold, a marvelous work is about to come forth among the children of men. Therefore, O ye that embark in the service of God, see that ye serve him with all your heart, might, mind and strength, that ye may stand blameless before God at the last day."*

•1 Nephi 3:7: *"And it came to pass that I, Nephi, said unto my father: I will go and do the things which the Lord hath commanded, for I know that the Lord giveth no commandments unto the children of men, save he shall prepare a way for them that they may accomplish the thing which he commandeth them."*

•D&C 112:14: *"Now, I say unto you, and what I say unto you, I say unto all the Twelve: Arise and gird up your loins, take up your cross, follow me, and feed my sheep."*

His letters home expressed respect for his companions and love for the people he was teaching and had baptized. He loved the Saints in the Utah Mission. He had love and respect for his mission president, Elden Cooley, and his wife, Sister Cooley. We were proud and happy with every letter Mark sent home. We loved to get his letters; he was so positive and happy.

Mark fell into a coma on 1 January 1978 in Vernal, Utah, where he was serving at the time. He was flown to Salt Lake City to the LDS Hospital. It was frightening to hear from the mission president about Mark's condition. He called five times that night and said Mark's condition was worsening and they didn't think he would live through the night. I thought at the time that he just couldn't die without my seeing him again.

The doctor didn't know what was wrong with him but took X-rays and performed other tests, including a spinal tap. The doctor determined Mark should have a biopsy of the brain and that was when an inoperable, fast-growing brain tumor was discovered. Mark spent three weeks in the hospital in Salt Lake and had all the radiation possible.

While Mark was in the hospital, President Eldon N. Tanner and Sister Tanner visited him, and President Tanner gave him a blessing. Sister Tanner was an aunt of Mark's father. Our bishop and stake president, the mission president, and many friends were a comfort during that time. Everyone was very helpful, attentive, and comforting.

We brought Mark home on 15 February. He lived for several more months, during which the mission president contacted us several times. Our precious son passed away on 21 June 1978. After his death we received a comforting letter from the First Presidency. The scripture in D&C 122 has been close to my heart during Mark's trials and through the years.

Elder Rex C. Reeve, Sr., of the First Quorum of the Seventy, among others, spoke at Mark's funeral. Elder Reeve was very comforting and came to our home to visit and have a prayer before the service. While he was in our home, Elder Reeve said that the Lord takes the very best to help Him beyond the veil. He has to have help there just like we need to have help here. Every time there is a tragic event when hundreds of people are killed, I think, "Oh, Mark's busy today."

The Lord knew what He was doing. He knows everything, and He knew it was time for Mark to go home. We're no different from any others who have lost loved ones in the mission field. We all experience the same sorrows, but we each grieve in our own way. There were no far-reaching events that occurred as a result of Mark's death. At the time, his brother Johnny cried, and said, "He's my only sibling."

Mark's patriarchal blessing is being fulfilled beyond the veil. There were so many promises that we thought would be fulfilled on earth, and now we feel they're being fulfilled beyond the veil.

Venna Tolman Hess

Born: 8 December 1908, Lava Hot Springs, Idaho
Parents: Rozilla Malisa Dalton Tolman and Lamoni Holbrook Tolman
Siblings: Elbert, Ellis
Spouse: Oel Clark Hess
Children: Venna Joleen, Dennis Clark, David, Loo, DeAnn
Missions: Texas, San Antonio 1962-1964, Missouri Independence
Time of service: November 1979 to 7 December 1980
Nature of death: Car accident during a snowstorm
Date and place of death: 7 December 1980, Council Bluffs, Iowa
Age at time of death: 72
Place of burial: Lava Hot Springs Cemetery,
Lava Hot Springs, Bannock, Idaho
Story related by: DeAnn Hess Franklin, daughter

VENNA TOLMAN HESS WAS BORN IN Dempsey Creek, Idaho (now called Lava Hot Springs). Her grandparents were early settlers in Utah and Idaho. She learned early the joy of working at home and magnifying her callings in The Church of Jesus Christ of Latter-day Saints. Her mother suffered from a lifelong illness, and Mom had to leave high school to care for her mother, which she did until Grandma's death in her 80s.

Mom married the missionary she had waited for, Oel Clark Hess, and together in Pocatello, Idaho, they worked hard to raise their four children and pay their tithing. She supported her husband in his Scouting calling, as a bishop, and as a high councilor. She taught us to never turn down a calling. She had many callings, serving as Relief Society and Primary president, and secretary in the MIA. She played countless hours as ward organist and accompanying soloists and small ensembles who were always practicing in our home.

Her father was struck and killed by a car a short distance from our home as he walked from a ward teaching assignment (now called home teaching), and I remember hearing Mom say, "What better way to die than while on the Lord's errand."

At the age of 44, Mom finished her high school education and went on to become a licensed practical nurse. After their move to Las Vegas, Nevada, in 1962, Mom and Dad served in the Texas San Antonio Mission. Mom loved the hymn: "I'll Go Where You Want Me to Go."

Not long after their return from Texas, Dad died from a fall off the ward chapel roof, where he was inspecting the air-conditioning system. Mom continued working as a nurse and was a teacher in Relief Society. She felt impressed to serve another mission in 1979. While preparing her possessions for storage, she labeled many items with the names of family members who should receive them in the event she didn't return. Much later, my husband told me she had confided to him that she did not expect to return from serving this mission.

Because of her love for Church history, Mom was pleased to be sent from her home ward in Las Vegas to Council Bluffs, Iowa. However, during the move there, she had injured her back and was confined to bed during the first weeks of her mission. Her early letters shared her earnest pleas to Heavenly Father for the pain to subside so that she would neither be a burden to others nor sent home, unable to complete her service as a missionary. Other letters expressed her gratitude for having been healed and her joy at being where she was supposed to be when she was supposed to be there.

Shortly after her one year mark in the mission, Mother was traveling to a Sunday meeting in a car driven by her 23-year-old companion, Sister Senitelela "Cindy" Tonga. Two miles north of Council Bluffs, the car skidded on ice, and the rear of their vehicle was hit by an oncoming car. Sister Tonga was pronounced dead upon arrival at the hospital, just two weeks before she was to have returned to her parents. Mother died about eight hours later while in intensive care. We were told she never regained consciousness and that she likely did not suffer after the impact, a blessing for which we are grateful. She would have been 72 years old the next day, 8 December.

The driver of the other vehicle was 19-year-old Denise McIntosh. Despite severe injuries to her right knee, she left the scene of the accident on foot and struggled three quarters of a mile through the snowstorm to reach help. Our family sent messages of love, concern, and gratitude to Denise and her family for her valiant efforts.

My family was attending meetings at home in Las Vegas. The bishop called my husband from priesthood meeting and gave him a number to call in Salt Lake. The General Authority on duty that day reported the details of the accident, saying that Mom was not expected to live. We left our meetings, went home, and phoned my siblings and extended family members. Mom died later that day.

Mother's body was flown to Las Vegas, where Elder Jacob de Jager, of the First of the Seventy, conducted the funeral service. He related a story told to him by her mission president: The evening before the accident, Mother and her companion had attended a cottage meeting where the film *Man's Search for Happiness* was shown. Mother had been asked to say the closing prayer. She stood to do so, but first bore her testimony, saying that everything the missionaries taught was true. She told those present that the 10th anniversary of her husband's death would be in two weeks, and she was absolutely certain that he was waiting expectantly for her arrival. She expressed gratitude for the gospel and its effect in her life and added, "I've been everywhere I want to go, and done everything I want to do, and if Heavenly Father sees fit to have me come home . . . ," she glanced upward and continued, "I'm ready to go whenever You are ready to have me."

We shed tears of loss, anticipated loneliness, and grief that Mother had died in the way she always feared: in a car on an icy road in the winter during a snowstorm, but we were comforted by her words when her father died, that there was no better way or time to go than while serving the Lord. The account of her last testimony and almost casual, direct statement to her Heavenly Father were so typical of the way she had lived her life and of her relationship with Him that we couldn't resist smiling during Elder de Jaeger's speech. My brother David commented, "Her life was a much greater testimony then her death, although that was consistent with her life as well."

Our family has been blessed with the opportunity to read the diaries of and memorials written for many of our pioneer ancestors, all of whom suffered severe trials. Mom lived up to their examples, which has given me a quiet satisfaction but also has caused me to hope I can do the same. I was not surprised that Mom died while serving a mission. We all witnessed her selfless care of her mother and heard her say that her sincere prayers to Heavenly Father were that she would not live to be a burden on her children.

We were touched by a letter from the presidency of the Quorum of the Seventy. We appreciated the many messages of condolence from members of the Church in Las Vegas. Even now, almost 30 years later, I still meet folks who knew my mother and remember that she died while serving a mission for the Church. Each one takes a moment to tell me something they remember about her, her faithfulness, and their admiration of her determination to live the gospel to its fullest.

I hope that other families who have sent missionaries "home" in similar circumstances have been bolstered by the spirit of comfort that comes from the Lord. I used to wonder if some of my peace came from the fact that Mom was 72 and ready to go home. Since then, two of my sons have served missions overseas, and while it brings tears to my eyes to think that they may not have returned to our home, I know they would have returned to their eternal home earlier than I might have expected. To others who are sending loved ones to serve the Lord, I would say, "Never fear."

Mom's story has been told at many family home evening gatherings, and our joy in her passing while serving the Lord has been shared with many generations of her posterity. One of her granddaughters, Norell Johnson, shared:

"In 1980, I was a senior in high school, looking forward to a great year. I planned to send my senior picture to Grandma Hess in November with my expression of love on the back, but I never got around to it. When I was told she had been killed in an ice storm, I was broken hearted and guilt filled my soul. I cried as I wrote my feelings on the back of that photograph, and although I wished I had sent it to her, I couldn't change what had happened. My mind was tormented by my neglect, and I prayed for peace and forgiveness.

"I carried that picture with me to the viewing and funeral. Before the casket was closed, I had my sister gently place my picture into Grandma's cold hands. I couldn't touch her, but I needed her to hold my photograph. Her hands seemed to accept and hold the picture, so she would see it when she woke from the dead. I left a piece of myself in the casket with her, and I found peace.

"Over the years I have looked back on that experience with gratitude for what I have been taught by my grandma from the grave. I learned to never delay or postpone acting on the inspiration of the Spirit. I had missed the opportunity to tell Grandma how much I loved her when I didn't mail the photograph; however, I freely and promptly tell those I love how I feel about them."

My siblings and I echo our mother's testimony: Our parents and other deceased members of our family are happily serving Heavenly Father to the best of their ability while waiting to be reunited with those yet to return.

Roger Todd Hunt

Born: 20 May 1967, Provo, Utah
Parents: Roger Todd Hunt and Mauna Sue Hawkes Hunt
Siblings: Rachelle, Kristina Marie, Tyler Lee,
Melanee Sue, Ryan Joshua
Mission: Portugal Lisbon
Time of service: 3 June 1986 to 11 February 1987
Cause of death: Shot in the head and killed by a gunman
Date and place of death: 11 February 1987,
in a suburb of Lisbon, Portugal
Age at time of death: 19
Place of burial: Bunkerville, Nevada
Story related by: Roger T. Hunt, father

As ROGER TODD HUNT WAS GROWING UP, our son was known as "Todd," to distinguish him from me, his father, who shared the same name. Todd was the beloved older brother, protector, and example to all of his siblings. In fact, many of the parents in his ward and stake where I was bishop and then stake president often used Todd as an example for their children.

Although Todd was born in Provo, Utah, while I attended Brigham Young University (BYU), he moved with his parents to Alexandria, Virginia, where I attended George Washington University Law School, and later to Las Vegas, Nevada, where Todd lived until he enrolled in BYU, prior to his mission for The Church of Jesus Christ of Latter-day Saints. He enjoyed hunting with his father and playing basketball and skiing. He aspired to follow me into the legal profession.

Todd was an Eagle Scout at the age of 14, was a member of the National Honor Society, and served in many Aaronic Priesthood presidencies and as president of his teacher's quorum. He served as the secretary of his elder's quorum at BYU. At a 1981 ward conference, Todd gave a talk entitled "How to Serve Ice Cream in a Celestial Family." The talk was later published in the January 1982 *New Era* magazine and was used at the time of Todd's death, and for many years after, in the Sunday School Course 16 manual.

Todd always wanted to serve a mission and was excited to be the first in his grandfather's family to be called to a foreign mission. During his time at the Provo Missionary Training Center, he witnessed a presentation on the martyrdom of the Prophet Joseph Smith, which touched him deeply. He poured his feelings into his journal and sent us a copy, asking us to gather the family together and read his testimony, which later proved to be prophetic:

"I sit and write these things that they may never be lost. . . . Joseph Smith died for his friends and for his God. Would we be able to do likewise? The kindness and love to give himself up in the middle of shooting so that his other two friends may be saved . . . Joseph knew he would die—what courage, what knowledge. . . . Joseph knew this, but his love was so great he willfully did it. . . . The Lord reaches out to all of his children who die and seal their blood to him. This experience tonight was great for my testimony of Joseph Smith. It grew tremendously. The Spirit was with me, and He would not leave me. I love that. I wish it was that way constantly. I wish my eyes were filled with tears constantly because the Holy Ghost was with me. . . . Oh my almighty God! I love him so. . . . After the video, the lights came on. . . . The narration was ended with a song. The last words of the song, 'Who will die? He said, I will.' My Lord, sweet Lord, you were there when all others were amiss. My Lord, my God, I love you so. . . . What more can be sung or said for righteousness' sake, or for Him or love can tell, than what we do for our brothers here, and we give them the way back home."

It was Carnival time in February 1987, and large numbers of people were celebrating the season with parties and fireworks. In most parts of the world, missionary hours are 6:30 a.m. to 10:00 p.m., but in Portugal, mission hours were 7:00 a.m. to 11:00 p.m. Elder Hunt was junior companion to the District Leader, and they had become good friends with two other elders who lived nearby. Elder Hunt and Elder Jorgensen were to be transferred the next day, 12 February, so that evening the elders went to one apartment where they wrote in one another's journals and were on their way to the second apartment to do the same.

A neighborhood security guard, carrying a gun, drove by the elders as they walked along. At some point along the way, a car pulled in front of the missionaries, its lights shining in their faces. They heard the car door open and an unseen man began yelling obscenities and shooting. The missionaries fled in different directions. Elder Hunt, the smallest of the four, wearing a knee brace from a surgical procedure, lingered behind, either to draw the attention of the gunman, or to try to dissuade him. Minutes later, the missionaries reported hearing another gunshot but did not know that it was Elder Hunt who had been shot. When the elders gathered at one apartment and then the other, they realized Elder Hunt was missing and went to search for him.

The elders met a policeman who told them to go to police headquarters, where they waited for several hours before learning that Elder Hunt had been shot in the head and had died. The chief of police owned the security company the guard worked for and had dressed the guard in a police uniform, trying to pass him off as a policeman. The missionaries later learned that the guard was the man who had shot at them and gunned down Elder Hunt.

The chief of police was reportedly the most powerful man in the city and used his influence to protect the gunman from any charges. Despite the efforts of the U.S. Embassy, the investigation into the shooting was eventually dropped. To deflect attention from the gunman, the missionaries were charged with trying to steal a car, and the police promoted anti-Mormon propaganda. When the case came to trial, the police were laughed out of the court by the jury. Prosecutors were startled when the missionaries testified of the events in fluent Portuguese. Their consistent testimonies turned the tables on the prosecuting attorney. At the suggestion of U.S. Embassy officials, the area was closed to avoid confrontation with city leaders, many of whom reportedly had ties with a communist party.

Our family did not file any personal claims. Todd really loved missionary work and the Portuguese people. He was teaching a message of peace and love, not an eye-for-an-eye. We felt that by pressing a claim, we would violate the memory of our son.

When the area reopened, the empathy of the Portuguese people toward the missionaries opened doors. People wanted to talk about the missionary who had been shot and the circumstances of the shooting. Membership in the branch jumped immediately from 25 to more than 90, and during the next three years, Church membership in Portugal grew from 12,000 to 34,000.

Leaders of other churches invited missionaries to speak to their groups, and many copies of the Book of Mormon were distributed as a result.

Elder Hunt's funeral in Las Vegas was attended by more than 1200 people, including many members of the press as well as community leaders. It was standing room only, and many people stood outside to listen through open windows and doors. A number of favorable news articles and editorials were written about Elder Hunt and Mormon missionaries. Elder DeVere Harris, of the Quorum of the Seventy, spoke. At the time, I was president of the Las Vegas Green Valley Stake and also had the privilege of speaking.

Todd's memory and example have been an inspiration to our family. Not dissuaded by his death, but inspired by their brother's life and example, both of Todd's younger brothers served honorable missions, Tyler in the California Santa Rosa Spanish-speaking Mission and Ryan in the Ohio Cleveland Mission, spending most of his time in the Kirtland area. The family all remain strong in the Church, serving faithfully in callings and in the temple.

Joseph Edward Hyde, Sr.

Born: 8 March 1842, London, Middlesex, England
Parents: John Hyde, Sr., and Martha Marmoy Hyde
Siblings: Henry James, John, Jr., William, Thomas,
Annie Martha, Eliza Amelia, LaVina
Spouse: Annie Loraine Farrell Hyde
Children: Joseph Edward, Jr., Ezra Taft,
George Lionel (died at one year), John William,
Lillie Annie, Mary Alice (died at one year), Emma Loraine
Mission: London, England
Time of service: 6 April 1878 to 5 July 1878
Cause of death: Illness
Date and place of death: 5 July 1878 on board the ship *Nevada*
in the Atlantic Ocean
Age at time of death: 36
Place of burial: Logan Cemetery, Logan, Utah
Story related by: Scottie Rappleye Munns,
great-granddaughter (from family records)

JOSEPH EDWARD HYDE, SR., WAS THE FIFTH SON of eight children born to John Hyde, Sr., and Martha Marmoy. He was baptized into The Church of Jesus Christ of Latter-day Saints 10 December 1850 in London by his father.

In 1853, at 11 years of age, Joseph left England on a sailing vessel (name unknown) with his older brother John, Jr., and his wife, LaVina Hawkins

103

Hyde. They came through New Orleans and Council Bluffs to reach Salt Lake City, being three months on the ship and three months on the plains.

A decade later, Joseph would discover that his future wife had left England on the ship *International* shortly before he did. As the *International* arrived in the harbor of New Orleans, it struck a sand bar and was stranded. Joseph's ship came along and passed by, sailing on up the Mississippi River.

In 1855, Joseph's brother, John, Jr., left his wife LaVina, whom he later divorced, and sailed back to England, never to return to America. It is unknown who looked after young Joseph, who would have been about 13 at the time and living in Salt Lake City.

At the age of 18, Joseph moved to Logan and operated a sawmill for Ezra Taft Benson, an early apostle at the time of Brigham Young. Joseph was also employed on the farm of N. W. Birdno of Logan.

Soon after his arrival in Logan, as he walked along First North Street, a huge dog came running from a house and growling toward him. Annie Farrell opened the door to call the dog back. By that time, Joseph had drawn a huge Bowie knife as protection. As he passed by, she noticed that he wore buckskin trousers, jumper, and a cap with a beaver tail. That was her first view of her future husband.

They were married 18 January 1863 [some sources say 7 January]. Annie Loraine Farrell, born 5 November 1839, was the daughter of William Farrell, Jr., and Alice Sadler Bird. Joseph and Annie obtained a lot on First South and built one of the first houses in Logan. They lived in that two-room cabin for many years with their five children (two had died in infancy).

On 4 July 1864, at a sunrise salute, Joseph met with an accident. He was playing in the band, when an anvil which was being used to fire cannon shots exploded and several pieces of steel struck him and pierced his body. He was ill several months and was troubled with pain that bothered him the rest of his life. Eleven years after the accident, one of the pieces of steel worked its way out of his shoulder.

Although Joseph never had much schooling, he became self-taught and began the study of many branches of learning. He became quite proficient in drama, music, bookkeeping, and carpentry, enough so that he taught school for several years. In 1868 he became a member of the Salt Lake Theatre Dramatic Company, performing with prominent actors of that day.

Joseph took a contract for grading on the Southern Pacific Railroad and was present at Promontory Summit on 10 May 1869 when the last spike was driven on the railroad by Leland Stanford. He was also employed as a bookkeeper by the Utah Northern Railroad in 1876.

Joseph was active in his religious duties, taught Sunday School in many different wards in Logan, and was secretary of the Cache Valley Sunday School for a number of years. His patriarchal blessing states: "For the eye of the Lord has been on thee for good and from everlasting thou shalt be a great and mighty man in the hosts of Israel, you shall have great faith to do any miracle; thou shalt confound the wisdom of the wise."

Apostle Orson Pratt set Joseph apart as a missionary to London, England, on 6 April 1878. Within the month, he said goodbye to his wife and five children, ages 2 to 14 years. Almost all in the town were at the depot to see him off. En route, he stopped to for a few days to visit his sister, Annie Hyde Marshall, in Galt, Ontario, Canada.

Joseph sailed from New York on 28 April 1878 to London. Upon his arrival in London, he became ill. He was able to visit his parents and family he had not since he was very young. His health, which previously had been impaired by the anvil accident, began to fail, and it was determined he should return home. He left England on 29 June on the ship *Nevada*, and passed away 5 July 1878, when he was 36 years of age. His body was washed, dressed, and carefully enclosed in a lead casket and taken to Logan by Elder Barnhard Schettler, president of the company of immigrants.

Funeral services were held in the Logan Tabernacle, to an overflowing crowd. Moses Thatcher, who later became an apostle, presided and delivered a sermon. Funds were contributed from all over Cache County to build an impressive monument in the Logan Cemetery. The inscription reads:

> "Life's duty done as sinks the day,
> Light from its load, the spirit flies.
> While heaven and earth combine to say
> How blessed and righteous when he dies.
> Amiable . . . he won all.
> Intelligent . . . he charmed all.
> Fervent . . . he loved all.
> Dead . . . he saddened all."

It is amazing to me the strength, especially spiritual strength, those early Saints had. Joseph obviously lacked in physical strength because of his accident, but in determination, he did not fail. He educated himself so that he could support his family, contribute to the community, and serve the Lord.

Despite his health concerns, and a young family, he answered the call of the Lord to go back to his native country to serve the Lord as a missionary.

> Much of the history of Joseph Edward, Sr., was written by his son, Ezra Taft Hyde (1865–1939). Birth dates and additional information were confirmed by research done by his granddaughter, Eiley Dunbar Rappleye (my mother), whose records are in my possession. I also have a journal of a trip Joseph made with wagon, mules, horses, and five other men to visit the southern portion of Utah Territory, 13 April to 7 July 1867.

Bradley Jay Isle

Born: 6 August 1985, Idaho Falls, Idaho
Parents: Kevin Isle and Sharla Isle
Siblings: Brandon Willis, William, Daniel Morgan,
Donovan Scott, Haley Dawn
Mission: New Zealand Wellington
Time of service: 12 October 2005 to 6 January 2006
Cause of death: Auto accident
Date and place of death: 6 January 2005,
Waitohi, Temuka, New Zealand
Age at time of death: 19
Place of burial: Tonaquint Cemetery, St. George, Utah
Story related by: Kevin and Sharla Isle, parents

IN 2003, BRADLEY JAY ISLE had graduated early from high school and began attending Brigham Young University (BYU) in Provo, Utah. He was there two weeks when a call came from Brighton Ski Resort near Salt Lake, informing his family in Las Vegas that Bradley had been in a snowboarding accident, had fallen, broken his right femur in two places, and dislocated his left hip. As Bradley went through therapy to learn to walk again, he told Kevin and me that he felt he wouldn't have a very long life.

Starting in September 2003, he spent two years at BYU–Idaho on the Fall–Winter track, working summers to save money. While there, he was a service coordinator for the "Happy Factory" project, collecting wood to make and paint toy cars which were sent to Third World countries. He learned leadership skills and made many friends.

He and his roommate became good friends and spent time with girls they knew who didn't have dates, watching movies, making ice cream, and playing games. The two young men decided to prepare to serve missions for The Church of Jesus Christ of Latter-day Saints and moved toward that goal beginning in 2005.

During Bradley's summer vacation, our family toured historic Church sites, including the Sacred Grove, the Joseph Smith home, the Angel Moroni monument, and the Palmyra Temple. Bradley knew his mission papers should be arriving at our home soon, and he became anxious to learn where he would serve, expressing a desire to go to New Zealand. When he opened his call, that is exactly where he was called to serve: the New Zealand Wellington Mission. Kevin and I began making preparations, and Bradley entered the Missionary Training Center in Provo, Utah, in October 2005 and was there two and one-half weeks.

He and the other missionaries bound for New Zealand flew first to Los Angeles to catch a plane to New Zealand. While in the L.A. airport, he was able to phone home. He was excited and ready to go, and he recorded the following in his journal: "The Elders I have been traveling with were all worried about making our flight in time. I reminded them a few times that we were missionaries, and if we needed to say to the [long line of people waiting], 'Be thou removed,' it would be. After a few more minutes, another line was opened, and we went in. We had enough time to grab a bite and phone our families."

Upon his safe arrival, his photo was taken with the mission president and his wife. He wrote to us weekly, always with positive things to say. He told us about the families he had met, the challenges he faced, and the love he was developing for the people in New Zealand. He and his companion were given bikes initially, but by 1 January, they were to have a car for two weeks. He wrote, "That will be nice to give our legs a rest."

On 9 November, Bradley wrote: "I dreamt that I was back at the MTC having a sleep-over. I was really tired, but people walked into the room where we were sleeping. I'm not sure who these people were, but I could feel their importance, and knew they were either Apostles or Angels, special witnesses of some kind. I was the only one who woke when they came, so I asked them what was important for me to focus on. One answered and said, 'The Atonement.' They held a small, dull, bluish-green statue and stated that with the Atonement, things become golden. (A lot of Kiwis say 'Good as Gold.') As they said this, the statue became brighter blue and had a blue glow. That person put his hand on my face and left. That is all I remember, but as I ponder it, I think it was a gift to me saying, 'I'm in the right place doing the right things, and I need to keep my focus, especially on the Atonement.'"

Bradley had been serving only eight weeks when tragedy struck. On 6 January 2006, Bradley's companion drove the two of them to a member's home for dinner. According to police reports, the missionary car was traveling over the speed limit when it went onto the shoulder of the road. The driver overcorrected and struck a car going the opposite direction, which caused the car to ignite, and Bradley was thrown from the car. Both missionaries were killed in Waitohi, Temuka, New Zealand.

Because of the time difference between our home in Las Vegas and New Zealand, Kevin and I were contacted at 2:00 a.m., so we wouldn't hear about the news before Church leaders could contact us. The bishop and stake president came to our home and were able to give us comfort through priesthood blessings. Kevin and I were advised not to go to New Zealand, as Bradley would be transferred home before we could make arrangements to travel there.

Within two weeks, the mortuary sent information that Bradley was sent home in a "hermetically sealed liner" because he was burned during the accident, and his body was placed in a wooden casket made from the Rimu tree, native to New Zealand. He was buried in that casket at the Tonaquint Cemetery in St. George, Utah.

People all over the United States and in New Zealand were sad to hear about Bradley's death. Well-wishers sent cards, flowers, and pictures of a boy in Christ's arms to us. Members of The Church of Jesus Christ of Latter-day Saints prayed in our behalf. Members of the First Presidency—Gordon B. Hinckley, Thomas S. Monson, and James E. Faust—sent a letter to us.

Bradley's mission president wrote: "Know that we loved Elder Isle. He was dedicated to serving the Lord with 'all of his might, mind and strength.' He fulfilled his covenant as a missionary and led others to fulfill theirs. He was not only obedient himself, but was a leader in obedience. At the point he was 'transferred' from this mission field to one on the other side of the veil, he was serving in Timaru and had won the hearts of the members there, notwithstanding the brevity of his stay among them." Bradley's mission president still keeps Bradley's picture on his desk.

Many people from the ward helped our family during this hard time. So many cards and letters were sent that we have filled three large white notebooks with them, along with the above photo of him taken at the Missionary Training Center.

In several of the letters we received, people commented that Bradley had told them his favorite scripture was Doctrine and Covenants 6:33–36, which states, *"Fear not to do good, my sons, for whatsoever ye sow, that shall ye also reap; therefore, if ye sow good ye shall also reap good for your reward. Therefore, fear not, little flock; do good; let earth and hell combine against you, for if ye are built upon my rock, they cannot prevail. Behold, I do not condemn you; go your ways and sin no more; perform with soberness the work which I have commanded you. Look unto me in every thought; doubt not, fear not."*

Bradley was the third child in a family of four boys and a girl. Bradley's death has helped our family strive to a higher expectation of each other. Many blessings have poured into our family as a result of this tragedy. One of the last things Bradley said to us as we traveled together to the MTC was that if he were to "go," meaning if he were to die at this period of time in his life, that it would be "ok," and he would be ready.

The letter from the First Presidency said: "We were deeply saddened to learn of the passing of your dear son, Elder Bradley Jay Isle, who was serving in the New Zealand Wellington Mission. We express to your family our heartfelt and sincere condolences. Please be assured of our love and prayers in your behalf. . . .

"The Savior knew the sorrow we would experience when our loved ones depart this life. Elder Isle has returned home to a loving Father in Heaven. There he is reunited with other loved ones who preceded him in death and will await the opportunity to once again be with others left behind. May you and your family be comforted and sustained at this tender time of parting and in the years ahead."

Ronald Brent Jack

Born: 4 October 1967, Farmington, New Mexico
Parents: Ronald Jack and Shirleen Zufelt Jack
Siblings: Jolynn
Mission: Portugal Porto
Time of service: 18 February 1987 to 26 November 1988
Cause of death: Car/train accident
Date and place of death: 26 November 1988, Coimbra, Portugal
Age at time of death: 21
Place of burial: Kirtland Cemetery, Kirtland, New Mexico
Story related by: Ron and Shirleen Jack, parents

RONALD BRENT JACK GRADUATED with honors in May 1988 from Kirtland Central High School. He participated in and loved football and track, lettering three years in each sport. He also enjoyed weightlifting.

After graduation from high school, Brent attended BYU–Hawaii. It was there that he gained a desire to serve a mission for The Church of Jesus Christ of Latter-day Saints. He was enrolled in an institute class taught by Brother Garth Allred. Brent loved the class, and his testimony really began to grow. He wrote a letter to David Heap, his former Kirtland Seminary teacher, stating: "The gospel is so exciting, I only wish that I could retain every word, every thought of every lecture that is presented, so that I'll be able to recall it in the mission field. I don't think there's one day that I have that class that sometime in the hour, I do not feel the Spirit at least once. I haven't missed a class yet. . . . This last Sunday I also received the Melchizedek Priesthood. . . . I'm now trying to get my mission papers filled out."

He was excited to serve in Portugal and to learn another language. His letters home were upbeat and filled with his experiences. He wrote about "the beautiful people in Portugal" that he loved, and we were happy to see him grow, line upon line, as he shared many spiritual experiences.

He and his companion opened a new area, and he wrote: "At the time it was opened, it had two active members, US (Ha!). The first Sunday, we had 8 in attendance and were confronted with various obstacles . . . which indicates the involvement of Satan. . . . So, faithfully and diligently we plowed until at last we received the promised harvest. This last Sunday we enjoyed having 147 active members and investigators in attendance—and a new chapel in our area is under construction. It's a little trying being the branch president as well as the district leader, but the challenge is what I enjoy."

At one time during his mission, Brent was very ill and missed a baptismal meeting. President Copeland went to visit Elder Jack, who was in the next room vomiting blood. He was taken to a hospital for treatment and then was moved to the mission home to recover. Brent had hepatitis, but told the mission president, "President, I can't have hepatitis! I can't stay in bed for three or four weeks, I just can't. I have to work." President Copeland related, "We gave a blessing to Elder Jack, asking for a miracle. Each time I entered his room after that, I found him kneeling and pleading with the Lord. After two days he said, 'President, I'm not staying, I'm going to work.' I couldn't make him stay. He was praying and fasting, got better, and returned to his work."

Elder Brent Jack and his companion, Elder Adam Koontz, had been called to serve as assistants to the mission president. The two had been in the Provo Missionary Training Center together and became great friends. They had kept in contact with each other during their time of service and hoped to serve together in the field. They had the opportunity to do so in Coimbra, Portugal.

Shirleen writes, "Our greatest trial came on 26 November 1988. Our daughter and her husband were home for the Thanksgiving break from BYU. The day after Thanksgiving, with Christmas on our minds, my daughter and I spent the day shopping for Christmas items we could mail to Brent. Later that night, my husband and I were alone when the doorbell rang. Standing on our porch were our stake president, Dan Sherwood, and our bishop, George House. They had come to tell us that Brent had been killed, along with his companion, in a car/train accident. The two missionaries had been made assistants to the mission president three days earlier. They were in a new and unfamiliar area and had to drive over a railroad track that rounded a blind curve.

The car stalled as it straddled the track, and the train, which was running 15 minutes behind schedule, slammed into the car. Both elders were killed.

"We knew that when our leaders came to our home that night, they did not come alone. The comforting spirit of the Holy Ghost was there, stronger than we have ever known it before. Before they left us, they gave each of us a priesthood blessing. As I have reflected many times upon that night, I still remember some of the things I was told in that blessing. The Holy Ghost was our constant companion and never left us throughout that week or the next.

"After they left, we sat and talked. We knew God had a plan; we knew He had a reason. One of us reflected back on a letter we had received just one week before, which Brent wrote on 13 November 1988: 'I love my mission. I wish it could last forever.' We knew he had been faithful in serving his Father in Heaven, and we knew he was granted his wish.

"The next morning, Brent's mission president, President Copeland, called us, and during the conversation he said, 'I want you to know that your son will be exalted on high!' I thought, 'Isn't that what we all want for our children and for ourselves?'"

Two days later we received a telegram from the American Embassy in Oporto, Portugal, confirming that Brent had died. We were given phone numbers of the Consulate in Oporto, where we could call for help and information, and we were informed that President Copeland was assisting in Portugal.

A memorial service was held in the Coimbra Chapel on 28 November 1988, presided over and conducted by President Copeland. He stated that along with the many authorities, missionaries and friends in attendance, Heavenly Father's Spirit was there, and also the spirits of Elder Jack and Elder Koontz. He stated, "Their suffering has already passed, and they are already at work and are close to us." President Aires, second counselor in the mission presidency spoke, saying, "Two missionaries are with our Heavenly Father and our Lord, and no one could want anything better for them than this. . . . They are continuing to preach the gospel to the people on the other side. . . . Their parents accepted their deaths and are strong members of the Church. I wonder if I could have accepted this if I were their parents."

The funeral was held Saturday, 3 December, in the Kirtland First, Second and Third Ward building, with Bishop George House officiating, and Elder Lloyd P. George of the Quorum of the Seventy presiding. Following the service, Brent was buried in the Kirtland Cemetery, Kirtland, New Mexico, where many of our family members and pioneer ancestors are buried.

Elder George sent a letter a few days later. He wrote: "I accepted this invitation with the thought in mind that maybe I could bear you up and strengthen you in the work of the Lord as one of His Brethren. Instead it was the exact opposite. I went away refreshed, happy, lifted up, and strengthened by being in your company and by the great spirit which I felt in you wonderful people. Long will I remember the calmness of mind and soul which you possessed amid this most traumatic experience. The Lord loves you and will sustain you. I am aware of this and the knowledge that you possess that our Heavenly Father lives and that this is His plan for that great Elder-son of yours."

We received a loving letter from the First Presidency—Ezra Taft Benson, Gordon B. Hinckley, and Thomas S. Monson. Elder Carlos E. Asay and the others from the Europe Area Presidency sent a letter of condolence. We treasure those letters as well as the many cards and letters we received from family and friends.

We decided after the funeral that we needed to attend the temple, and we traveled to Provo to do so. After a session, we walked into the celestial room. Within seconds, we were the only people in the room. For about 20 minutes, we were able to sit in silent prayer and feel the peace of our Father in Heaven's love for us. We know that time was given to us to strengthen our spirits and give us understanding. We love the temple and know we can receive answers to our prayers by going there.

When Brent's personal things were returned to us, we had the privilege of reading copies of the weekly letters he wrote to his mission president, which brought us so much joy. Excerpts from those letters read, "President, I am so happy. . . . President, we are not going to quit, we are going to continue this work that is so important. . . . President, you can have confidence in me because I will do it."

The Lord helped us defeat discouragement as we prayed and received priesthood blessings. We were blessed to have the Comforter as our constant companion. We read scriptures to gain understanding. We attended the temple, and there we found peace. President James E. Faust's words have also been of great comfort: "Some of [our] healing may take place in another world. We may never know why some things happen in this life. The reason for some of our suffering is known only to the Lord."

We enjoyed having the full-time missionaries in our home when Ron served as a bishop of the Kirtland 5th Ward. We felt it was a great privilege to have them there, presenting the missionary lessons to investigators. We love missionary work and are pleased to think of our son, Brent, continuing that work in his new field of labor.

114

Bryan Thomas Johnson

Born: 16 July 1940, Salt Lake City, Utah
Parents: G. Mahlon Johnson and Eventa D. Johnson
Siblings: Larry M., Susan J. Beck
Mission: South Australia
Time of Service: October 1960 to 13 May 1962
Cause of death: Auto/train collision
Date and place of death: 13 May 1962, between Ballarat and
Muklura, Australia
Age at time of death: 21
Place of burial: Salt Lake City Cemetery
Story related by: Larry M. Johnson, brother

BRYAN THOMAS JOHNSON ATTENDED East High School in Salt Lake City and then went on to attend the University of Utah (U of U). While there, he was active in sports and joined the Marine Reserves.

Bry had some concerns about going on a mission. He talked to his father and prayed a lot about whether or not he should go, but he finally came to the conclusion that this was something he should do.

On 30 August 1960, Elder Bryan Thomas Johnson received his call for The Church of Jesus Christ of Latter-day Saints to the Southern Australian Mission. In that call, Bryan was promised that the Lord would reward the goodness of his life and that he would enjoy greater blessings and more happiness than he had yet experienced.

While Bryan was in Australia, he was able to convey the Lord's message to many. On one occasion, he spoke at a Rotary Club meeting in Port Augusta. The following is a newsletter quote from that organization, dated 12 September 1961: "Elder Johnson's very sincere and enthusiastic attitude to his work impressed all of his listeners with a number of questions put to the speaker before the meeting concluded."

Bryan and his companion, Elder Steven LaMar Denney, were the district leaders in the State of Victoria. At 5:10 p.m. on 13 May 1962, they were returning from meetings in Mildura when a diesel locomotive struck their car, throwing both elders from the car. They were killed instantly. Elder Bryan Thomas Johnson's remains were flown home to Utah.

President Henry D. Moyle came to see his parents and me, offering words of comfort. President Moyle told us that all was well with our son and brother, and from all the reports he received, Bryan was an honorable missionary. Apostle Spencer W. Kimball spoke at Bryan's funeral service held at the Monument Park 5th Ward in Salt Lake City. Both of these servants of the Lord helped Bry's parents deal with the loss of their son. Bryan is buried in the Salt Lake City Cemetery near his grandparents and other family members.

Letters of condolence were sent from many parts of the world to Bryan's parents. Many were from those whose lives he touched while on his mission, and many came from people who wanted Bryan's parents to know of their love and support for them.

As President Moyle said, "The Lord will bless you for your son, for what he has done and for that which he shall yet do." Those blessings have indeed followed Bryan's family for all these many years.

Wesley Brian Johnson

Born: 18 July 1955, Logan, Cache County, Utah
Parents: Charles L. Johnson and Ellen Diane Jorgensen Johnson
Siblings: Denise, Laura, Rodney, Clyde
Mission: Germany Hamburg
Time of service: 22 March 1975 to 18 December 1976
Cause of death: Severe cerebral hemorrhage (aneurysm)
Date and place of death: 18 December 1976, Hamburg, Germany
Age at time of death: 21
Place of burial: Treasureton Cemetery, Treasureton, Idaho
Story related by: Charles and Diane Johnson, parents

WESLEY BRIAN JOHNSON GREW UP on the Stock Valley Ranch in Treasureton, Idaho. There, he enjoyed the companionship and love of his parents, siblings, cousins, a grandpa and grandma, and an aunt and uncle.

Wes was always interested in what was going on at the ranch; even as a child he wanted to do what his dad was doing. Throughout his teenage years he rode motorcycles and snowmobiles, played church basketball and school football, and had several very close friends. He participated in track and set records, made many batches of cookies, and loved deer hunting and fishing. Each summer from the time Wes was six or seven years old, he and his father and young cousin Randy camped and fished near Palisades, Idaho.

Wes graduated from high school and seminary in Preston, Idaho, and then spent his freshman year of college in Laie, Hawaii, where he lived with an aunt and uncle and attended The Church College of Hawaii, now BYU–Hawaii. That summer he worked as a horse wrangler at Jackson Lake Lodge in Wyoming, taking "dudes" on rides and cooking breakfast for them. He earned additional money for his mission in the late fall working with his dad for Utah Power Company.

Elder Wesley Brian Johnson was called to serve a two-year mission for The Church of Jesus Christ of Latter-day Saints in the Germany Hamburg Mission on 21 January 1975. He had hoped for a foreign mission and was pleased to receive his call to Germany

Leaving for his mission was quite overwhelming. No doubt, his favorite scripture story, the stripling warriors, strengthened him when he left home and family. His mission journal and notes indicate he had a great struggle with homesickness, but his letters home were mostly upbeat.

Beginning in late November 1976, Wes began to suffer painful head-aches centered behind his eyes, and he was having difficulty seeing. At times the pain was immense. The evening of 3 December, when some expected in-vestigators did not show up to watch the Church video "And Should We Die," the missionaries decided to watch it themselves. While standing to offer a closing prayer, Wes collapsed.

His mother, Diane, says: "President Glenn M. Roylance, mission presi-dent, phoned to tell us our son was in the hospital. He had suffered a seizure, tests were being run, and he was in great pain. In a follow-up call, President Roylance informed us that a cerebral aneurysm had been found and that a protective clot was preventing further bleeding from the leaking artery. Also, the doctors were trying to avoid anything that might make Wes's heart beat faster and thus perhaps dislodge the clot. Wes was not well enough to speak to us on the phone.

"Later, arrangements were made for him to talk to us prior to a delicate and complicated operation. But when our phone rang, it was not our son calling. It was President Roylance sadly relaying the tragic news that the fragile clot had dislodged, allowing further hemorrhaging, that Wes had suf-fered another seizure and was now brain-dead. President Roylance asked about removing the life support. I asked him what he would do if it were his son, and he replied that when life is gone, we should let them go and that is what he would do. President and Sister Roylance promised to be with Wes when life support was removed, but before the appointed time, the doc-tor phoned to tell them that Wes had passed on. President Roylance said he had prayed that Elder Johnson would be released before it was his duty to order the life support removed. President Roylance could not have been more kind and helpful. He kept our family well informed throughout the experience."

Charlie, Wes's father, had a personal experience while he and his wife waited to hear of their son's passing: "One morning before daylight, I lay in bed thinking about Wes. The bedroom lamp came on. I thought it was very strange because that light has a twist switch and it had never come on suddenly before, or since. About thirty minutes later, when the President called to report Wes's death, I thought that somehow Wes had been able to come home and put that light on. I think Wes came home the instant he died and put that light on. He surely did. We received comfort from that."

Charlie also says, "President Roylance told us Wes's name had rested on the altars of all the Church temples and he had been blessed and administered to several times; however, after each blessing Wes's condition worsened. As I pondered that, I thought, 'All that was to no avail; the Lord had decided to take him home. That was all there was to it.'"

Sometime in late November, before the family learned of Wes's illness, his mother had experienced two unusual dreams; and his oldest sister, Denise, who was attending BYU at the time, experienced some unusual thoughts. Diane says, "In the first dream, I saw Wes sitting on our couch enjoying some memorabilia from his room. I knew he was home early, but it seemed okay since he hadn't been sent home. In the second dream, other family members and I were in the field. Wes entered the field from the gate by the round shed. We saw him walking fast, coming to greet us, and he looked very happy. We were happy to see him, but knew he was home early. When Denise came home for Thanksgiving vacation, she told our family, 'I cannot stop thinking about Wes. I have thought and thought about him; he is on my mind all the time. I'm not especially worried, but I wonder why this is happening.' Later, we understood. My dreams and Denise's thoughts began occurring in the same time period that Wes was beginning to suffer vision problems and severe headaches. The Lord was preparing us."

Charlie said, "There can be a lot of 'red tape' involved with getting a body home from a foreign country, but the Church was able to bring Wes home six days after his death. Our local mortician, a long-time family friend, went to the Salt Lake Airport 24 December to receive Wes's suitcases and his body, which arrived in a welded metal container."

Charlie shares some of his thoughts as he viewed his son's body later that Christmas Eve night: "My first thoughts were: 'His hair has really darkened. He left a boy; he has returned a man.'" Diane expresses her thoughts this way: "On Christmas Eve, we went to the funeral home to see Wes. It may sound strange, but I couldn't wait to see him and have him home again. On the other hand, we had to face the fact that he had passed away." She adds, "When we first learned of Wes's illness and then his death, we were shocked. We thought that since he was in the service of the Lord, he would have extra protection. Later, we came to the understanding that our son was at the most spiritual time of his life, and he went back to Heavenly Father ready for his next assignment." When they held Wes's Book of Mormon sometime later, they noticed that the Book of Enos was marked with a ribbon. Charlie says, "We felt it marked the place where Wes had been studying and pondering before he could no longer do so. Our attention was drawn to Enos 26 and 27, which Wes had underlined."

"And I saw that I must soon go down to my grave, having been wrought upon by the power of God that I must preach and prophesy unto this people, and declare the word according to the truth which is in Christ. And I have declared it in all my days, and have rejoiced in it above that of the world.

"And I soon go to the place of my rest, which is with my Redeemer; for I know that in him I shall rest. And I rejoice in the day when my mortal shall put on immortality, and shall stand before him; then shall I see his face with pleasure, and he will say unto me: Come unto me, ye blessed, there is a place prepared for you in the mansions of my Father. Amen."

Diane speaks of some of the comfort and support they received: "The Germany Hamburg Mission sent a tape recording of the memorial service held for Wes, as well as the memorial book full of written memories of Wes prepared by district members. Our family was comforted by the special gifts from those who knew Wes during his mission. Throughout this difficult time, we received many cards, letters, and phone calls from people expressing their love and sympathy. President Roylance sent many wonderful letters. Expressions of comfort and love came from the First Presidency— Spencer W. Kimball, N. Eldon Tanner, and Marion G. Romney. Elder Joseph B. Wirthlin, the Europe Area Supervisor, and members of the Missionary Executive Committee—Thomas S. Monson, Bruce R. McConkie, and David B. Haight—sent letters of condolence. Mrs. Harold B. Lee personally called to convey her love and extend comfort. Elder Carlos Asay, of the First Quorum of the Seventy, spoke at Wes's funeral."

Charlie and Diane believe that "reading Wes's patriarchal blessing had proved to be a great blessing for us and our children. Though a patriarchal blessing is primarily a personal guide, we learned from Wes's that it can serve as a source of comfort to others during difficult times. Our son's blessing comforted us. The Lord blessed our other children with the opportunity to be sealed for time and eternity by a temple marriage here on earth, but Wes's blessing was different." Charlie explains, "We have come to understand that the Lord had not blessed Wes with the opportunity for a temple marriage as a mortal, but, instead, his blessing blesses him in the hereafter rather than here on earth."

Diane says, "We have kept Wes a part of our family. Even children born after Wes's death feel they would know him if he walked in. Wes had a great sense of humor. I can easily say to my family: 'Since Wes left us like that, he'd better run for the hills when he sees me coming!' They laugh, and I'm sure he laughs loudest."

Robert Wayne Kinghorn

Born: 7 July 1944, Idaho Falls, Idaho
Parents: Ronald J. Kinghorn and Dorothy Harrison Kinghorn
Siblings: R. Brent, Janice Lee
Mission: Mexico Hermosillo
Time of service: July 1964 to June 1965
Cause of death: Automobile accident
Date and place of death: 21 June 1965, near Santiago, Mexico
Age at time of death: 20
Place of burial: Sugar City, Idaho
Story related by: R. Brent Kinghorn, brother

ROBERT WAYNE KINGHORN GREW UP in Sugar City, Idaho. He graduated from Sugar-Salem High School as co-valedictorian in 1962. In high school, he was a state champion debater and an accomplished pianist, and he sang with a popular quartet. He attended Ricks College in Rexburg, Idaho, and graduated in 1964 with high honors.

Wayne had always planned to serve a mission for The Church of Jesus Christ of Latter-day Saints and had saved appropriately. He studied two years of German at Ricks and hoped to serve in Germany, as that was where I served my mission. He was very surprised to receive a call to Mexico, having never studied Spanish. Wayne was fair skinned and blonde and knew he would really "stick out" as a gringo, but he accepted his call with the attitude of, "If this is where the Lord wants me to serve, then this is where I will serve."

He epitomized the scripture found in 1 Nephi 3:7: *"I will go and do the things which the Lord hath commanded, for I know that the Lord giveth no commandments unto the children of men, save he shall prepare a way for them that they may accomplish the thing which he commandeth them."*

Wayne was a very sensitive young man and especially struggled to leave his grandparents, with whom he was very close. Our mother was a school teacher, so Wayne stayed with our grandparents all of his growing up years. Ironically, our grandfather died just two months before Wayne was killed. Wayne took his grandfather's passing very hard and sent a very kind and loving note to Grandmother expressing his great love for her and his deep sorrow at Grandfather's passing.

Wayne was very organized and very clean, and when he arrived in Mexico, he struggled because conditions there were neither clean nor organized. Initially, Wayne found it difficult to love the people and to cope with the poverty and living conditions. In his patriarchal blessing, Wayne was told he needed to overcome pride, learn to love all people, and to become more humble and faithful. Many times he wrote explaining how he was trying to do those things. As the months went by, it became evident in his letters that he had learned to look past all his concerns and simply love the people.

A month or so prior to his death, he developed a serious illness and was transferred to the mission home to recuperate. During that time, Wayne developed a close and loving relationship with President and Sister Turley. A few weeks later, he was called to be the Mission Sunday School President.

In his new calling, he and another elder accompanied President and Sister Turley on a mission tour, visiting several branches. At that time the mission comprised the entire western side of Mexico and was about 2,000 miles in length. At Tepic, Mexico, which was about 1,000 miles from Hermosillo, they conducted a meeting after which President and Sister Turley headed home, leaving Wayne and his companion to continue traveling toward the southern tip of the mission.

The next evening during a rainstorm, near Santiago, Mexico, at about 9:00 p.m., Wayne's companion was at the wheel and drove around a curve. A truck was coming toward them on their side of the road. Their car veered off the road and rolled, and Wayne was thrown out and killed instantly. His companion was not injured. When police officers came to investigate, the companion told them Wayne had been driving, a wise thing to do, because in Mexico, at that time, drivers involved in fatal accidents were always arrested and held for several weeks while the accident was investigated.

Wayne's companion arranged for two elders from Santiago to stay with Wayne's body, and he contacted President Turley to inform him of the accident. At that time in Mexico, bodies were not embalmed, and the law required burial within 24 hours of death. President Turley instructed the elders not to allow the body to be buried, but to tell authorities that "his father" was coming to claim the body. The Turleys then drove continuously for 26 hours to get to Santiago to claim the body. The elders had secured a casket, which was loaded into the Turley's station wagon. President and Sister Turley drove to the U.S./Mexican border, where they were able to have a United States mortician prepare Wayne's body before putting it on a plane to be flown home.

When President Turley had learned of Wayne's death, he immediately called the Missionary Department in Salt Lake, asking them to notify our family. He explained that he had a race against time to retrieve Elder Kinghorn's body and that he would get back to them as soon as he could. There was no air transportation between Hermosillo and Santiago at that time, and the roads were narrow and winding. There were few telephones in the rural parts of Mexico and no cell phones. It was a long and difficult week of waiting for our family.

Wayne was killed on 21 June; his body arrived in Idaho on 26 June. We were told that his body was in very poor condition, and the casket would have to remain closed for the funeral. This added to our sadness, because we didn't have the closure we longed for. Wayne had been gone from home for one year, and his passing became a very surreal experience for us.

Elder Marion D. Hanks of the First Quorum of the Seventy represented the Church and spoke at Wayne's funeral. He showed us great concern and was very kind to us. My parents were taking a temple preparation class at that time; I was a returned missionary and had recently married. Elder Hanks phoned me to talk about what the Church could do to help my parents. He was so kind and thoughtful, and his words were just what my parents needed to hear. That November, my parents were sealed in the Idaho Falls Temple and I was able to serve as proxy for Wayne.

President Turley phoned several times and spoke with my parents, showing kindness and sensitivity for our family's needs. He held a memorial service in Mexico for Wayne so that missionaries and local members could pay tribute to him. We received photos from the service and copies of the talks that were delivered. He also gathered up and sent home Wayne's personal effects. We especially appreciated receiving Wayne's journal, which my sister transcribed and copied for all our family. We were deeply touched to read

Wayne's last entry. He quoted Alma 29:1—*"Oh that I were an angel, and could have the wish of mine heart."*

We sensed that Wayne was a faithful, humble, and righteous missionary, and our feelings were confirmed from letters we received from his mission president, President George Turley, and from a few of his fellow missionaries. Later, at the Church-run Benemerito Academy in Mexico, we met Elder Lino Alvarez, who became a member of the Second Quorum of the Seventy. He told us that he had served with Wayne in the West Mexico Mission, and he told us that Elder Kinghorn carried a special spirit with him.

My brother's death has had a significant and positive impact on our family. Our father, who has now passed his 91st birthday, is very proud of his family, especially of Wayne. Until Mother passed away in 2001, she and Dad remained faithful in the Church. My wife and I are the parents of six sons and four daughters (one who died in infancy). All of our sons served missions, and all of our daughters married returned missionaries. My sister and her family have also been fortunate to have their four sons serve missions, and their daughter married a returned missionary.

During the year of Wayne's death, President and Sister Turley had arranged for their 16-year-old daughter, Linda, to complete her last year of high school in America, studying the organ, under the direction of Sister Ruth Barrus, at Ricks College. That year, Linda stayed with my parents and younger sister, which became a wonderful blessing for her and for our family. Linda still comes to Idaho to visit with my dad and stays for a few days each year. Her parents also came to visit and have maintained a long and true friendship with my parents over the years.

I served as president over the Albania Tirana Mission with my wife at my side, for three years. We drew much strength from Wayne's spirit during our service. We shared his story with our missionaries and feel it strengthened them. One of our sons served in the California Los Angeles Mission, serving with the Hispanic people. He told us he often felt Wayne's spirit close to him and felt he was able to complete some of the work Wayne started among the Mexican people.

Wayne has been gone over 40 years now. We have since met a few other families who lost missionaries that were serving. In every case, the missionary was faithful and seems to have completed his/her mission and was called home. We feel that missionaries are protected by the Lord and that when a missionary dies, it is the Lord's will, and those missionaries continue their service to our Father in Heaven and His children in the spirit world as described in Doctrine and Covenants 138:57.

Matthew Lawrence Knoop

Born: 23 February 1988, Salt Lake City, Utah
Parents: David Walter Knoop and Kaye Ann Cowan Knoop
Siblings: Marnie
Mission: Brazil Salvador
Time of service: 19 June 2007 to 21 April 2008
Cause of death: Hit-and-run auto accident
Date and place of death: 21 April 2008, Salvador, Brazil
Age at time of death: 20
Place of burial: Historic Park City Cemetery, Park City, Utah
Story related by: Kristine Cowan Prince-McStotts, maternal aunt

WHEN MATTHEW LAWRENCE KNOOP was just a little boy, he proudly announced to everyone, "I want to go on a mission." From the time he was young, Matt had a close relationship with his Heavenly Father and a sure sense of his purpose in life. He toted his Book of Mormon with him wherever he went, even on vacation and soccer trips. Throughout the remainder of his life, he never wavered on that decision. A classmate remembers that on the first day of school, the fifth-grade teacher asked each student to bring something to school that would tell a little about themselves and the things that were important to them. The children took out pictures, games, and toys to show to the class, but when it was his turn, Matthew opened his paper sack and took out a copy of the Book of Mormon and told his friends that he wanted to be a Mormon missionary when he was old enough.

Matthew was the firstborn child of David Walter and Kaye Ann Cowan Knoop. His parents were thrilled with their new little son and began making plans for the experiences and opportunities they could provide for him: schooing, travel, sports, biking, hiking, and college education that included playing soccer, which was his father's passion. However, Matthew inserted himself early in the decision-making about his future and talked of his desire to go on a mission for The Church of Jesus Christ of Latter-day Saints. This information was perplexing to his parents. His father, an honorable man, was not a member of the Church, and his mother was not active in the Church at that time. They often wondered where his desire and spirituality came from at such a young age. Quite simply, he was born with it. Because of his strong interest in spiritual matters, Kaye began taking Matthew and his sister Marnie to the local LDS ward.

Matthew was a beautiful boy with bright blue eyes, fair skin, freckles, and blond hair. In the ensuing years, Matt grew physically in stature to 6'4", while at the same time his testimony of the gospel grew in depth.

Matt participated in youth soccer leagues and on the Olympic Development Team in Salt Lake City, and soccer became one of his passions. He became an outstanding soccer player. He played for Park City High School, and during that time the soccer team won the state championship all four years. Matt was named to the All-State soccer team the year he graduated, 2006. He was contacted by several universities and colleges that offered him scholarships if he would play soccer for them. He was thrilled, but when he told them he would need to take two years off to fulfill an LDS mission, their interest waned. They feared he would lose his abilities and skills in those two years. His father encouraged him to accept one of those offers, but there was never any hesitation from Matt, never a waiver. Although he loved soccer, he wanted to serve a mission more. When Matt's father realized that his son was determined to serve a mission, he lovingly supported him in his decision, even though he didn't quite understand it.

When Matthew submitted his mission papers, he told his family that if he could choose anywhere in the world to serve a mission, it would be Brazil. In February of 2007, he went to Temple Square in Salt Lake City to open the envelope containing his mission call. In that sacred place, he read that he was called to the Brazil Salvador Mission.

A few weeks before entering the Missionary Training Center, while dining with his family at a restaurant in Park City, he saw Apostle Dieter Uchtdorf seated at a nearby table. Unable to contain his excitement, Matt went to Elder Uchtdorf's table and introduced himself. His face gleaming with excitement and happiness, he told Elder Uchtdorf that he was leaving on a mission to Brazil in a few weeks. Elder Uchtdorf shook Matt's hand, congratulated him and wished him well. It wouldn't be the last time their paths would intersect.

Elder Knoop left Salt Lake City on 19 June 2007. He hugged his parents and his sister goodbye at the airport and started to walk down the ramp. He turned suddenly, walked back, and hugged his mother again, saying, "Mom, you are going to need to be strong." He took a few more steps, turned a second time to embrace her and whispered in her ear, "Mom, you are really going to need to be strong." And then he was gone.

He proved himself a leader at Missionary Training Center in São Paulo and was asked by the mission president to be zone leader of a group of new missionaries. After four months in the mission field, Matt was called to be a senior companion and a district leader. After eight months, he was called to the sacred position of training new missionaries. Once in a while on his Preparation Day, he joined children in a game of soccer on the street, showing them some moves and leaving them amazed at how this tall, blond American shared their passion for the game.

Matthew loved being a missionary but found it to be considerably harder than he anticipated. Because he had immersed himself in scripture study for years prior to his mission and had developed a strong testimony of the gospel, he thought he was adequately prepared. But he slowly realized that what he had developed was strength of character and the self-discipline needed to be a successful missionary. He was able to handle disappointments when baptisms didn't come easily. He could laugh off people who threw things and called him an "American Pig." He dealt with homesickness and pushed through discouragement when he felt the language was coming too slowly. His inner strength helped him bear deep disappointment when investigators knew the gospel was true but were unable to abide by its precepts. He grew in devotion to his Heavenly Father and to missionary work.

On 26 February 2008, he bore his testimony to his family in the following email: "Being on a mission has been great some moments and heartbreaking at others. Great, in the fact that I love the mission, and really hard because sometimes I feel like stopping and crying because it's so hard. . . . I have put my entire soul into this work, and I have learned so much, especially faith, and also that I can never give up . . . never. When I want to stop after walking 10–15 miles during the day and just break down . . . I teach one more lesson, I do one more good work, one more contact, and I go one step at a time. I have been here for eight months. The time has flown. I have learned more in these eight months than in my entire life. My body is tired, and I have baptized very little, but I have never been so happy. I have such clarity in my life, and I feel blessed. The other day I realized that one day I would leave this place, and I don't know why, but I felt such a deep pain in my heart. The only conclusion that I can come to is that it is because in these eight months I have learned to forget about me. Day upon day, difficulty after difficulty, and blessing after blessing, I have changed. This truly was a defining moment in this mission and I will never forget. I can only hope that I will continue on like this, that I will be the Lord's servant until the end, that when I return to the temple in Salt Lake, that I may kneel down and offer this work that I have done, and that I may feel the sweet confirmation of the Spirit touch in my heart, as it so often does, to tell me that He accepts, that this work I do is accepted by my Father. . . . I do not know what is in store for me, but I would like to think that I, too, would be able to glory in my tribulation in the last day. My testimony is simple, but it does not have a shade of doubt. I know with all my heart that these things are true."

President Sousa knew only his very strongest missionaries could survive in the small city of Catu, which had the reputation of being one of the most difficult in the mission. Elder Knoop was called to serve in Catu, and although it was difficult and frustrating, he gave his soul to the work. The tone of his emails became more serious and reflective. On 18 March 2008, after a particularly difficult week there, he wrote these words to his family:

"Tonight I read my patriarchal blessing. Never before had I noticed something so obvious in it. It repeats a few times that he [the patriarch] is prompted to tell me that Satan knows who I am, and he tells me all the things I need to do to keep on going. Truly that night, the blessing was the only thing that kept me from breaking down. For the first time, my mission made sense. I understood why things are so difficult. . . . Satan knows who I am, but . . . I will be led to the honest in heart . . . to people who really are prepared. . . . I told my companion that I feel like this place is my big test. . . . I'll either fall or rise here in this city."

After four long months in Catu, Matt hoped for a transfer. He felt the power of Satan working to discourage him, even destroy him. He had worked hard and was tired. But when he knelt to pray, he felt God's supreme love for him and confirmation he was doing the right thing. Transfers came in early April for many other missionaries, while a disappointed but ever faithful Elder Knoop was left in Catu. He wrote, "I guess God has other plans for me."

Elder Knoop and his companion, Elder Michael William Sides, took a 10-year-old boy to Church on Sunday morning, 20 April. Brother Andre

Lima, second counselor in the bishopric, noted a glow about Elder Knoop as he helped the young boy sing from the hymn book. After the meeting, the two elders walked the boy safely home and then made plans to visit and teach him later in the week.

Their next appointment was several miles away, and they visited as they walked along the road. In the middle of a conversation, they were struck from behind by an automobile which had veered off the road, hitting them both. Neither elder saw the car coming and had no time to dive for safety.

Witnesses stopped to call for help, and both elders were taken to a small medical facility in Catu. Elder Knoop's injuries were too severe for doctors in the clinic to treat, so he was taken by ambulance to Aliança Hospital in Salvador, two hours away. He was conscious during the entire ambulance ride, talking about his family and little sister Marnie, saying how much he loved and missed them. He expressed his gratitude for his home in Park City, Utah, and talked about everything near and dear to him, as if reviewing his life. He knew his injuries were life threatening and that he was in very critical condition, but his soul was pure, and he was never more spiritually prepared to meet his Savior.

Matt was met at the hospital by his mission president and many of his fellow missionaries. He asked for and received a priesthood blessing and was promised that "everything would work together for his good." Immediately after, and in spite of his injuries, he provided an update to his zone leader on the number of contacts and lessons taught that week.

His family at home were sitting down for dinner when the stake president and bishop knocked at the door to inform them of Elder Knoop's accident. Arrangements were made for Elder Knoop's parents to fly to Salvador, Brazil, to be with their son. They were in the process of submitting the necessary paperwork at the Brazilian Consulate in Los Angeles, when they received the call informing them that their son, Matthew, had passed away, a little over 24 hours after the accident. They were devastated and decided to return home to be with their daughter and family members—they could do no more for their son.

In his final letter to his mother, for her birthday, a month before he died, Matt wrote: "I have learned that we don't need to understand everything, but we do need to accept what we have been given and make the best of it."

Friends, family members, and hundreds of missionaries in Brazil had been fasting and praying for Elder Knoop's recovery, and doctors worked feverishly to save Matthew's life. He had remained very calm in spite of his pain, his eyes closed, except for the times he opened them and looked directly up, as if he was seeing someone or something. His eyes remained fixed on what he was seeing. He peacefully, and without fear, began to say to those with him, "I am dying, I am dying." We believe he saw heavenly visitors from beyond the veil who had come to escort him back to his heavenly home. He died Monday, 21 April 2008, at 2:10 p.m., Brazil time.

A viewing was held on Sunday evening, 27 April. Elder Knoop's body lay peacefully and serenely in his white temple clothes, his missionary name badge on his shirt pocket. The freckles still danced across his nose and cheeks, his eyelashes long, but his beautiful blue eyes were now closed forever in mortality.

The funeral was held on Monday, 28 April. The stake center in Park City was overflowing with people who had loved Matthew. Copies of the Book of Mormon, with Elder Knoop's testimony pasted on the inside front cover, were available to any who wished to have one. To the family's surprise, President Dieter Uchtdorf, now a member of the First Presidency of the Church, walked into the Relief Society room where Matt's casket lay. He remembered his conversation with Matt one year before in a Park City restaurant and recalled Matt's excited announcement that he was going on a mission to Brazil.

Upon the completion of his mission, Matthew had planned to return to the Salt Lake Temple, where he would kneel and offer the work he had done, hoping that he would feel the sweet confirmation of the Spirit touch his heart, and he would know that his work was accepted by his Father in Heaven.

President Uchtdorf spoke at the funeral, stating, "I don't believe in randomness; I don't believe in coincidences." He explained that there was a reason he and Matt had met months ago, perhaps so that when he was asked to speak words of consolation to the family, he would know personally of whom he spoke. He referred to Matt as a bright-eyed, beautiful young man, pure and innocent, who wanted so much to please his Heavenly Father. Then, he looked directly at Matt's parents and confirmed that Matthew's work is accepted by his Father and that Matthew is worthy to enter into the celestial kingdom of his Father to enjoy all of the blessings and privileges of those righteous spirits who dwell in the kingdom of the Father.

Matt was laid to rest in the historic Park City Cemetery, surrounded by the beautiful hills he loved. His gravestone reads: "Elder Matthew Lawrence Knoop, Returned with Honor, 23 Feb 1988 to 21 Apr 2008," followed by an inscribed quote from Orson Pratt: "My body sleeps for a moment, but my testimony lives and shall endure forever."

Within days of Elder Knoop's death, two missionaries unexpectedly appeared at the door of a family member who had been inactive in the Church and said they had experienced a strong feeling as they walked by the house that they should talk with the family. The missionaries were unaware of any connection between the family and Elder Knoop's death, but they knew the burning impression of the Spirit. As a result of their visit, two of Matt's cousins who lived in that house were baptized six weeks later, both of them saying they felt Matt's presence with them as they entered the baptismal font.

A friend phoned Matt's mother to tell her that after years of her working with a small town in Germany, officials there were now beginning to turn their records over to the Church. The name of Knoop was included in the list of names. Truly, Elder Knoop continues as a missionary.

Family members have felt Matt very near. He has spoken spiritually to his mother, Kaye, and has asked her to seek out family names of those who had not been taught the gospel here on Earth, while Matt works on the other side of the veil. Kaye walks by Matt's picture in the living room every day and hears him say, "We've got a lot of work to do, Mom."

Several weeks after his passing, Matt appeared to a family member in a vivid dream, with a message for his family. He wanted us to know that he is fine, that he is very busy, and very happy; his death was not premature, and it was "supposed to be." He is aware of our suffering and grief, which saddens him, and he wants us to continue to live our lives and to be happy; he is waiting for each of us.

Our family has been forever changed by this experience. We now realize that Matthew was a special gift to our family, a loan from our Heavenly Father. We thank God for sending this valiant young son to our family and allowing us the privilege of nurturing him and watching him grow. He embodied the very best of our family's core values. We have been given a marvelous spiritual experience, both in watching him live and in understanding the meaning of his death. The greatest challenge of losing Matt is to turn our sadness into something good, to service for others and into love in our own lives. It is also our greatest opportunity. We have lost Matthew for a short while, but we know that we will see him again in eternity, and he will be ours forever. He lives on through the things he taught us. God did, indeed, have other plans for him. He was transferred, just as he had prayed for, only this time, he is serving his mission in the spirit world, and it is glorious.

Arnold Joseph Kunzler

Born: 2 March 1896, Rosette, Box Elder, Utah
Parents: Jacob Kunzler and Louise Ott Kunzler
Siblings: Bertha, Louise, Pauline, Mary Elizabeth, John Henry,
William Jacob, Charles Edward, Tina Matilda,
Harold Lorenzo, Emma Alvena, Gladys Julia
Mission: Central States Mission, Independence, Missouri
Time of service: April 1917 to 8 October 1917
Cause of death: Complications of typhoid fever [phlebitis]
Date and place of death: 8 October 1917, Springfield, Missouri
Age at time of death: 21
Place of burial: Park Valley Cemetery, Park Valley, Box Elder, Utah
Story related by: Judy L. Nielson, great-niece

ARNOLD JOSEPH KUNZLER WAS THE NINTH child of Jacob and Louise Ott Kunzler. He was described as a quiet, sweet young man with a kind disposition. Arnold was 21 years old when he received his mission call from the Prophet Joseph F. Smith of The Church of Jesus Christ of Latter-day Saints to serve in the Central States Mission. He wrote his first letter from the mission home in Independence, Jackson County, Missouri, on 14 April 1917, describing Sunday dinner with a member family as the best since he arrived.

His letters described the costs of serving in Missouri in 1917. He needed additional money from his family to cover expenses of an upcoming conference in Independence. "I have about $15 left ... so I wish you could send me some more. ... It has cost me about $27 for books and a grip and tracts.

$15 for a suit, $9 for a rain coat, and about $6 a week for board, room and washing and what other little expenses I have."

In his 30 May letter from Springfield, Missouri, where he had been transferred, he wrote that he and the other missionaries had to register for the military draft when they were in Independence. The draft was a concern to Arnold as he had not applied for an exemption, and he asked if his brothers had been required to register.

He and two companions rented a big room in a house for $10 a month. They reduced their expenses by fixing their own meals, mostly bread, milk, and mush for breakfast. Costs were defrayed by picking peas and turnips out of a member's garden.

Mission President S. O. Bennion wrote the following to the family: "Elder Kunzler is doing good work in this mission, having received a good start in Kansas City and now working in a good field where they had several baptisms last Sunday. He is earnest and sincere and will no doubt do much good in this great work."

Arnold wrote to his family that he enjoyed the work, but explained: "The people are such awful tobacco users. Women come to the door with a big chew of tobacco in their mouths and with their lips dobbed up. It almost makes a fellow sick sometimes. They are also quite handy with the pipe."

On 30 August 1917, Arnold's companion, Elder E. J. Curtis, wrote the following letter: "By request of your son and a duty I owe as presiding elder of this branch, I will inform you that he is ill. He has been failing in his appetite the past two weeks and has not done any work since the 23rd of this month. He stayed in the room a day or two but did not seem to improve, so I thought it best to procure a doctor. He was undecided just what was the matter, but he has symptoms of typhoid and in order to give him the best of attention, the doctor suggested that he be removed to the hospital. Now I don't want you to worry about him, for he has every comfort possible and will be cared for the same as if he was home. Please send him $25 direct at earliest convenience. I will inform you each day how he is."

The Kunzler family felt helpless and looked forward to the postcards from Elder Curtis; he sent nine to the family during the month of September informing them of Arnold's condition. On 21 September, he wrote that although Arnold had been well, his fever had returned and was quite high, requiring that he be moved to a private room with a nurse, which would be quite expensive. Arnold's mother was making plans to visit him, but Elder Curtis wrote that it was unnecessary and that Arnold would be coming home as soon as he was able to travel, possibly another three weeks. The hospital bill was $10 per week, but doctor's fees were not known. He added that Arnold was content with what he had to bear.

Days later Elder Curtis wrote the following. "Arnold's case is an unusual one and it is hard to tell what the outcome may be. . . . The doctor says he is very sick and it is hard to tell how the case may terminate. . . . Several more doctors say nothing more could be done for him than is being done. . . . Arnold had a light case of typhoid, but it's the effect it has had upon his legs. His system is full of poison, and it brings on chills which he has about every 5 or 6 hours . . . and his temperature goes up to 106. . . . This has caused blood clotting . . . poor circulation and an amputation then follows. . . . My advice to you is to catch the first train that comes this way. Telegraph me when you leave so I can meet you at the depot. Arnold does not know I am writing this letter. He might object if he did, but he does not realize how sick he is. Now Dear Sister I hope you will act promptly. . . . I think all will be well if you come at once."

Five days later Elder Curtis wrote: "He has been rational all the time. . . . I wired the mission and conference presidencies. . . . President Gardner was here in a few hours. He expects to stay till the danger is passed. . . . The doctor calls the disease fleabitis [phlebitis]."

Arnold died on 8 October 1917. His father, Jacob Kunzler, arrived in Springfield a few days prior and was at his son's bedside when he died. He accompanied Arnold's body home on the train. Arnold's sister, Louise Kunzler Pugsley, wrote: "Arnold was on his mission about 6 months in Springfield, Missouri; he had typhoid fever, was getting along all right at first when gangrene set in. Father was sent for and went to his bed side in the hospital. Arnold died while father was with him. He was brought home and buried in Park Valley, Utah. . . . Arnold died October 8, 1917, services in Rosette Ward, buried in Park Valley Cemetery."

Elder Curtis wrote a final letter to Arnold's mother on 10 October, writing in part: "I am indeed proud to have had the privilege of laboring as a companion with him, for he proved to be honest to himself, unto his fellowmen and unto his God, and indeed a credit unto his community and worthy of the love and confidence of every one whom he ever met. . . . What more could we ask than this? And why should we feel bad when we know the purity, honesty, and integrity of a child of the Lord's as indeed this Dear Son and Brother was. He has proved himself worthy of the highest exaltation in Our Father's Kingdom and has been called to work in that heavenly home. . . . May the Blessings of the Lord be with you always is ever my prayer. From your Dear Friend and Brother, Elder E. J. Curtis."

Mosese Kotoisuva Maiwiriwiri

Born: 22 December 1928, Kabara Lau Island Group, Fiji
Parents: Ropate Jone Maiwiriwiri and Noame Vuto Maiwiriwiri
Siblings: Temalesi, Volai, Amelia, Olivia, Lebai, Salote,
Volai Tagi, Sekope
Spouse: Jese Edwina Tavo Maiwiriwiri
Children: Navita, Susu, Mere, Ephraim, Ropate, Rosalinli, Susu Jr.
Mission: Fiji Suva
Time of service: January 1984 to 8 October 1984
Cause of death: Heart attack
Date and place of death: 8 October 1984, Malau, Labasa, Fiji
Age at time of death: 55
Place of burial: Somosomo, Taveuni
Story related by: Jese Maiwiriwiri, wife

MOSESE KOTOISUVA MAIWIRIWIRI was a quiet person and did not show his feelings very easily. He was a very kind person, a good father and husband. He was the last member of our family to be baptized into The Church of Jesus Christ of Latter-day Saints. His desire to be baptized was a big surprise to me and the children, and to the elders. That day he told me he was taking two weeks' leave from work and going to live at an estate his uncle managed, and would I please ask Elder Brekterfield and his companion to come to Salialevu to baptize him.

The day of his baptism we prayed for the heavy rain to stop. The Lord was generous and by 10:00 a.m. the rain had stopped. We walked up a hill to a little waterfall where Mosese had chosen to be baptized. I shall never forget that day; I was so happy and felt the Spirit and the Lord's love for our family. The Lord had brought the head of our household to take up his responsibility in order to complete our sealing ordinance. It was the greatest blessing a family can have.

Before he became a member, Mosese was very supportive of all church activities. When the little branch in Somosomo closed due to the lack of missionaries, our Sunday School was held in our home. Mosese helped set up chairs but left to attend his Methodist Church on Sundays. Things began to change when he was baptized.

Our little branch started off with only 10 in attendance when Mosese joined the Church. Brother Walter Smith was our first branch president, assisted by Brother Vilikesa Bautarua. The Smiths played a major role in the conversion of Mosese. He was touched by their hard work and dedication to the work of the Lord. I give them all the credit. They were the backbone and pioneers of the Church during our time in Taveuni.

We moved to the city of Suva in 1975. Mosese continued to be active, not missing any meetings. His resolution every year was to be punctual to his meetings.

Our desire to serve a mission came from a very personal reason. We raised a grandson from the time he was five months until he turned seven years old. His paternal grandmother came from Philadelphia, USA, to visit in Fiji and asked if she could take little Aaron back to the States for his education. This was a hard and emotional decision for Mosese to make, but we agreed. Mosese's life was not the same, and Aaron's absence was hard to bear. We fasted and prayed for his safety and became close to the Lord. We humbly decided to serve a mission.

When we learned we would serve in Fiji, we were not surprised, for we didn't expect to serve anywhere else but among our own people, and we were happy. We needed to find someplace to store our meager belongings, and Mosese found a little piece of land where he built a lean-to; all our things fit into it. Our young daughter, Susu, Jr., went to live with my sister Lydia, and the others moved in with relatives. We did not have much financially, and Mosese used his retirement money from the police force to get us in to the mission field. We planned to live in the village, fishing and farming to keep us going after our mission.

His favorite scriptures were Amos 8:11, which talks about the Lord sending a famine of hearing the words of the Lord, and Jeremiah 2:21, which he quoted to the youth a few hours before he passed away.

137

Our son Ephraim and cousin Simi were preparing to leave for Sinai in the Middle East with the Fijiian Military. Mosese sent me to see them off and to tell them that if something happened to either of us, they were not to return to Fiji, but to stay on and take care of their duties. Ephraim said, "Why did he say that?" I answered, "Son, you know that we do not know what will happen today or tomorrow or next week. Just be prepared and remember what he said." Mosese passed away two weeks after they left, and they both stayed to attend to their duties. When they returned home, my son Ephraim told me that while they were parading on the grounds, he blacked out and fainted, and that was the day his father passed away.

We were assigned to accompany our branch for a picnic to Malau in Labasa, but I was not very happy about making the trip. I was afraid for the safety of the children, and for some reason I felt uneasy all day, with a chilling fear in me. The day was joyous for the youths and for Elder Maiwiriwiri, as they liked fishing; there were a lot of fish, and they filled the buckets.

When it was time to return home, some of the youth decided to swim to the boat instead of waiting for the punt to ferry them. One young man called for help, for he was having a cramp in one of his legs. Elder Maiwiriwiri swam back to the boat, put his left arm around the boy's neck and began swimming with his right hand. The boy, about 12 years old, was big and tall. It was too strenuous for Elder Maiwiriwiri, and he called for help. A brother swam over and grabbed the boy, and we all noticed that Elder Maiwiriwiri was struggling to keep afloat. He made a few backstrokes, and then lay motionless on the surface of the water. Efforts to revive him were in vain.

I started to scream, and I began asking Heavenly Father to take me with my husband. Elder Andrew Jackson tapped me on the shoulder and slowly said to me, "Sister Maiwiriwiri, the Spirit told me that the Lord needs Elder Maiwiriwiri on the other side." That message helped me throughout the ordeal. The young man that my husband had saved began screaming hysterically. I went over to him and said,

"My boy, please stop crying. I want you to know that today is Elder Maiwiriwiri's day to leave us; when it is time to go, he will have to go. Please do not blame yourself." He seemed to calm down, and I know that the words of truth are a soothing balm to the soul.

Elder Jackson dreamed about Elder Maiwiriwiri that night and came to tell me early the next morning. He saw my husband taking some Fijiian men into a big Fijiian Bure (thatched house). Their faces were painted black and they wore skirts made from leaves. I visualized that meeting in my mind. My cousin also dreamed about Elder Maiwiriwiri after our mission. She was not a member of our church, but her dream left an impression on her, and she later joined the Church and served a mission.

Elder Wilbur Woolf was our mission president, and he wrote in his journal, "We had just gone to bed when the phone call came from President Naga of the Suva Fiji Stake, informing me that Elder Maiwiriwiri had died at Labasa. Elder and Sister Maiwiriwiri were the very first older native couple that ever served a mission. President Naga didn't have a lot of details but said Elder Maiwiriwiri had died of a heart attack. . . . I then spent the next hour getting in contact with Church authorities to let them know of his death. . . . We made reservations to leave for Suva the next morning to help with the funeral preparations as well as family and missionary problems associated with the sudden death of Elder Maiwiriwiri. . . . It was decided to fly the body to Suva for a funeral, then fly the body to Taveuni to his native village for burial. . . . [There needed to be] a certain traditional ceremony so the family could accept the body and make a proper disposition.

"The funeral was in the Suva 2nd Ward. I was instructed by assignment from the First Presidency and the Quorum of the Twelve to express their sympathy and condolences from all the General Authorities of the Church to the family. . . . I reported on the good work Elder and Sister Maiwiriwiri had done while on their mission, and I bore my testimony about the reality of the resurrection. All the elders in the Suva Zone acted as pall bearers . . . and looked so good in their white shirts and ties. . . .

Everyone . . . was impressed with their dignity and bearing as they carried their fellow elder in and out of the funeral to a small Fiji Airline plane. It was a trick to put the casket in the plane, then Sister Maiwiriwiri and one son. . . . When we arrived in Taveuni . . . a flatbed truck waited to carry the casket to the village. . . . We drove . . . to the village of Somosomo. Sister Maiwiriwiri was presented to the village chief . . . and she was wrapped in tapa cloths. . . . Then we proceded to the burial place on top of a beautiful hill overlooking the Somosomo Strait."

My husband's casket was carried up a steep hill. . . . President Naga was asked to dedicate the grave by the authority of the Melchizedek Priesthood. . . . I said goodbye to my eternal companion. I am looking forward to the day when I shall be with him and our family forever.

There were 80 baptisms in our mission before Mosese died.

I asked President Woolf for two weeks off from my mission but wished to finish the two months left in our mission. He told me I could stay, and after completing the traditional requirements of my late husband's funeral, I was assigned to serve in Somosomo, where my husband is buried.

There were many from our family and from the village who served missions. The branch has grown from 10 members to 904, and the Church has purchased a piece of land for a real LDS chapel. Although Elder Mai-wiriwiri will not be physically there when the chapel is built in Taveuni, I know he will be present spiritually. He had served a mission and had given his life to save a young soul, a son of God.

I strongly believe that this mission helped him to prepare for a new calling. He had been nourished by the good word of God. He had an opportunity for growth and training in the work of the Lord. I can not think of a better way to enter the spirit world than when you are on a mission, fully occupied in the work of the Lord.

Our grandson Aaron served in the U.S. military for four years and returned from Iraq. He is now happily married to a wonderful girl. Their wedding celebration was held in Fiji, and in a full traditional way.

I, Sister Maiwiriwiri, went on a second mission, to Scotland in 2001–2002. I am now ready to go on my third mission, waiting for the Lord's time and place.

Kenton Leigh Martin

Born: 23 February 1978, Rexburg, Idaho
Parents: Don Martin and Linda Martin
Siblings: Shane, Kari Ann, Kelby, Amber
Mission: Florida Tallahassee
Time of service: 17 June 1997 to 27 March 1998
Cause of death: Vehicle/bicycle accident
Date and place of death: 27 March 1998, Blountstown, Florida
Age at time of death: 20
Place of burial: South Jordan Cemetery, South Jordan, Utah
Story related by: Don Martin, father

KENTON LEIGH MARTIN WAS A VERY SHY young boy and was a deep thinker, both spiritually and intellectually—incredible with mathematics and statistics. At the age of five, he could instantly add and subtract five digit numbers in his head. He memorized names of NFL players, team rankings, stats and game scores, and he could recite the action of entire games, years after he had watched them.

Kenton was in the first graduating class of the new Copper Hills High School in West Jordan, Utah, where he was an Honors and AP student, and the school's first Science Sterling Scholar. He maintained nearly a 4.0 GPA. He attended Ricks College in Rexburg, Idaho, on two scholarships, majoring in pre-medicine with the hope of becoming a medical doctor.

Kenton had always planned to serve a mission for The Church of Jesus Christ of Latter-day Saints and was thrilled to be called to Florida since a brother, uncle, and grandpa also had served missions in the South.

His missionary scripture was 2 Nephi 31:20: *"Wherefore, ye must press forward with a steadfastness in Christ, having a perfect brightness of hope, and a love of God and of all men. Wherefore, if ye shall press forward, feasting upon the word of Christ, and endure to the end, behold, thus saith the Father: Ye shall have eternal life."*

He had a great sense of humor and often found humor in small things other people might miss. The first two words of his first letter home from Florida were, "Holy humidity!" It was 90% humidity and over 90 degrees! In spite of that, he enjoyed his mission, his companions, converts, and the Saints in Florida. He served in Pace, Tallahassee, and for eight days in Blountstown.

On the morning of 27 March 1998, I attended a workshop at the University of Utah, learning what I could to help Kenton get admitted to medical school. Kenton's mom, Linda, received a call indicating that Kenton had been in an accident and had a broken arm, but the nurse was unclear about "further injuries." We later learned that Kenton lost his life by turning his bicycle in front of an oncoming 16-wheel empty gravel truck which neither he nor his companion had heard. Linda frantically tried to reach me, and in the midst of her desperation, our stake president, President Hall, arrived at our door, followed by our bishop and his counselor.

Campus police were finally able to locate me, and I phoned Linda and then frantically drove home as fast as I dared with tears streaming down my face. I prayed aloud to the Lord: "If he is in pain, please allow Dad (Kenton's grandpa who passed away in 1992) to be there, to comfort him." At that moment, my father spoke to my mind, "Donald, he is not in pain." A huge knot formed in my throat as I realized what this must mean.

I arrived home and found Linda frantic. The stake president advised us to make a decision quickly regarding harvesting Kenton's organs. We prayed and then made a call to the waiting surgeon. He informed me that Kenton was unresponsive to all seven neurological tests performed on accident victims. He said he knew we were good Christians, as he was, and that his advice was to remove the respirator and allow Kenton to go peacefully, that if he were the father, that was the decision he would make. Shaken to the very core of my being, I gave the OK to remove the respirator. I pray fervently that it was the correct decision.

A letter from Kenton, mailed a few days before his death, arrived the day of the accident. He encouraged us to read Moroni 7 in the Book of Mormon. We opened our scriptures and read the heading: *"An invitation to enter into the rest of the Lord."* We shed some tears and later read the entire chapter. It has become our favorite, encompassing the gospel of faith, hope, and charity.

We were struck with disbelief, asking how could it have been Kenton? He was so athletic and so bright; we were sure it was a case of mistaken identity. Then, his body arrived at the mortuary and shock began to settle in. It took every ounce of energy we had just to stand and move. The spirit of the Second Comforter was in our home for the next few weeks, and our senses were on overload. Colors were much brighter and we were aware of the slightest sounds. I became aware of the birds singing at 4:00 a.m., and although I was totally exhausted, I had to get up because I knew the Savior was there, and perhaps Kenton was as well. I woke the family to have them enjoy the wonderful Spirit and the unusual beauty of the sky, the moon, and the stars.

As we were leaving for the viewing, the phone rang. President Gordon B. Hinckley had phoned to tell us that people all over the world were praying for our family. It was so comforting to hear his voice and know of his love and concern. We shared our love with him. We arrived a few minutes early for the viewing and found the funeral home already packed. We greeted friends, family, and wonderful people for over five hours. We met other families who had also lost missionaries, and new friendships were formed.

Elder David B. Haight of the Quorum of the Twelve Apostles, spoke at the funeral and later invited us to spend an afternoon with him. We developed a great love for Elder Haight, and he and I gave Linda a blessing. We also spent an afternoon with Elder Henry B. Eyring, of the Quorum of the Twelve, and again we gave Linda a blessing. We were so touched by their willingness to spend time with us, and they shared many gospel insights that have blessed our lives.

We have since attended several missionary viewings and funerals and have discovered a common thread among all the missionaries: they are all select, bright, and talented individuals with outgoing personalities and an ability to reach people.

Some of our family members have had vivid dreams of visiting with Kenton. He has said, "I am perfectly happy. I'm doing everything I ever wanted to do." He has told us about his current calling, about the accident, and he has been natural, happy, and laughing. These conversations are sacred to us, and we have promised to share any glimpse we have of him with others in our immediate family.

We traveled to Florida to meet the converts, members, and missionaries Kenton served with. At first, the mission president hesitated to allow us to come, but with some urging, he agreed, and we made the trip to Florida. We visited with Elder Tim Moser, Kenton's companion at the time of the accident. He had been extremely upset at the time but decided to complete his mission. Had Elder Moser been in the lead on his bicycle, he said he would have been the one struck, but Kenton had gone first. We visited with converts and members, all of whom spoke of Kenton's deep spirituality and love for the Savior, adding that he was unlike any other missionary they had seen. We made several new friends, many who have since visited in our home.

We met with Brother Sutton, a member of the Blountstown bishopric who was working at the hospital when Kenton was brought in. He took care of Kenton's personal belongings and clothing. He said something significant to me that I have thought of often: I did not have the power to rewind the clock and save Kenton from losing his life. Were we given the power, we might have changed every wrong to right, including the martyrdom of the Prophet Joseph Smith, or the crucifixion of the Savior. However in doing so, we would have changed the history of the world.

We were shocked and amazed at the response from around the world, from members of the Church and those of other faiths, and we thank God for all the wonderful people on this earth. We received poems, songs, and a few dollars accompanying their heartfelt sympathy and love for missionaries and for us. Friends from my hometown in La Jara, Colorado, and Linda's in Rexburg, Idaho, were wonderful to us. Members of the Glenmoor 6th Ward and South Jordan West Stake huddled around us, and although we all felt a great loss, we were comforted and cared for.

Not a single day has gone by since the accident that we do not think of Kenton. He pops into our minds often at odd times, and we feel him close to us. Everything in our life changed on that day, including how we think and view the world. Our focus is now on eternal life, and living worthily. We have had many ups and downs since losing Kenton. Parents and siblings have passed through the veil, and Linda and I have had serious physical ailments. Kelby, Kenton's younger brother, has completed a mission and is now married. As to how we are, the simple answer is, OK. Even on the hard days, we are simply OK. We think of and discuss the love of our Savior, and our love for Him, the Atonement, the wonderful resurrection day, and the beauty of earth life. Our testimonies and the testimonies of many others have been strengthened through this experience.

Fortunately, Kenton was a voracious writer. He kept a detailed journal of his missionary activities and corresponded with family members and with 20 friends serving missions. He wrote his feelings about what he read each day in a Book of Mormon journal. A few minutes prior to his fatal accident, he wrote, "I cannot remember living with the Savior, but I am preparing to return to him instant by instant."

Kenton's missionary plaque still hangs in the foyer of our chapel. It was presented at a homecoming meeting we held for him after all of his friends returned from their missions. We wonder what he would have done with his life had he lived, but we trust in the Lord and look forward to a great reunion with our son. Our lives are focused upon Christ and his wonderful atoning sacrifice. Because of Him, we will be made whole again. Our testimonies of the gospel are stronger than ever, and we pray that upon our Savior's return, we will be found serving Him.

Ella Adelia Williams Moody

Born: 31 October 1874, Spanish Fork, Utah
Parents: David Daniel Williams and Rosina Allen Williams
Siblings: Loran, Loris, Orville David, Lillian, Lillie, Elizabeth, Rosina, Dora, Semoa, Beatrice, Guenna, Estalla, Nellie, David
Spouse: William Alfred Moody
Children: Hazel Moody, born in Fagalii, Samoa
Mission: Fagalii, Upolo Island, Samoa
Time of service: 12 October 1894 to 4 June 1895
Cause of death: Complications of childbirth
Date and place of death: 24 May 1895, Fagalii, Upolo Island, Samoa
Age at the time of death: 20
Place of burial: Fagalii, Samoa
Story related by: William A. Moody, husband

ELLA ADELIA WILLIAMS WAS BORN in Spanish Fork, Utah, to David Williams and Rosina Allen. The Williams family moved to Thatcher, Arizona, where Adelia met and married William Alfred Moody.

In his autobiography, William Moody describes Adelia as being "gentle and good, intelligent, amiable and cheerful, trustworthy and kind. While she was naturally quiet, she was also affectionate. One evening after we had returned from M.I.A., we sat together on a trunk and I asked her to be my wife, and she accepted me. The days that followed were wonderful beyond description."

On 4 June 1894, Ella Adelia Williams, aged 19, became the bride of William Alfred Moody at the home of her parents. William called Delia the "cherished bride of my youth" and describes their early life together as sweet, their future bright and full of promise. William was well established in the shipping business and owned some 80 acres of land. He became very prosperous, realizing profits at every turn.

At this point in his career, he received a letter from "Box B" of The Church of Jesus Christ of Latter-day Saints and was called to serve a three-year mission in Samoa. William states in his autobiography that he was torn between accepting the call and continuing in his opportunity to get rich. He wrote: "I was painfully aware that I was standing at the forks of the road, one way leading upward toward a life of virtue, respect, and esteem, with service in the work of the Lord and salvation and an eternal life of joy as its goal. The other path would have plenty of hazards, but it was reasonable to presume that it would bring wealth."

He and Adelia earnestly and humbly prayed for an answer. Adelia was expecting their first child and had misgivings at the thought of William leaving. They concluded that the call came from the Lord and he should go. On 24 September 1894, they left the little depot in Thatcher together, planning to travel as far as Salt Lake City, where they would be endowed and sealed. Delia would return to Arizona to live with her parents while William was away.

Before they made it to Salt Lake City, a letter from Church headquarters reached them, telling them that the mission needed a sister and Delia could accompany her husband to Samoa. They were overjoyed but did not have enough money with them to pay both fares and added expenses. William told Delia the Lord would provide, and they would go as far as their money lasted and trust God to open the way. William wrote: "Without hesitation, she lifted her sweet face to me and said, 'we will go. I trust you, and the Lord will be with us.' . . . As I write this, I marvel now at our child-like faith in undertaking a trip thousands of miles long without sufficient funds, with my wife on the way to bearing a child, and with no slightest knowledge of what conditions we should find in Samoa . . . as isolated from our home as another planet seems today."

They reached Salt Lake City on 9 October. Two days later they were endowed, sealed, and set apart for their missions on 12 October. They headed to San Francisco, and the Lord truly opened the way for them financially. When they arrived in Samoa, they still had nine dollars.

Delia was very ill during the two-week journey and became emaciated and weak. She and her husband remained at the mission headquarters with

President Thomas Hilton and his wife Sarah. Delia soon regained her health, and they learned to love their new life, in spite of the climate and cockroaches.

William and Delia had been married six months that November and looked forward to the birth of their child. They talked often of their plans for the future when their missions were complete. William wrote of their idyllic life, surrounded by tropical beauty, their mutual trust and love, and unity in laboring for the gospel.

On 27 March 1895, President Hilton and his wife, Charles R. Thomason, and two missionary sisters from Tonga, Maggie Durham and Luella Adams, left for their homes in Utah. They had been released as missionaries, and "with prayers and tears we bade them farewell," wrote William.

Delia was a little concerned that she was now the only woman missionary on the island and would not have the help of her friends when her baby came. Her husband wrote, "She silently yielded to a trying situation and clung to me still more closely as she looked toward an uncertain future. . . . Every detail was as carefully planned as possible for the safe arrival of our baby and the preservation of the life and health of the mother. No word of mine can overstate our anxiety as the hour approached."

On 3 May 1895, a tiny baby girl was born to the couple, and they named her Hazel. Adelia was unwell following Hazel's birth, and William wrote: "Our joy was short-lived, and the days that followed took my faith through the most crucial test it ever had. For three weeks, I abandoned everything else to the care of my wife. . . . I can still hear the tick of the clock which marked the hours of my lonely vigil, as night after night, in silence, I watched the life of my beloved ebbing away.

"Hitherto, God had answered my prayers and administrations in her behalf and that of others, but He seemed now to have forsaken me. Adelia had a vision of heavenly beings standing near her bed and called my attention to them, friends and relations from the spirit world who appeared to have come to welcome and guide her to them.

"She asked for her baby, once more to hold her in her arms clingingly, then on May 24th of 1895, she closed her eyes to everything mortal. I must have felt much as Jesus did when, upon the cross, he was impelled to cry out, 'My God! My God! Why hast Thou forsaken me?'

"The light of the whole world went out of my life when she was taken. I feel sure now that heavenly angels accompanied her spirit to her heavenly home, where, if I can only remain faithful to the end, I shall meet her, know her once more, and continue to lavish upon her my undying love."

Ella Adelia Williams Moody, aged 20, was laid to rest in the midst of a coconut grove on 25 May 1895, in Fagalii, Upolo Island, Samoa. Others were buried in the same area—President Ransom Stevens and three of the children of Thomas H. and Sarah Hilton. William arranged with Mrs. Bell, a school teacher from England, to care for Hazel while he continued his mission and traveled where he was assigned.

William wrote: "The anguish of my heart and the hopes buried beneath that coffin lid had better remain further untold. . . . I found it very difficult to accept my new situation. . . . My outlook appeared to be dark and largely without incentive. My one gleam of interest was now centered in my baby. I must save her and love her, so that, through her, I might see something of Adelia. In the course of time, nature began to bring about a gradual return of my spirit for the duties and environment surrounding me and to create a new interest in life. Yet even then, I felt a protest at my return to normal living, as though it were a disloyalty to my wife, leaving in the background my great love for her.

"In my heart and soul, I nursed a grievance against God for His dealings with me. I also nursed my grief, much to my own detriment. I should have known that God is always just and never cruel. He could not be God and be otherwise. Withal there was something within me that led me to be faithful to my missionary work and to make a success of it. I prayed earnestly in the hope that God would somehow make the whole matter clear to me and re-store my confidence and faith. I had to wait a year, however, during which time I carried both my wounded feelings and my work as a double burden."

Hazel was ill off and on during the time her father served, and finally William sent her home when she was a little over a year old. Three months after he carried her onto the ship, William finally learned that she had arrived safely. She thrived with her grandparents, grew to be a lovely woman, marrying and raising a child of her own.

On the night of the first anniversary of Adelia's death, William experi-enced what he called a vision; at its conclusion he wrote: "I was now wholly reconciled to my bereavement. My soul was full of trust and faith in God."

William Moody was honorably released on 17 May 1898. He arrived home at Thatcher, Arizona, on 18 June 1898, after being away for 3 years, 9 months, and 24 days. He was met by his father, his daughter Hazel, and other family members. William outlived three other wives before his death on 19 January 1967. He is buried in Salt Lake City, Utah.

Source: William A. Moody, *Years in the Sheaf* (Orem, UT: Granite Publishing Co., 1959). Dorothy Ostegar Busath and Mary Jane Carlyle Heider submitted the autobiography.

Lorin Lee Murdock

Born: 3 August 1956, Driggs, Teton County, Idaho
Parents: Lorin Andrew Murdock and Dorothy Lee Hutto Murdock
Siblings: Kerry Ray, Dorothy Cherie, Kelly Ann
Mission: Texas San Antonio
Time of service: 27 September 1975 to 6 December 1975
Cause of death: Deliberate auto/bicycle hit-and-run
Date and place of death: 6 December 1975, Portland, Texas
Age at time of death: 19
Place of burial: Bates Cemetery, Driggs, Idaho
Story related by: Dorothy Murdock, mother

LORIN LEE MURDOCK WAS BORN 3 August 1956 in Driggs, Teton County, Idaho, in the beautiful valley of the Teton Mountains. His birth was not an easy one. The nurse told his father, Lorin, "If you want this child, you had better get on your knees in mighty prayer." In doing so, Lorin expressed to Heavenly Father how much he wanted this son—never even thinking the baby would not be a boy. Father said, "You cannot have him. I need him here with me." Lorin pled and finally [understood Heavenly Father to say], "You can have him until he is grown." Lorin did not tell me of that experience until later. In the joy and happiness that comes with a baby, those special feelings were forgotten or put aside.

So we were privileged to have Lorin Lee come to our home for 19 years. When he was two years old, he began asking over and over again, "Mama, why did you wait so long to have me?" and I repeatedly answered, "I had you as soon as I could, Son."

He seemed to be an especially pure and happy child, easily entreated. Through the years of growing up and while on his mission for The Church of Jesus Christ of Latter-day Saints, when anyone was rude or hurtful, he wrote: "I just smile at them and go on my way."

During his formative years, our family lived in the beautiful pine woods of East Texas, where Lorin became especially close to his Hutto grandparents, aunts, uncles, and his Grandpa Murdock, who spent many months of the year with our family.

In 1964, in the Beaumont Stake Conference, Spencer W. Kimball was the visiting apostle. He called the 8- to 10-year-old boys to the pulpit and gave each one a dollar bill to start a mission fund. Lorin Lee was 8, and that was a powerful moment in his life! Elder Kimball's teaching that these young men should become missionaries was sealed in Lorin's heart and mind forever.

Our family moved to a cattle ranch in 1972 in Leadore, Idaho. Later, Lorin Lee attended Ricks College one year before his mission and could hardly wait to turn 19 so he could go on a mission. He received a letter signed by President Spencer W. Kimball, dated 19 August 1975, calling him to serve in the Texas San Antonio Mission. He was happy to serve in Texas, where he had lived at one time. His dad had served in the Texas–Louisiana Mission some 25 years earlier.

He entered the mission home on 27 September 1975. It was a joyous day for Lorin, but a hard day for me. I had a distinct and powerful feeling that I would never see him again. After many tears, peace returned and I passed off my fears to having my firstborn leave home. We had taught him all his life the importance of serving a mission, and now it was right that he should leave home to do so.

Lorin's joys as a missionary could not be contained. His reports and letters were full to overflowing with his love for missionary work, and for his companion, Elder Michael Averett from Utah. He loved his mission president and the people of Portland, Texas. After one month he wrote, "I thought I was happy before, but I guess I didn't know what happiness is." He loved the temple and counseled his cousins to serve missions if they had the opportunity and not to marry anyone who could not take them to the temple.

He wrote that he learned that if he did exactly as instructed, the Holy Ghost would help him learn his lessons quickly and easily. If he deviated in any way, he could tell he did not receive the Lord's help. He also stated, "I surely do miss everyone, but I have my Father to be with me. I know I do not do everything He wants me to, but He still loves me."

On Saturday, 6 December 1975, Elder Murdock and Elder Averett taught Brother Ben and Sister Barbara Davis and family, who were to be baptized the following week. Sister Davis wrote: "Elder Murdock is such a pure, happy elder with spiritual depth. He seems to have a glow, a light around him." They left the Davis home about 6:15 p.m. on their bikes to return home. Five minutes later, Elder Averett heard a crash and saw a red pick-up truck whiz by without stopping. He administered to Elder Murdock, but said he knew the Lord wanted Elder Murdock; it was the Lord's will and he could not change it.

Our family was returning from a wonderful day of shopping in Idaho Falls, 125 miles from our home. We had already sent Lorin Lee's packages, including the homemade bread he had requested. We were so happy because he was so happy, and we laughed and sang all the way home, feeling life was good.

We stopped at Lorin's sister's home in Mud Lake. She said our stake president, Joe Proksch of the Salmon Stake, was trying to reach us. When we arrived home, President Proksch was waiting for us. He struggled to tell us our son had been killed by a hit-and-run driver. The police said it was deliberate and called his death "murder."

We couldn't believe it was true! The Lord watches over His missionaries, and our son was serving the Lord! But it was true. Lorin's sister and family came to be with us, to love us, and strengthen us. There are no words to express the depth of pain, grief, sorrow, and shock we felt. We could not understand how someone could deliberately take the life of our son because he was a missionary of The Church of Jesus Christ of Latter-day Saints, who testified of Jesus Christ and gospel truths.

Four days later we saw our son, lying peacefully as though asleep. My husband said, "Well, son, we did not expect you to come home this way." We both felt our Father's love in abundance, to overflowing, and an abiding peace that cannot be described came to us. I knew at that moment that had Heavenly Father asked me, "Dorothy, I need your son here to help me; may I have him?" I would have said, "Yes."

We learned, five years later, that a detective from the Portland Police Department was determined to have justice done no matter how long it took, telling us that he had visited with and loved "those boys." A witness came forward and described the deliberate hit and run by a prominent citizen of the town who was driving a red pick-up truck. Before the driver could be arrested, he choked on some food, slipped into a coma, and died a year later. The officer said, "There is a higher power than me, and He took care of it." We are blessed to feel no ill will or animosity toward the driver.

Funeral services were 11 December 1975, with President S. Dilworth

Young of the Quorum of the Seventy representing the Church. He brought love, comfort, and assurance that our son, who died a martyr to the Lord, was now in Heavenly Father's presence; that he would continue to serve and teach as a missionary in the spirit world. We are so grateful for his presence and his message from our prophet and from our Father in Heaven.

President Ronald Loveland of the San Antonio Mission wrote us that he found Elder Murdock to be a "very, very special young man . . . very wholesome, clean, and pure . . . with extraordinary spiritual depth." He added that Elder Murdock and Elder Averett were "a powerful team." Elder Murdock testified that his companion, our son, knew the gospel better than any other companion he had.

A letter signed by President Spencer W. Kimball, N. Eldon Tanner, and Marion G. Romney, the First Presidency, stated: "We trust that you have faith and assurance that your son is not lost, but that he has merely gone home to continue his mission in preparation for the future work and happy reunions which await him."

We received many additional letters and expressions of love and concern from family, friends, and others that had experienced the deaths of missionaries. The blessings of strength, love, and support of family members, of our ward and stake family, and our community cannot be counted or measured.

And so it is. This is our faith. We know where our son is, and we desire to live our lives so we can be with him in Heavenly Father's presence. His death did not deter our second son, a daughter, cousins, or us, his parents, from serving missions. I received assurance from the Lord that our second son, Kerry Ray, would return to us following his mission. We suffered our hardest years in work and financially while he was gone, but the test was complete. Words cannot describe my joy when he arrived safely home. We suffered similar tests and joy when our daughter Kelly Ann served a mission.

I was privileged to visit with Lorin Lee from the other side of the veil. He assured me he is very happy and continuing his service as a missionary, teaching our Father's children. It was a very sacred experience to be with him and to feel of celestial love.

It has now been over 30 years since Lorin Lee died, and we still miss him. Christmastime is hard, yet at the same time, very wonderful, because of the sweet assurance we have of the birth, Atonement, and Resurrection of God's beloved, only begotten Son and His gospel plan of eternal life.

We found our son's favorite scripture among his belongings: Psalm 106:1 *"Praise ye the Lord. Oh, give thanks unto the Lord; for He is good: and His mercy endureth for ever."* And so we do.

Gary Lane Nielson

Born: 9 February 1958, Delta, Utah
Parents: Vern S. Nielson and Clara Anderson Nielson
Siblings: Steven, Roger, Virginia, Nola, Elaine, Dorthy
Mission: Hawaii Honolulu
Time of service: 10 March 1977 to 2 August 1977
Cause of death: Hit-and-run bicycle/auto accident
Date and place of death: 30 July 1977, Guam
Age at time of death: 19
Place of burial: Oak City, Millard County, Utah
Story related by: Virginia N. Peterson, sister

GARY LANE NIELSON WAS THE YOUNGEST of eight children and was preceded in death by his oldest sister, Jerrlyn, who died at birth. In 1977, Gary, a young farm boy from Oak City, Utah, left his parents, brothers, sisters, nieces, nephews, and grandparents at home to serve a mission for The Church of Jesus Christ of Latter-day Saints in the Hawaii Honolulu Mission. Ten exceptional young men his age from Oak City all served missions.

Gary loved his nieces and nephews, and he made them feel special, even letting them hang out with him when his friends were around. He had many close friends and was nominated "Preferred Man" in his senior year at Delta High School. He was special to all who knew him. Gary's future plans always included a mission, and he was very excited about his call to Hawaii.

At that time, the Hawaii Honolulu Mission included the district of Micronesia, which included the island of Guam, that consists mostly of a United States Naval Base. Soon after Gary began his mission, he was transferred to proselyte in Guam. President Huber Butler presided over the six elders assigned to Guam. President William W. Cannon was president of the Hawaii Honolulu Mission.

On Wednesday, 3 August 1977, the following message was sent to the missionaries in the Hawaii Honolulu Mission:

"And they were all young men, and they were exceedingly valiant for courage, and also for strength and activity; but behold, that was not all—they were men who were true at all times in whatsoever thing they were entrusted." (Alma 53:20)

"This scripture was the theme for the devotional, Saturday, July 30, 1977—Pioneer Week, and describes the two thousand stripling soldiers led by Helaman. This scripture also characterizes a modern stripling missionary, Elder Gary Nielson. Since arriving in Hawaii on March 24, 1977, Elder Nielson averaged 68 proselyting hours per week and [was] partially instrumental in bringing a substantial number of people into the Church. He was concerned that he had taught only seven discussions when he wrote in his mission journal on July 16, 'this week has been sort of slow as far as teaching goes.'

"July 23 he wrote: 'It has been raining quite a lot this week. . . . Despite the rain we were still able to keep our total proselyting up to 67 hours. . . . We have two families that are near baptism. . . . We also have several individuals that are promising. We hopefully will baptize Terry Glaze next Saturday.'

"Saturday night, July 30, Terry Glaze was baptized and confirmed by Elders Campbell and Nielson. As they were riding toward their apartment on their bicycles following the service, a car hit both Elder Nielson and Brother Glaze. The driver sped off without stopping. Brother Glaze is now in the hospital with back injuries. Elder Nielson had severe head and internal injuries and never regained consciousness following the accident. He returned to our Heavenly Father at 10:30 p.m., August 2, 1977, Guam time."

Elder Nielson and his companion, Elder David Campbell, and a Navy man, Terry Glaze, whom they had just baptized, were riding their bicycles home. As they passed a car that was backed into a driveway, it pulled out and drove directly into them. Gary was the back rider and was hit first, then Terry Glaze was hit. Elder Campbell was the lead rider and was not hurt.

155

Gary sustained head and internal injuries and was hospitalized until his death four days later on 2 August 1977. Brother Glaze was in the hospital for two months with back injuries.

Shortly after the accident, President Cannon and an assistant had given Gary a priesthood blessing. President Cannon talked with Gary's parents on the telephone about Gary's passing and the accident, and helped them work through all the arrangements that had to be made. President Thomas S. Monson from the First Presidency also talked with them on the telephone and shared a great deal of comfort and strength with the family.

A plaque was given to the family in memory of Gary by the members of the Waipahu Hawaii Stake, quoting Doctrine and Covenants 50:5: *"But blessed are they who are faithful and endure, whether in life or in death, for they shall inherit eternal life."*

During the time Gary was in the hospital after the accident, there was always someone from the Waipahu Hawaii Stake by his side. Many volunteers took turns serving their dear friend.

An article published in the *Pacific Daily News*, in Agana, Guam, dated Friday, 5 August 1977, reported the accident, featuring a picture of Elder Nielson and his friend Kathy Murdock, taken before he left home in Utah. The headline reads, "His Mission Cut Short, Gary Nielson Goes Home," and continues: "Gone, but not forgotten. Gary Nielson hadn't yet discovered his calling when he posed with Utah friend, Kathy Murdock, for this portrait. The Mormon Church Elder died a victim of a hit-and-run accident as he pedaled his bicycle after the baptism of a friend."

The whole town of Oak City rallied around the family. Elder S. Dilworth Young of the Quorum of the Seventy spoke at the service and said many consoling words that helped the family. The Holy Spirit was very close to Gary's parents and siblings and brought much comfort through a very hard and trying time.

Brother Terry Glaze has kept in touch with our family through all these years. He and his wife live in Tennessee. They were sealed in the temple for time and all eternity; their children are grown and have all been active in the Church. Brother Glaze has served as a branch president and as executive secretary to his stake president. Although Brother Glaze doesn't recall the accident because he was so seriously hurt, he loved Gary and has had much concern for his family and has kept in touch by letter and telephone through all these years. He has been a wonderful blessing to our family. Mom and Dad were always happy to hear from him.

At the time of this writing in 2007, we have seen many changes in our family. Gary's nephew, Scott J. Peterson, filled a mission to Hawaii in 1985–1987. He said people there still remembered Gary, as his death had left such an impact on them. Scott also said that he felt Gary's influence with him many times. Gary's mom, Clara, passed away 18 October 1999, and his dad, Vern, passed away on 10 April 2007 at the age of 90. Also a nephew, Matthew Kapler, passed away on Christmas Eve of 2003. None of us knows why we are tested to the limit sometimes, but I'm sure the Lord has His reasons and we will understand someday, when we can see the whole eternal scheme of things. We are very thankful for the gospel that gives us such great comfort during our stay on this earth.

Gary was one of the stalwarts and always showed great respect and love to his parents and all those that were associated with him. Gary progressed so much spiritually during the last six months of his life and gained a real and true testimony of The Church of Jesus Christ of Latter-day Saints. He loved his work and enjoyed serving his Heavenly Father. He worked hard and had great success for his 4 ½ months of service. I truly know Heavenly Father was helping him to prepare for something greater through this experience in his life. His death has strengthened my testimony and faith in God. The only way one can make it through such a difficult time is with the help of our Heavenly Father.

Gerald Lee Ockey

Born: 10 October 1935, Salt Lake City, Utah
Parents: Henry DeWitt Ockey and Alice Winn Ockey
Siblings: Blaine, Robert, Norman, Gail, Thomas
Mission: Australia
Time of Service: 5 March 1956 to 5 September 1957
Cause of death: Struck down by a pick-up truck
Date and place of death: 5 September 1957,
New South Wales, Australia
Age at time of death: 21
Place of burial: Wasatch Memorial Park, Salt Lake City, Utah
Story related by: Thomas Dee Ockey, identical twin brother to Gerald

GERALD LEE OCKEY CAME FROM a family of six boys, twins Gerald (Jerry) and I being the last. On learning that twins were joining our family, our dad said, "When they start doubling up on you, it's time to quit!" Our three older brothers, Blaine, Robert, and Norman, all served in World War II. Less than a year after Gail was born, Jerry and I made our debut, and the three of us grew up together, following each other through the ranks of the Aaronic Priesthood and other church activities. We all received our Eagle Scout Awards on the same day in 1950.

In 1955, Gail was called to serve in the East Central States Mission, and one year later, Jerry and I were called to serve in the Australian and South Australian Missions, respectively, having a joint farewell in February 1956. Prior to his mission, Jerry completed two years of study at the

University of Utah and had been provisionally accepted to a dental school in the Midwest. He was engaged to be married upon his return from Australia. He enjoyed swimming, tennis, hiking, and playing piano duets with me.

Jerry always wanted to serve in the mission field for The Church of Jesus Christ of Latter-day Saints. He had been encouraged by his priesthood leaders, family, friends, and fiancée. His decision was made early, and he never wavered. Seventeen missionaries from our ward had already been called to serve throughout the world. Jerry had a vibrant testimony of the gospel and of the Savior, Jesus Christ, and he was eager and excited to be on his way. His example evidenced his beliefs!

The call to serve in Australia, however, was a total surprise. Jerry had a rudimentary knowledge of the French language and had a neighbor serving as the mission president in the Netherlands, so he thought France or Holland would be possibilities. Australia had never been considered, and we didn't know anyone serving there. Jerry and I opened our mission calls together, and, as the shock settled in, the only comment Jerry made to me was, "Well, Tom, at least we'll be serving together on the same continent for two years." Leaving home was tough, but Elder Ockey was committed to the mission experience. The fact that we were sailing together softened our departure somewhat; we would have at least 17 days together on the ocean.

One of his favorite scriptures which he had memorized early in life was Philippians 4:13: *"I can do all things through Christ which strengtheneth me."* He quoted it often as occasion and circumstance arose. Every member of our family was familiar with the power and promise of that scripture.

His letters home to our family and to me in Australia were always optimistic, up-beat, and positive. He loved to tell about his tracting experiences and also of the people he shared the message with. He felt they were "the ones" that would come into the Church. He seldom gave up hope for their eventual baptisms and never gave up the enthusiasm that had taken him to the land "down under." As we served with all our hearts, Elder Ockey and I began a friendly competition as to the number of contacts made, cottage meetings held, hours tracting, service time given, etc., which served to inspire us both.

Elder Ockey was serving in the Blacktown Branch, where he was to be sustained branch president. He willingly accepted his responsibilities and was pleased to build our Father's kingdom there.

At approximately 6:20 p.m., on Thursday, 5 September 1957, Elder Ockey and his companion were riding their motorbikes on the Windsor Road, towards Richmond. Upon nearing an airfield, they had pulled off the side of the road to watch a plane land. As they prepared to leave, a truck, driven by an intoxicated driver, came down the road; and the driver, seeing the reflector on Elder Ockey's bike, swerved toward it, hitting Elder Ockey and throwing him over 100 feet down the road. His companion had not been touched, and he ran to Elder Ockey, only to discover that elder Ockey had died. The driver was arrested on the spot, declared legally drunk, charged with manslaughter, and served a short time in prison. I have never met the man who killed my twin brother. I know his name, but often forget it. I hold no animosity or anger toward him, just pity.

The news of my twin brother's death reached me in Melbourne, Australia, where I served in the mission office. When my companion and I arrived at an appointment, we were told by phone to return to the office at once. I turned to my companion as we rushed back and said, "It's my twin brother! I know it!" The mission president broke the news to me.

The next day, I received a call from my family in Utah and was deeply strengthened by their faith, courage, and acceptance of what had happened, and their determination to "carry on" in spite of all that had transpired. I thanked my Heavenly Father for His blessings of comfort to them and to the Saints back home.

With my mission president and his wife, I flew from Melbourne to Sydney to attend a funeral service for my brother. It was a particularly difficult time for me, but again, the Lord granted me a sense of serenity and peace as I enjoyed the sweet spirit of that service.

His body was flown home, accompanied by an elder from his mission. I remained in Australia for the next six months to complete the missions we had begun. Another funeral service was held for Jerry in our home ward in Salt Lake City. Among others, Apostle Hugh B. Brown, spoke, saying in part:

"This is, in a real sense, a missionary farewell. It is somewhat different from most, but the same facts are prevalent. Before, Jerry was called by the president of the Church. This time he has been called by the Master. . . . He responded then cheerfully and heartily, and he responds thus today. It is more difficult this time, because it is a longer mission, but he is closer to you now than he was [in Australia]. Let us all leave this building today, not trying to answer the question 'why?' but being reconciled to the fact that God our Father is our Father, that He loves and knows us better than we know ourselves, and that all that He does is for our good."

Both my brother and I had met Elder Brown in our respective missions. He related that he first met Elder Ockey in South Australia and had talked with him and heard his testimony. Knowing Elder Brown was going to Sydney, Elder Ockey told him, "You will meet a better Elder Ockey when you get there." Elder Brown continued, "When we did go North and met Elder Ockey, I thought it was the same one I had met in Melbourne and asked if he had come to another mission. He said to me, 'You saw a better Elder Ockey in Melbourne; I'm his twin brother.' The expressions of those two young men and their attitudes and personalities stood out, so that when we heard a week ago yesterday from President Erekson that he had lost one of his best missionaries, I felt I knew before I learned the elder's name, because he told me repeatedly this was one of the best elders he had.

"I would not undertake to answer 'why.' I shall not undertake to tell in detail just what is happening Over There. But this I know: there is an Over There, and what has happened to this young man has not robbed him of consciousness, personality, or individuality. He still lives Over There. Just as we know that God our Father is in charge of things over here, so I can say with certainty that He is in charge of things Over There.

"Brother and Sister Ockey asked some years ago for a choice spirit to come into their home, and God sent them two. What a blessing. How kind God has been to you. Now He has said: 'Let Jerry come and Tom remain, because I need Jerry.' We are richer if, as we pass through these experiences, we do not allow them to embitter us. There is something purifying in sorrow. Of all the virtues I think of, there is none more admired than humility. And every person in this House, today, feels humble."

Relative to my brother's passing, I have never asked myself the question "Why, why Jerry?" But the one question I did allow myself to ask is this: "IF one of us had to go, why couldn't it have been me?" The answer to that question has been my personal revelation, and as the years advance, I've come to clearly understand the answer.

I named my son Gerald Mark, in honor of my brother. My son and my daughter know about their missionary uncle and of my love and respect for him. They have both served honorable missions themselves and have tried to pattern their lives after the stories I related about him. What greater tribute could a father ask?

Great responsibility is laid upon each one of us to preserve and acknowledge the legacies left for us by such remarkable servants of the Lord.

Dale Lynn Olson

Born: 4 January 1955
Parents: Glen I. Olson and Margaret Olson
Siblings: Wanda, Marilyn, Brent, David, Bill, Steve
Mission: Alabama Florida
Time of service: 2 February 1974 to May 1975
Cause of death: Bicycle/auto accident
Date and place of death: 22 May 1975, Huntsville, Alabama
Age at time of death: 20
Place of burial: Memorial Garden of the Wasatch, South Ogden, Utah
Story related by: Margaret Olson, mother

DALE LYNN OLSON WAS BORN on 4 January 1955, in Sacramento, California. We and two sisters welcomed this delightful little boy into our home. When the nurse brought the baby to me, she said, "Here is your little dimples." He had a dimple in his chin and a dimple in each cheek, short blond hair, and the most beautiful blue eyes. He was the cutest little boy I had ever seen. He grew to be a happy, curious child who wanted to learn everything, "right now!"

Dale happily learned about the gospel as he attended Primary. He was baptized and confirmed a member of The Church of Jesus Christ of Latter-day Saints when he was 8 years old. I was impressed and surprised when Dale stood the following Sunday to bear his testimony. We were proud and happy when Dale later received his Duty to God Award.

When Dale was 11 years old, we moved to Poughkeepsie, New York, where his father had accepted a job to work for IBM. While there, with Utah plates still on our car, we put our five children in the car and drove to the Joseph Smith home in Palmyra, New York. The missionaries there gave us a special tour of the site, including the outside well dug by the Smith Family, and suggested we watch for a special "friend" while we walked to the Sacred Grove. On that lovely autumn day, the children happily and excitedly discovered that "friend," a raccoon washing a fish in the creek for his lunch.

We were alone in the grove, chatting and laughing, when the Holy Ghost prompted us all, including our two-year-old son, to stop and whisper. We knew we were on sacred ground, and that experience became a blessed testimony for our family.

After Dale graduated from high school, his uncle invited him to join his family on a fishing trip to Canada. Dale stayed with them the entire summer at their home in Wyoming, helping fix up a house his uncle planned to rent. When Dale returned home, he went to see the bishop, who gave him a recommend for a patriarchal blessing, and the papers to fill out for a mission call. Dale was called to the Alabama Florida Mission.

We went to the temple with Dale when he was endowed, and while there I had a sweet experience. My mother had recently passed away and had not received her endowment nor been sealed to my father, who was still living. As I helped Dale, the spirit announced to my mind, "Your mother is here." I was filled with joy and happiness knowing Mother was in the temple with us that day. The stake president set Dale apart as a missionary, telling him that as he walked down the streets, people would approach him and ask questions because the gospel would be shining from his face.

Dale entered the Mission Home on 2 February 1974 and arrived in the Alabama Florida Mission on 8 February. The following December, Dale's uncle asked Dale's father to come to Wyoming to baptize his wife. After spending the summer with Dale, and knowing he had chosen to serve a mission, they wanted to find out more about the Church and asked to be baptized.

Dale loved the Lord, loved the people, and loved his service as a missionary during the year he had served. His letters were full of happiness. He was excited to share how the blessing from his stake president as well as promises from his patriarchal blessing had been fulfilled.

Dale's mission president, Spencer H. Osborn, phoned my husband at his office to tell him there had been a terrible accident. My husband did not phone me but planned to tell me in person when he returned from work.

President Osborn phoned our home later, asking to speak to my husband. When I informed him my husband had not arrived yet, he said he would call later. I asked him to tell me what had happened, but he did not want to tell me. When I asked again, he told me that Dale and his companion were riding down a hill on their bicycles when a car, driven by a young woman, made a left turn in front of Dale. He was thrown against the windshield and bounced off the car. His companion was ahead of him and was not involved in the accident. There had been a prayer circle around Dale, anointing his shoulder since he had suffered a serious head injury. In our home, my two sons and I knelt and prayed for Dale, for ourselves, and for our family that was not yet home.

We traveled to Alabama to be with our injured son. Dale was still alive when we left Bountiful, but died while we were en route, on 22 May 1975. There was a memorial service held in Alabama, and it was there we met the family of the young girl who had hit Dale. I felt very sorry for that young woman, feeling I would not want to trade places with her.

We returned to Utah with Dale's body, and with his spirit aboard the plane. Dale's spirit told me that he would be able to help motivate my father to go to the temple. On April 14, 1977, I was sealed to my mother and father in the Ogden Temple, a miracle Dale performed in only two years' time.

President Spencer W. Kimball, and his counselors, N. Eldon Tanner and Marion G. Romney, sent a letter of condolence, dated 22 May 1975, stating: "Like the Master whom he served, your son went about doing good, and in the performance of duty he gave his life. He might have lived many years, but he could never have been engaged in a more worthy service or in one more acceptable to the Lord than that in which he was laboring when he died. To mortals his going has seemed untimely, but mortals do not know the will and providence of God. We trust that you have faith and assurance that your son is not lost, but that he has merely gone hence to continue his mission in preparation for the future work and happy reunions which await him."

Spencer H. Osborn, Dale's mission president, wrote the following in a letter sent to our home on the day Dale passed away: "The tragedy that claimed the life of your son, Elder Dale Lynn Olson, has left us numb with grief and sorrow. We send you our heartfelt sympathies and share with you the pain of his loss.... If I had received yesterday a divine mandate to transfer to our Father's heavenly service the purest and most saintly missionary among the 240 of the Florida Tallahassee Mission, that transfer would have gone to Dale, as indeed it has."

Sister Osborn wrote her feelings about Dale. "He was a real joy to us, and each zone conference when we visited with him, he would express his love for, and pride in, his family. . . . Dale has been a real inspiration to all of us in this mission, and we are confident that his assignments from now on will be even greater. . . . We love Dale so very, very much and appreciate his influence in our lives. I am sure that you have felt that there was something special about him as you have watched him grow up. We felt it here."

We received many letters from Dale's former companions, all full of sweet tributes to our son. He was known for giving 100% to the work, for his loving example, and for his Christlike love. A check in the amount of $5.00 was sent to give to the Latter-day Saints missionary fund from the First United Methodist Church. I was raised in a Methodist town in Colorado, and to have them remember the Latter-day Church was very touching to me and our family.

President A. Theodore Tuttle of the Quorum of the Seventy was asked by the First Presidency to speak at Dale's funeral. Along with many comforting words, he stated that no one should worry about a wife for this young man. Although President Tuttle said he could not do anything about the situation, he knew Someone who could.

On a bright and sunny Monday in June 1981, while my husband and I tilled the garden, I shaded my eyes and saw Dale and a young woman standing in the air above the grapevines, their arms around each other. I received Dale's message, spirit to spirit: "We came to tell you as soon as we knew for sure." It was as if I had been invited to their wedding. The girl had recently died, and her funeral had been held on Saturday. Although she and Dale stayed only a brief moment, I had never felt Dale so happy. Tears streamed down my face, and I knew that in Heavenly Father's Plan of Happiness, an earthly Mother matters very much. The grapevines have become my own personal "Sacred Grove."

Sometime later, President Tuttle spoke in our ward. I pondered if I should tell him of the visit from my son and the young woman. Following the meeting, I made my way to the front of the chapel. President and Sister Tuttle remembered me from the funeral. As I shook his hand, a shock went through me, and I knew President Tuttle felt it too, because he looked at me with a surprised look. He turned to everyone still in the chapel and for several minutes, shared his witness that young men and young ladies are meant to be together forever. I was filled with love for President and Sister Tuttle, who love and serve the Lord, as the tears coursed down my cheeks.

We were comforted through this difficult time. Because of my testimony of the Atonement and the Resurrection of my Savior, Jesus Christ, I was able to bury that handsome body of my son.

William Seldon Owens
Carol J. Owens

Born: 14 May 1926, Boise, Ada, Idaho
Parents: Alice Elvaretta Harris Owens and Joseph Alma Owens,
"Elva & Alma"
Siblings: Marva, Joseph Lyle, Clarita, Robert Terrence, Karen
Spouse: Carol Diane Jensen Owens
Children: Richard Seldon, Jonathan Lyle, Diane, James Robert,
Fredrick Dean, Marianne, Gary Lynn, Christine, Catherine,
David Alma, Rebecca, Deborah, William Andrew
Missions: Western States Mission 1947 to 1948,
New Hampshire Manchester, September 1991 to 1992
Time of service: 18 September 1991 to 18 September 1992
Cause of death: Heart attack
Date and place of death: 18 September 1992, at the mission office
in Bedford, New Hampshire
Age at time of death: 66
Place of burial: Orem City Cemetery, Utah
Story related by: Fredrick Dean Owens, son

WILLIAM SELDON OWENS WAS BORN to an active LDS family of
pioneer heritage. He grew up in the small railroad town of Glenns Ferry,
Idaho, where his father worked as a railroad mechanic and his mother took
in sewing. The parents were an integral part of the Church congregation,

and the whole family helped to build the first chapel there. Seldon learned to work hard from early on: he delivered newspapers, along with his brother ran the town's bicycle repair service, milked the family's cow, and worked many long hours helping to raise the family's summer food and winter supply in the gardens. He studied hard, even teaching his own physics class when there was no teacher qualified to teach it; he lettered in three sports, participated in high school dramas, and was high school valedictorian.

Three months after high school, he was inducted into the U.S. Army, served during the final part of World War II, among other things receiving a Purple Heart for wounds to his leg during the battle of Okinawa, and spent his 19th birthday recuperating in a hospital in Guam and then was part of the peace-keeping forces in Korea.

Seldon was always active in The Church of Jesus Christ of Latter-day Saints. Soon after his military service, he began his first full-time mission, 1947 to 1949 in the Western States Mission. His assignment was mostly to keep the small branches going in order that there be hope for the children growing up in less-than-diligent LDS homes there.

He majored in biology at the University of Utah, starting in fall 1949. He paid his way with the GI bill, driving the bloodmobile for the Red Cross and doing other jobs related to his chosen field of medicine. He married Carol Diane Jensen in the Salt Lake Temple on 31 August 1950, received his bachelor's degree in 1953, and entered the U of U medical school. Carol's father was a cement finisher; Seldon learned this skill and worked summers as a cement finisher to help with the costs of his education. When he received his M.D. degree, spring 1956, the birth of their fifth child was imminent; this was the largest family of any in his graduating class, yet through this couple's frugality, he was also the only new doctor to graduate debt-free.

After a one-year internship in general medicine at St. Benedict's Hospital in Ogden, Utah, Seldon entered family practice at a clinic in Layton, Utah, where the family lived for 13 years. He was recruited to help pioneer 24-hour emergency service at Utah Valley Hospital in Provo, Utah, on New Year's Eve as 1970 began. That summer the family moved to the home in Orem, Utah, which would be their permanent place of residence.

Back in 1947, when the doctor performing the pre-mission physical exam for Seldon had learned of the reason for the exam, he refused payment. When Seldon became a physician, he felt that if a non-LDS doctor had done this for him, he certainly could and should do the same. No record was kept of how many hundreds or thousands of future missionaries received a no-cost physical exam from Dr. Seldon Owens.

His family, the Church, and service to others were the center of his life. He served several stake missions, including service as stake mission president in both Layton and Orem. He always told his children from early on of the importance of serving a mission. Of his 7 sons, all 6 who grew up served full-time missions, as did 2 of his 6 daughters, plus so far some 14 grandsons and a granddaughter.

He and his wife, Carol, had always spoken of serving a mission as a couple. When their last son left on his mission in spring 1991, they pre-pared their own mission papers; their call came with very short notice. Their mission began on 18 September and was the opportunity to form greatly cherished friendships with other senior missionaries they met during the MTC training period. When most of their children were present at the MTC to say good-bye to Seldon and Carol, at least two of the daugh-ters felt that this would be the last time they would see Seldon alive; one of these two commented that by a certain look in his eye, she felt he was feel-ing the same thing too.

Seldon and Carol served as an office couple in the New Hampshire Manchester Mission, Carol as secretary to the president and Seldon at dif-ferent times in charge of fleet vehicles or apartments, or materials, etc. They also worked with activation and rendered many kinds of service to mem-bers and investigators. One very meaningful experience for Seldon was to teach a terminally ill brother about the phase of our existence which follows earth life and to help him prepare for that transition; the increased knowl-edge and testimony this brother received were a great comfort to him, and he departed this life at peace and ready. Seldon honored his request to speak at the funeral. Little did anyone realize that all this teaching of and testify-ing of the plan of life and death would soon have personal application— some two or three weeks later when Seldon himself was suddenly called home to his Maker.

On the morning of 18 September 1992, one year to the day from when they had begun their 18-month mission assignment, Seldon awoke very early, around 4:00 a.m. He told Carol, "I'm all slept out; I'm going to go in early to the office and get some things going." Carol would finish her night's rest and then call him when breakfast was ready. Seldon advanced a lot of the paperwork needed for transferring his current office task to the next person, as the president felt it was time to trade assignments around. After a nice breakfast together, Seldon and Carol went to the office and began a normal morning's work. Around 10:00 a.m., Carol was typing at the computer, and Seldon was off to one side behind her, making photocopies. Carol heard a thud, and the other senior sister in the office exclaimed, "Elder Owens!" Carol turned and saw Seldon lying there and immediately began resuscitation efforts, in the meanwhile looking up and around, wondering from what vantage point Seldon was looking down on them working over his body. A massive heart attack had in an instant sent him beyond the veil.

Carol accompanied the emergency vehicles to the hospital, where it was determined that he was indeed gone. She called home to have one of the family members notify everyone else. Then she returned to the office that afternoon and the next morning to get everything in order for her to be able to be away for several days. The next day, Seldon's body was flown back to Utah, and Carol also flew home to her children in Orem, Utah. The funeral was held during the next week, and Carol dealt with insurance and other paperwork, relishing time with all the family, including their missionary son who came home for 40 hours to attend the viewing and funeral, before returning to finish his other six months. After two weeks at home, Carol returned to New Hampshire and finished the other six months of her mission. She said, "This is what I was called to do, and this is what Seldon would have wanted me to do."

A scripture included in the funeral program, which has given the family much comfort: *"I beheld that the faithful elders of this dispensation, when they depart from mortal life, continue their labors in the preaching of the gospel. . . of the Only Begotten Son of God"* (D&C 138:57). We as a family have much faith in this and in the fact that we can again be together after we all depart this life. While we were all together around the time of the funeral, at least a couple of the grandchildren reported seeing their grandpa looking in through the dining room window at the family gathering. At the funeral, much of the extended family joined the ward choir to sing "The King of Love My Shepherd Is"; though both the family and our ward choir have some considerable musical talent, including current and former members of the Tabernacle Choir, never had we performed that song so gloriously; even the Seventy who spoke at the services said, "I have never heard such beautiful music rendered by the choir." A daughter-in-law in the congregation reported that when she looked up and saw the ward-family choir filling the entire choir area, she saw in the air above us another choir, singing with full heart, Seldon in the front and center, with a great big smile on his face. Though most of us have not seen him, his nearness has been felt. We hope to continue on with the same diligent labors in missionary work and the Lord's service which Seldon showed, and we look forward to our reunion with him.

During the two-week hiatus Carol spent at home for the funeral, a beloved neighbor brought her a quote from Apostle Bruce R. McConkie: "This was talking about Seldon": "Everyone in the Church who is on the straight and narrow path, who is striving and struggling and desiring to do what is right, though is far from perfect in this life; if he passes out of this life while he's on the straight and narrow, he's going to go on to eternal reward in his Father's Kingdom."

Sometime after Carol finished her mission, one of their sons asked her, "Since Dad's life ended without his having seen any of his children or grand-children during the last year, do you regret having gone on that mission, or do you think Dad would have regretted it?" Her immediate and firm reply was, "Not in the least. Not for one moment have either of us ever regretted having gone on that mission. It was the happiest year of your father's life, and by far the happiest year of our marriage."

Christian Glenn Packer

Born: 26 February 1976, Salt Lake City, Utah
Parents: Gary Lowell Packer and Paula Pearson Packer
Siblings: Thomas, Kathryn, Laura, Mark
Mission: LDS Church Welfare Square
Time of service: 1998 to 1999
Cause of death: Auto/pedestrian accident
Date and place of death: 5 October 1999, Salt Lake City, Utah
Age at time of death: 23
Place of burial: Brigham City Utah City Cemetery
Story related by: Gary and Paula Packer, parents

CHRISTIAN GLENN PACKER WAS BORN to us, Gary L. Packer and Paula Pearson Packer, as the second of our five children, on 26 February 1976. He was named Christian after a dear friend who was baptized during Gary's mission in France and Glenn after his maternal grandfather, Glenn L. Pearson. The patronymic name, Packer, stretches from humble beginnings in England through courtiers of King James I to an indentured servant to a Quaker Family in Pennsylvania, and to the Nauvoo Era convert and Mormon pioneer stock.

Christian's first year seemed quite normal for this beautiful, healthy boy, but soon it was apparent that his motor and speech skills were developing slowly. An intensive preschool medical exam diagnosed cerebral palsy, most likely caused by brain injury during his difficult, instrument-aided birth. His doctors and therapists were doubtful that he would walk normally or enjoy normal physical activities like bike riding. It was unlikely he would read or write.

As his childhood and youth progressed, Christian grew into a handsome, strong, tall, and healthy young man but slow in his educational development. His friends and classmates loved him because of his friendly, caring, and mild nature. He loved riding his bike and was an expert at video games. He was raised on a small farm in Honeyville, Utah, and lived with his family for three years in Germany during his late teens, where he attended German public school, learning to communicate in a second language. He also worked part time at the U.S. military commissary at a Burger King Restaurant in Frankfurt.

Although mentally disabled, he was compensated with unusual gifts and abilities. He had many childlike attributes contained in his six-foot-two-inch-tall frame. He learned to perform nearly normally physically and to read and write. He had an unusually developed memory for names of people, places, and street names. He was determined to learn to sing and persevered until he was able to sing solos at family Christmas advent programs.

Upon returning to the U.S., the family settled in Farmington, Utah, where Christian graduated with his special education class from Viewmont High School. He was unable to serve a full-time proselyting mission but was able to work part time at a local grocery store and fast food restaurant, and he was known for his "ready-aim-fire" handshake offered to everyone he met.

In the spring of 1998 he was extended a mission call from his bishop to be a service missionary for The Church of Jesus Christ of Latter-day Saints at Welfare Square in Salt Lake City. He was so proud to serve. A young woman in the ward, Summer Fowers, had a special connection to the family and was working to receive her Young Womanhood medallion. She approached Christian's mother, Paula, to see if she could help Christian. Summer and Paula spent weeks riding the bus with Christian, teaching him how to make the right connections to his place of service. Elder Packer enjoyed his associates and his service, which was stocking shelves at the bishop's storehouse. He loved to be called Elder Packer and wore his black and white badge with great pride.

On a crisp, October morning in 1999, after completing 18 months of his two-year mission, Elder Packer walked down from his home on Compton Bench to the bus stop. While crossing the highway at the intersection, he was struck by a car. Heroic efforts were made by witnesses, emergency medical technicians, and the life-flight crew who flew him to the LDS Hospital in Salt Lake City.

When we, his parents, arrived at the hospital, we were met by our bishop, Rockie Dustin, and counselor, Brad Davies, who administered a priesthood blessing. The head and brain trauma was severe, and prognosis was poor. Much fasting and many prayers were begun by family and friends. Immediate contact was made through the two bishoprics to the driver of the car, expressing our concern for her. It was important for us to let her know, as soon as possible, that this was an accident and that we included her in our prayers as well.

That night as the family left the hospital, Paula decided to go home to console Christian's siblings, and Gary would remain at the hospital. A small room near the ICU was provided where the night was spent in prayer. During that night an event occurred which is of the "unspeakable" sort, which gave us great comfort and knowledge that made it possible to deal with the events of the following week. By that we knew that Christian had died at the accident scene, which made it easier to remove life support a few days later. We also took great comfort that his donated organs gave life to other individuals, including a mother of young children.

During the days between the accident and funeral service, there was a great outpouring of concern from family, friends, and others. A wonderful missionary couple representing the Missionary Department stayed quietly in the background offering condolence and support. The mortuary and chapel viewing was of great solace, as hundreds came, each with a story of how Christian had touched their lives. Hundreds of people we had never met came; classmates, fellow workers, school and UTA bus drivers, fellow bus passengers, bishops' storehouse personnel, and many others offered their love and concern.

The sight of the filled chapel, overflow, cultural hall, stage, and hallways at the services was overwhelming. Several General Authorities were in attendance, and Christian's great uncle, President Boyd K. Packer, presided and spoke. A home teacher, Jim Robertson, spoke, and Christian's sisters, Kathryn and Laura, sang a hymn.

Although his missionary name badge that he wore on his work clothes and burial suit states "Elder Packer," Christian died as a priest, not having his temple ordinances completed. Our bishop obtained special permission from the First Presidency to have his temple work done immediately, rather than waiting the normal time following death. His elder brother Thomas stood as proxy for his ordination and other vicarious ordinances.

During his life, his mother had the overwhelming desire to truly know Christian and her other children. Talking with them about personal feelings and beliefs became precious to her. She was unable to do this to the extent she wished with Christian, as he was simple and pure as a child. After his death, a picture of Christian was enlarged to be shown at the viewing before the funeral. When the wrapping was taken from the portrait of her son, an amazing thing happened. It was as if an electrical shock ran through her body as she gazed into the eyes of her son. Christian appeared to her behind his mortal portrait. He emanated deep love for his mother and conveyed to her that he was a magnificent, intelligent, celestial being who loved and cared about his mother, and his smile told her he was happy and right where he was supposed to be! What comfort, what unspeakable joy this was for a mother who had just lost her precious child.

At the time of this writing, it is now seven years from the time of Christian's "transfer." Since then, joining his older brother Thomas and himself as missionaries were his sister Kathryn's fiancé, now husband, Bryan Roberts. Christian's younger sister Laura and his brother Mark have also served full-time missions. One year after our youngest child returned from the mission field, we, his parents, departed to serve the first of our senior missions. We are dedicating the first to Christian and are writing this memorial while serving as ordinance workers in the Johannesburg, South Africa Temple.

Our hope in sharing this tribute to our missionary son is that others who have lost, or will lose, loved ones while serving will likewise receive the same comfort we feel.

Bryan Ward Peck

Born: 27 July 1877, Thatcher, Franklin, Idaho
Parents: Hezekiah Hatch Peck and Mary Susannah Nowlin Peck
Siblings: Hezekiah Hatch, Jr., Horton Franklin, Cecil Nowlin,
Guy Ion, Elzo Dean, Mary Gineva, Ivy May, Nellie Rose,
Susan Elizabeth, Gineva Fern, Iris Peck
Mission: Southern States (Tennessee)
Time of service: May or June 1899 to 27 February 1900
Cause of death: Measles or pneumonia
(according to various sources)
Date and place of death: 27 February 1900, Ai, Putnam, Tennessee
Age at time of death: 22
Place of burial: Unknown by this source
Story related by: Rhonda Nanney Stohl (my maternal grandmother,
Ardell Tanner Nanney was Elder Peck's niece.)

UNFORTUNATELY, LITTLE IS KNOWN about Bryan Ward Peck's life prior to his mission, other than the cold, hard facts contained on the family group sheet for his father and mother. Bryan came from a large family of 11 children. It is not known what the profession of his father (Hezekiah Hatch Peck) was, but he may well have been a farmer. Much has been written about his grandfather, Martin Horton Peck, who was among the first members of The Church of Jesus Christ of Latter-day Saints who were called on several missions and who performed many healings for members of the family and others. Bryan's mother, Mary Susannah Nowlin, also came from

175

a family of early converts. Her father, Bryan Ward Nowlin, II, was converted while living in Tennessee.

It is likely that the example of Martin Horton Peck, Bryan's grandfather, had much to do with Bryan's decision to serve a mission himself. It is unknown by this author whether his father or any of his brothers served missions, but given the high level of activity and commitment to the gospel by the family, it seems entirely possible.

Bryan's mother's family originally came from Tennessee, as did his grandfather, Bryan Ward Nowlin. We believe he would have been pleased to be called to the Southern States Mission. All of what we know about his experiences as a missionary in Tennessee are taken from letters which he personally wrote from Tennessee to two of his sisters, Nellie Peck Tanner and Ivy Peck Tanner. These two sisters were just older than Bryan, had apparently married brothers, and were living in the same household. The earliest of Elder Peck's letters is dated 21 June 1889, written a short time after Elder Peck arrived in Tennessee.

In that letter, he wrote that he had experienced some delay and confusion upon his arrival, before the days of smooth transfers and convenient transportation: "We left to go to our field of labor and got this far and did not meet the elders as we expected. Elder Decker has got to go with me to find our companions. We expect to walk 10 miles to where they have been laboring."

He found his companion and wrote to his sisters a few days later: "I am on the trump at present and have been up in the morning at about 7 o'clock and out until 10. We left Franklin and walked 17 miles without any dinner or supper. The next morning we got breakfast and walked 12 miles without any dinner, but had supper." Later they met one of the few Saints in Tennessee, "and when he invited us to go to his house and spend the night with him, you can bet we accepted the invitation with gladful hearts."

Bryan apparently had difficulty adjusting to the heat and humidity of the South. He says in that same letter, "It is awful hot, about 90 degrees. . . . My clothes are wet with sweat every day but that does not matter for it's an Elder's life for me with its trials and trouble and dinners free."

On 12 August 1899, Elder Peck wrote to his sisters his observations regarding the religious conditions of the people in the area. "Well, if you could just see some of these churches here and how they are conducted. Everyone has his own ideas in regards to what is right, so that there is no one who knows what the whole church does believe in. About every tenth man is a preacher and presents a different road to heaven so there is a road for all. If one does not suit you, you can find one that does."

The next letter, written 9 September 1899, finds Elder Peck still suffering from the heat, and from hearing strange ideas about Mormons. He wrote: "We are having a hot time. If you do not think so, you had better come and walk 16 miles in the sun when it is 104 degrees in the shade. It has been up to 119 in the shade. . . . You people at home can talk about fulfilling a mission, but down here it is different, so you had better take out that old Bible of yours . . . and be able to preach to the people. . . . We are accused of baptizing a lady and telling her man that she is as much our wife as she is his, but that is not so, as we have not baptized any lady at all yet, so you can see what we are thought of in here."

The last letter from Bryan to his sisters is dated 21 November 1899. He expressed the discouragement many missionaries feel from time to time: "I have not baptized anybody yet, nor do I know whether I have been the means of bringing anybody to a knowledge of the truth of the gospel."

The final letter in my possession, dated 20 March 1900, is from the woman and her daughter who took Elder Peck in when he fell ill and in whose home he died. It is signed by Lizzie Vaughn and her daughter. Sister Vaughn expresses her sympathy to Bryan's sisters and expresses her love and appreciation for Elder Peck.

"We thought he [Elder Peck] was such a good boy, he seemed like home folks to us. . . . Your brother bore his sickness the best I ever saw and never complained. I would of been glad if he had come to our place sooner, thinking it would of been better for him. When he was first taken sick he was caught in a rain or two which of course made it worse for him. . . . He called Elder Brimhall to the bed a few hours before he died and ask him what he thought of his case, and put his arms around the elder's neck and told him that he looked like one of his brothers. . . . We sent for Pres. Allred on Monday before he died on Tuesday. They arrived but a few hours before he died. We ask them to administer to him. They were very cold and did not administer right then for they did not think that he was so bad. He said, 'Hurry Elders. I am so sick.' I will have to close for this time.

"From your sister in the Gospel, Lizzie Vaughn and daughter"

Sadly, I don't know if Elder Peck was administered to, and I don't know the exact cause of his death. It may have been measles, as mention is made in an early letter about another elder who had died of measles. It is more likely, based on the description of his illness, that he died of pneumonia.

Elder Peck's mission was only a matter of months in duration, but he gave the ultimate sacrifice and remained faithful until the end. He was greatly missed by his friends and large, close-knit family.

Jasper Peterson

Born: 6 June 1847, Moderup, Odense, Denmark
Parents: Rasmus (Pedersen) Petersen and
Ane (or Anna) Jespersen Petersen
Siblings: Hans Peter, Niels Christen, James, Mette Marie
Spouse: Anne Louisa Maria Jensen Peterson
Children: Jasper Peter, William, Anne Maria, James Christian,
Anne Catherine Josephine, Emma Elizabeth Christina
Spouse: Christina Larsen Peterson (divorced)
Children: Louis Christian, Charles Christian
Spouse: Evelyn Floyel Peterson
Child: Axle Edward
Mission: Southern States, Scandinavia
Time of service: 1 November 1886 to April 1887,
then 26 April 1887 to 23 June 1887
Cause of death: Illness
Date and place of death: 23 June 1887, Odense, Odense, Denmark
Age at time of death: 40
Place of burial: Odense, Odense, Denmark
Story related by: Lorin Lee was Forest Peterson, grandson

JASPER PETERSON WAS BORN 6 June 1847, the eldest child of Rasmus
and Ane Jesperson Petersen, in Maderup, Odense, Denmark. In 1860, Jasper
and his father's family were converted to The Church of Jesus Christ of Latter-day Saints by an Elder Peterson and Elder Hans Brown.

In 1863 at the age of 16, Jasper immigrated to the United States, traveling alone to Utah, wishing to provide a livelihood so his father, mother, and five siblings could follow. Jasper's first destination was Mt. Pleasant, Utah, where he lived with the Hans Brown family, Elder Brown having been one of the elders who had converted his family. Many Danish converts had also settled in that area.

Three years later in 1866, his father, mother, and brothers and sister (Hans Peter, 16; Niels Christen, 13; Jens, 3; and sister Mette Maria, 18 mos.) left Denmark to sail to the United States. After many weeks on the ocean, they arrived and joined the Abner Lowery Company for the trip across the plains to Salt Lake City, Utah.

Not long after beginning their journey, Jasper's father, Rasmus Petersen, contracted cholera and was left behind, dying a few days later. Soon after Jasper received this information, his mother, Ane Jespersen Petersen, also passed away. She was wrapped in a blanket and buried along the wayside, near Illinois. A few days later, son Niels Christen also died. Jasper was the eldest of the children. Of the 300 people who started in the company, over 100 died before reaching Salt Lake City. The three surviving children of the Peterson family were reunited with their brother Jasper in Mt. Pleasant, where they all lived with the Hans Brown family.

On 19 April 1867, at the age of 25, Jasper married Anne Louisa Marie Jensen, a Danish girl who also settled in the Mt. Pleasant area. They had five children in Mt. Pleasant and one in Castle Dale, Utah. In 1877, Brigham Young encouraged 75 or so of the young men in Mt. Pleasant to create a settlement in Emery County where there were three streams of water and plenty of unsettled land.

In October of 1867, Jasper and 10 other men left Mt. Pleasant in five covered wagons, headed toward Castle Dale. Their families were left behind, and they took only what was necessary to form a settlement. The trip on a good saddle horse usually could be made in one day, but the company had to rebuild the road and finally arrived 14 days later.

The winter of 1878–1879, Jasper and Anne Louisa Marie lived in a dugout. In March of 1878, Jasper then homesteaded 160 acres along Cottonwood Creek and laid out land for the settlement of southwest Castle Dale. He and Justus Seely set to work digging a dirt ditch to bring water to their land. A settlement sprang up with many Danish immigrants carrying on the work of building homes and working the land.

That winter, Jasper and others wrote to the Post Office Department in Washington D.C., petitioning for a post office to be opened at "Castle

Vale," but the papers came back calling the new town "Castle Dale." On 7 October 1878, wards were formed, and Jasper Peterson was ordained bishop of the Castle Dale Ward. At this time, all the homesteaders on Cottonwood Creek were in the Castle Dale Ward.

In 1886 while Jasper served as bishop, he was called to serve a mission to Alabama in the Southern States Mission. After six months in that area, Jasper became ill with chills and fever. Mission supervisors thought it best to send him to a cooler climate and transferred him to the Danish Mission in Aarhus and Odense, where he had been born.

Jasper arrived in Copenhagen as a missionary to Scandinavia. Upon his arrival on 26 April 1887, he was apparently healthy and was assigned to labor in the Aarhus Conference, but soon afterward while on the Island of Fyen, he was attacked with chills and fever. His health worsened until his earthly career was terminated, 23 June 1887. He was buried in Odense on 28 June 1887.

On the morning of Jasper's death, his wife, Anne, and his family in Castle Dale, Utah, knelt in family prayer. Upon rising, Anne announced to her children, "Father died this morning," which proved to be correct.

Garth Vinton Pierce

Born: 10 June 1954, Salt Lake City, Utah
Parents: Ephraim Claire Piece and Myrle Long Pierce
Siblings: Brent Claire, VerJean, Colleen, Jan Lee
Mission: England Central Mission
Time of service: 18 July 1973 to 15 October 1974
Cause of death: Auto/truck accident
Date and place of death: 15 October 1974, Aberystwyth, Dyfed, Wales
Age at time of death: 20
Place of burial: Wasatch Lawn Cemetery, Salt Lake City, Utah
Story related by: Myrle L. Pierce, mother, and Colleen Pierce, sister

GARTH VINTON PIERCE WAS BORN 10 June 1954, in Salt Lake City, Utah, the third of five children. Garth was born with little crooked toes and with tufts of brown hair on the front and sides of his head, which became very curly like his mother's hair. He remained small in stature and was usually the smallest among his peers.

He was quiet when he was with other people, but at home he was very lively. He liked to tease his brothers and sisters, making them angry one minute and laughing the next. His sense of humor was one of his greatest traits. He made life fun, could laugh at himself, and found humor in many of life's exasperating experiences. Our family enjoyed many activities together, including basketball, football, camping, hide and seek, flashlight tag, and bike riding everywhere, with our dog, Princess.

Garth's childhood memories centered around his grandparents, Lee and

Adelia Pierce, and Rufus and Lettie Long. Grandma Pierce wrote: "To Garth Vinton Pierce: Keep those curls and smiles always for your Grandmother Pierce, but share that humorous attitude with those you meet, and you will always have friends, for you will draw them close to you."

Garth was active in Scouting and was faithful in The Church of Jesus Christ of Latter-day Saints. He received many individual awards and his Duty to God Award.

During his high school years, Garth worked for the Cottonwood Hospital, in the X-ray department. He was dependable and a good worker. Everyone who worked with him admired his quickness, efficiency, sense of humor, and ability to get things done. Although he was a "cut-up" around people he knew well, others considered him to be an extremely shy person. He kept his feelings and ideas mainly to himself.

Garth was a very determined young man. Once he had made up his mind, no one could persuade him to change it. He had a very difficult time deciding whether he should serve a mission for the Church, wanting to be sure he had a true testimony of the gospel. He spent some time by himself, reading the scriptures and praying, staying at his Grandma Long's house while she was away. When he came home, he got in touch with the bishop right away and said he wanted to serve a mission.

On the 16th of June 1973, Garth received his call to serve as a missionary for the Church to the Central England Mission, later called the England Birmingham Mission. His mission President was Reed L. Reeve. Garth put his whole heart and mind into being a good missionary and set goals for himself to accomplish this. His mission president related the following excerpt from a letter he received from Garth:

"He asked himself these questions: (1) What can I do to grow closer to the living Christ? Answer: Keep the commandments, study them, live them, love them and people. (2) How can I be a better companion? Answer: Empathy, help, understanding, show that I care by loving him. (3) What do I need to do to be a better builder of my branch? Answer: Never tear down, build up, help strengthen not only the individuals but the leadership, and show and be a support. (4) What do I need to do to be a better missionary? Answer: Study, know more, care about people so they may understand that I know they are important and that the Gospel is true, application, and hard work."

Garth's missionary journal shows that when he and his companions were teaching investigators the gospel, they witnessed the change in them when the Holy Ghost bore witness that the missionaries were teaching the truth. On one occasion he and his companion taught a young couple with four little children. When the missionaries first met them, this family were all drifting apart. The father said all he looked forward to was a couple of beers every night. The father related that he wasn't interested when the missionaries first came, but their spirit made him want to learn more. The family became faithful members, and the father served as a counselor in the bishopric of his ward.

On another occasion, Garth helped teach a family with five children. For years, the mother had been turning the elders away. She said, "I know Elder Pierce was sent to teach us the gospel because when he talked to us that night, I knew he was telling us the truth, and I couldn't send them away." Garth was thrilled to see this special family join the Church. A few months after Garth's death, they had a new baby. The mother wrote and said, "We have named him Garth Vinton after your dear son whom we all love and were so glad came into our lives to teach us the true gospel of Jesus Christ."

From these and other experiences, Garth strengthed his strong, firm testimony of the gospel. He was thankful he could represent the Lord Jesus Christ in teaching His gospel to the people in that part of His vineyard.

Early in the morning on 15 October 1974, Garth and his companion left the town of Aberystwyth, Wales, to go to a Zone Leaders meeting at the mission home. They were just a few miles out of town when they were involved in a truck–car accident. Garth was instantly killed.

That same morning in Utah, our family was busy getting ready for work and school. The bishop phoned and asked if he could come see the family. Colleen answered the phone and had the feeling that it was something to do with Garth, and she asked her mom to wait for the bishop. The family saw all three members of the bishopric walking down the road, dressed in their suits. Garth's dad had already gone to work at Hill Air Force Base, so the bishop first talked to Garth's mom and told her of Garth's death, then told the rest of the children. The bishopric brought Garth's dad home from work. The news was quite a shock to the family, but the Holy Ghost surrounded us and brought great comfort and peace into our home, which we and others who visited felt.

On 14 October 1974, Garth sent his family a postcard saying that he and his companion were going to present a *Meet the Mormons* book to the mayor of Aberystwyth. After Garth's death, his mother received a letter from Philip Davies, who was the clerk of the Aberystwyth Town Council. He wrote: "Dear Mrs. Pierce,

"I count it a special privilege to have your son call upon me in connection with the presentation of a suitably bound volume on the Mormon Church to our Town Mayor.

"Your son's passing over following the accident has been mentioned by a number of our residents who had become aware of his activities in connection with the establishment of a Mormon Church in this district and, personally, I experienced grief and great sympathy with you and your family in your bereavement.

"We proceeded with the presentation of the volume as arranged between your son and myself for we thought that it would also be his wish that this should be done. I was advised by Mr. Gregg, the local representative, accordingly and we are hoping that there will be some publicity with a picture in our local newspaper of the presentation.

"Of your son I can say that he impressed me greatly as being a young man of tremendous sincerity, filled with dedicated purpose and so very humble. The world can ill afford to lose young people of such splendid calibre.

"The Mayor, Mayoress, and all concerned join with me in this expression of sympathy with you and your family in your bereavement and we trust that you will be blessed abundantly so that you may be fortified to meet the trials of such great grief as has befallen you all.

"Yours sincerely, Philip Davies"

The family received many other letters from people in England and from members of the Church around the country. There was a great outpouring of love from many people to the Pierce family.

Garth's body arrived in Salt Lake on 18 October 1974. His mother's birthday was 14 October, the day before he died. She received a card from him in the mail, and it was addressed to "The Best Mother in the World." Garth's funeral was Monday, 21 October 1974, and he was buried at the Wasatch Lawn Cemetery in Salt Lake City, Utah.

Elder Paul H. Dunn of the Quorum of the Seventy was sent by the First Presidency of the Church to speak at Garth's funeral. He brought a letter written and signed by the First Presidency which brought us great comfort. In part, the letter stated: "Missionaries are so dear to the entire Church that the loss of one is felt deeply by all who know of it, and so we extend to you, not only our own sympathy, but that of all of those who support the missionary cause throughout the world. That the peace and comfort of our Father may come to your rescue at this time of trial and sustain you in the future is our sincere and earnest prayer. Spencer W. Kimball, N. Eldon Tanner, Marion G. Romney"

Although Garth's death was a great loss to us and his friends, we were assured that he was with the "faithful elders of this dispensation" whom Joseph F. Smith saw preaching the gospel to the spirits beyond the veil (Vision of the Redemption of the Dead, verse 57).

184

Coltan Duke Potter

Born: 27 February 1988, Coalville, Utah
Parents: Rene Wilde Potter and Sharlen Draper Potter
Siblings: Kaitlin, Cierra, Savanna
Mission: Portugal Lisbon
Cause of death: Auto accident
Date and place of Death: 28 August 2007, Chalk Creek Road,
four miles east of Coalville, Utah, a few days before he was scheduled
to enter the Provo Missionary Training Center (MTC)
Age at time of death: 19
Place of burial: Upton Cemetery, Chalk Creek Road, Upton, Utah
Story related by: Rene Wilde Potter and Sharlen Draper Potter, parents; and
Kaitlin, Cierra, and Savanna Potter, sisters

THE WORLD OF COLTAN DUKE POTTER was a good one. He was happy, and the grin on his face proved it. He was our only son, and the only paternal grandson carrying the Potter name. He was well loved by Potter and Draper family members, and we all affectionately called him "Buckwheat." We live in the rural township of Upton, 15 miles above Coalville, on the isolated, winding Chalk Creek Road that leads to the Uintah Mountains, where he fished, hunted, camped, caught frogs and snakes, shot clay pigeons, and set off fireworks in our own backyard. There was no other place Coltan would rather be.

Coltan was a wrestler, starting his career at the age of three, on the floor with his dad. When he was 17, he was determined to take the state championship and would not be deterred. Tragedy struck during the meet when his grandmother who was sitting in the stands suffered a heart attack and died at a nearby hospital. Her husband had died six weeks earlier. Coltan dedicated the rest of the meet to the memory of his grandparents, and he wrestled his way to the state title in his weight category. He had completed a perfect season and felt he could accomplish anything.

He was offered several wrestling scholarships around the nation, and after fasting and praying he felt the best fit for him was Utah Valley State College in Orem. He wanted to be close to home, and he wanted a school that would allow him to leave for two years to serve a mission for The Church of Jesus Christ of Latter-day Saints. He moved to Orem, training and wrestling in earnest, and soon began to focus his energy toward a mission.

He received his call to serve in the Portugal Lisbon Mission on 12 September 2007 and was beside himself with anticipation. His friend Skyler Burton was scheduled to leave for his mission to Santa Maria, Brazil, on the same day; he lived with our family that summer, and he and Coltan prepared together to serve. They talked about their missions every day, studied the scriptures and *Preach My Gospel*, and tried to teach themselves Portuguese!

Coltan was endowed in the Ogden Temple on Saturday, 25 August.. His mother, Sharlen, shares her feelings: "As we waited for Coltan in the Celestial Room, my heart was full of happiness. When he walked in . . . I wrapped my arms around him, hugged him, and whispered to him that when we died and came through the veil . . . the ones who love us most would be there waiting to welcome us, just like when he entered the room. He smiled, and I wondered why I had mentioned that. . . . How did I know what it would be like when we passed through the veil? I shrugged it off. I had had a lot of strange thoughts lately."

We headed home to prepare for the farewell dinner the next day. Coltan still needed to write his talk. Even though he was pressed for time, Coltan took his sister Kaitlin to a wedding reception that evening where they stayed for hours, laughing and dancing together. The two were great dancers and had won some dance competitions together. On the way home, Coltan gave Kaitlin a squeeze and said, "I'm glad we had this one last time together. That was a good way to say goodbye. Thanks."

Coltan's farewell meeting was the next day. Our small chapel was filled to overflowing. Coltan was adamant that the musical numbers include "If You Could Hie to Kolob" for the opening song, "We'll Bring the World His Truth," and "God Be with You 'Til We Meet Again" for the closing song. He said he wanted everyone "to know I love them and want them to be safe until I see them again." Within a few days, it became evident that he chose those songs with good purpose. In my heart I know he knew we would need the comfort the lyrics would bring us.

On Tuesday, 28 August, Coltan prepared to leave for his last day of work. He was happy and lighthearted, looking forward two weeks to when he would enter the MTC. Sharlen remembers, "I suddenly said, 'Buckwheat! Stay home with me today.' He asked, 'Why, what's up? Do you need something?' I paused and wondered why I had said that. 'No,' I replied. 'I just want you to stay home and talk with me.' He said, 'No, Mom, not today. Today is my last day to drive down this road and work for Justin. Every day after this I'll be working for the Lord, and I can't wait!' I thought, 'Every day after this? What about just for the next two years?' I almost corrected him, but something told me not to. His face was glowing and a bright light emanated from him. I began to realize our time was almost over. . . . He smiled at me and hurried out the door. He yelled, 'Bye Mom! I love you! See ya later!' I called out that I loved him, the door slammed, and he was gone. . . . I realized that if I hurried I could help my daughter, Cierra, with her class schedule. . . . I drove down Chalk Creek Road to the school. Just as I arrived, my cell phone rang, and I learned that Coltan had never made it to the job site. I hadn't seen him anywhere along Chalk Creek Road.

"I began making phone calls, trying to downplay my feelings. His father, Rene, told me he would call the Summit County sheriff and the Highway Patrol and then would leave Salt Lake and head home, looking for Coltan along the way. I left a message on Coltan's phone and then forced myself to focus on Cierra's class schedule. I told Cierra that Coltan was missing, but that there was probably nothing to worry about.

"By 1:00 p.m., I could no longer believe nothing was wrong. Two sheriff's vehicles raced past, their lights flashing. I silently prayed, 'Please, dear God, don't let those officers be racing toward my boy!' The next events were the nightmare of a lifetime."

Coltan's truck was finally spotted off the road. The truck had traveled 300 yards with no brake marks into the guard rail, which acted as a ramp, launching the truck into a tree that grew along the river. Coltan had died immediately of a skull fracture. He had no other broken bones, and no cuts or lacerations, even though he had to be cut out of the truck. The police had blocked the road above the accident and we couldn't go home, so we were taken back to the school, where we notified our daughters and loved ones of the unthinkable news. The community immediately rallied around us. My parents had just arrived back home after attending Coltan's farewell, but my dad changed his clothes and climbed back on a plane to return to us.

The days became a blur as we planned his funeral. Friends embroidered Coltan's favorite scripture, Psalm 18:30, 32, inside his casket. We were overwhelmed by the numbers of people who came to share their love and condolences. Flowers, phone calls, messages and even fireworks arrived, literally from around the world. Wrestling and football teams in Utah sent floral arrangements and beautiful messages of tribute and love. We received a loving letter from members of the Church Missionary Department. President Craig B. Terry of the Lisbon Portugal Mission called and testified that although he had not been able to personally meet our son, from what he had read and heard of Coltan's accomplishments and work ethic, he knew he had hit the ground running on the other side of the veil.

We sang the same hymns for the funeral that we had sung six days before at Coltan's mission farewell. We all knew Coltan had joined the Army of Helaman, the Stripling Warriors, and every other army God had ever organized. Coltan was buried at the Upton Cemetery on a hill overlooking the valley he loved so much, on Saturday, 1 September. The North Summit wrestlers wore their team jackets, with embroidered ties, claiming Coltan as their champion. We know Coltan was touched and honored to be so loved.

The next day, our young neighbor knocked at the door and said, "My mom told me I had to come tell you what I saw at the funeral. Coltan stood right next to where you were sitting. He looked around at everyone with a big grin on his face. When we sang, 'God Be with You 'Til We Meet Again,' I looked at his face, and his lips were moving. He sang the same words we were singing."

One morning two weeks later, Rene woke to say, "I saw Coltan last night. I was sleeping, but not asleep, and was aware I was lying in bed. Suddenly I was in a beautiful room more beautiful than any I had been in. I asked, 'What is this place, Buckwheat; what are we doing here?' Coltan appeared, looking more beautiful and perfect than I had ever seen him. He spoke to me with his thoughts, *In my Father's house are many mansions. If it were not so, I would have told you. I go to prepare a place for you.'* Then I was back in bed, alone, in that state between sleep and consciousness. When I woke, I opened my scriptures to Enos in the Book of Mormon, verse 27. *'And I soon go to the place of my rest, which is with my Redeemer; for I know that in him I shall rest. And I rejoice in the day when my mortal shall put on immortality, and shall stand before him; then shall I see his face with pleasure, and he will say unto me: Come unto me, ye blessed, there is a place prepared for you in the mansions of my Father. Amen.'* We sobbed with grateful hearts."

Our lives, our world, our thoughts, our sleep, and our tomorrows, all have been forever changed. So many have reached down to lift us up. We have felt the most breath-robbing pain, despair, and black moments, and yet, at the same time we have never been closer as a family, been more loved, or experienced a greater relationship with our Heavenly Father and the Savior. We are blessed to have raised Coltan as ours. He blessed us in life, and the blessings continue. We choose, as a family, to stand as witnesses of God at all times, in all things, and in all places. We refuse to be as we were before August 28. There is no vice, habit, or weakness we are not willing to cast off or give up, in order that we might stand with Elder Coltan Duke Potter before the pleasing bar. What a grand reunion that will be! May God grant us the strength to fulfill our missions in mortality, with the kind of faith and love that our Buckwheat shared with everyone he met. He exemplified for us a perfect season in his 19 years, 6 months and 1 day. Not because he was perfect, but because his heart was pure.

Joshua Matthew Prymak

Born: 5 March 1977, Kingston, New York
Parents: Rostislaw Prymak and Nancy Prymak Pratt
Siblings: David, Eric, Ian, Megan, Alexandra, Sasha
Mission: Spain Canary Islands
Time of service: June 1998 to January 1999
Cause of death: Swept off a cliff by a tidal wave
Date and place of death: 18 January 1999, Tenerife, Canary Islands
Age at time of death: 21
Place of burial: Manassas, Virginia
Story related by: Nancy Prymak Pratt, mother

JOSHUA MATTHEW PRYMAK WAS BORN 5 March 1977 in Kingston, New York. Before his birth, I had a strong impression that I was asked if I would be willing to have a child who would die. I was very fearful, but said I would, and I then felt this would not be required of me. When he was born, he was very sick, and we were afraid he might not live. He was finally diagnosed with celiac disease, and after placing him on a special diet, he grew and was healthy.

When he was nine years old, he had a serious bike accident and was sent to Fairfax Hospital Shock/Trauma Department in very critical condition. I was at work when I got the call and asked a friend to give him a blessing, and Joshua had a miraculous healing. He gained a true understanding that God loved him. Doctors paraded into his room and told him that he was a miracle. When we left the hospital, we learned that the entire hospital had heard about his miraculous healing.

Joshua was a fine young man. He had a 4.0 average in school and was captain of his high school wrestling team. There was never a doubt that he would serve a mission for The Church of Jesus Christ of Latter-day Saints, and after completing his first year at Brigham Young University, majoring in mechanical engineering, he submitted his mission papers. He was very knowledgeable about Church doctrine, and he always knew the Church was true. He loved to sing the song "Armies of Helaman," saying it inspired him.

Joshua was eager to go, and when the call came to the Canary Islands, we were happy to send him on his way. His letters home were enthusiastic. He loved his mission and was a little upset because he spent two weeks answering phones in the Missionary Training Center instead of going directly to the Canary Islands.

I spoke with Josh on Christmas Day, 1998, during his semi-yearly phone call. He told me of a dream he had in which the Lord asked if he would be willing to be involved in something violent to benefit the Canary Islanders. He told me that in the dream, he said, "Yes."

Josh and the missionaries in his district spent their Preparation Day at a tourist attraction in the Canary Islands, visiting a lighthouse. Josh was running along one of the high cliffs when a wave hit him. Another elder, Jaarl Papenfuss, searched the water, hoping to see Josh, and he was hit by a wave which washed him out to sea. The wave injured several of the other missionaries who were there as well. Jaarl and Joshua were not found right away but their bodies were recovered a couple of days later. Contrary to what some may believe, they were not swimming.

I received a call from my stake president, our friend, who asked if he could come to my home, and he asked if my children could also be there. The news was devastating, and especially upsetting not to know where his body was. I envisioned that he was alive and was swept out to sea. I was actually grateful when his body was found.

At first I thought that God had failed to keep the promise made when Josh was healed after his bike accident. Then I was told that Josh was no longer a child. I began to realize that Josh had been kept alive to fulfill his mission, and I came to know that God is involved with our lives. I can't be mad at God, although He was the one who took my son, and I know that if I surrender to His will, I will become what I was sent to earth to accomplish, and that I was learning lessons I could not learn in any other way.

The day Josh died, my daughter called me from BYU to tell me she had dreamed she was crying. Her deceased father came to her and said, "Yes, this is hard, but you will get through it." She didn't know what the dream meant, and at that time, neither did I. We realized later that she dreamt this shortly after Josh died.

It took a few weeks for his body and personal effects to be sent home. Bishop Richard C. Edgley of the Presiding Bishopric spoke at the funeral. We received calls from other General Authorities, and from the mission president, all expressing their sympathy. Joshua was loved by many, and many people have told me that they felt Josh helping them, even though he had passed on. His best friend, who is not a member of the Church, gave the eulogy at Josh's funeral, and he told me later of a dream in which he experienced the blessings of the "Mormon priesthood." He hasn't been baptized yet, but believes he will someday join the Church. I also have experienced the feeling that Josh told this friend that he would look after him all the days of his life.

Josh was buried next to his father, Rostislaw Prymak. After the burial, a friend came to me with tears in her eyes. She had been excommunicated a few years before and told me that Josh had appeared to her and told her it was time for her to be rebaptized, which she did about a month later.

For a while, I had to deal with people who thought Josh had been disobedient because his death was ruled a drowning. Many people who didn't know the circumstances said very hurtful things, until the stake president put a stop to it all.

Josh's paternal grandmother died two weeks after Josh. Later, when we were doing her work in the temple, Josh was at the baptistry and in the sealing room, which was an intense experience. I knew then that the world of spirits is very close, and I am much more aware of that. Having a husband, a daughter, and a son in that spirit world has made me feel that when things are difficult, I have assistance which I never had known until they entered that world. My children, especially my daughters, have struggled; although they have testimonies of the truthfulness of the gospel, they still have very tender feelings about losing their loved ones.

I miss Josh very much, and I dreaded the date he was to have returned from his mission. Something very strange happened that day. Our dog began behaving very strangely, staring at a space in the air in the kitchen, her tail tucked between her legs, and she continued to whine for about an hour, then stopped. The same behavior happened the next day and for an additional two days, causing the dog to have a seizure. I felt as if Josh had been near, and the dog had sensed his presence.

To those who are sending loved ones to serve, I would say that missionaries are in God's hands. I have a grandson who will be serving a mission in a few years, and I look forward to having him go.

I have been comforted and blessed in spite of the fact that I miss Josh very much. I feel that it was Josh's time to go, and I have had a lot of spiritual comfort that has helped me accept his passing. I feel lucky that I had the privilege of raising him. There is no fear where he is now, and I am motivated to join him when it is my time to leave this earth.

Gordon Myrl Quigley
Renee Lamb Quigley

Born: 24 April 1936, Salt Lake City, Utah
Parents: Joseph Phillip Quigley and Myrtle Gustaveson Quigley
Siblings: Barbara
Spouse: Renee Lamb Quigley
Children: James, Paul, Cheryl
Mission: Church Education Mission, Leeds England
Time of service: 10 August 1998 to 12 November 1999
Cause of death: Acute pancreatitis
Date and place of death: 12 November 1999, Leeds, England
Age at time of death: 63
Story related by: Renee Lamb Quigley, wife

GORDON MYRL QUIGLEY WAS BORN on 24 April 1936 in Salt Lake City, Utah, to Joseph Phillip Quigley and Myrtle Gustaveson Quigley. He had one older sister, Barbara. His parents and family were active in The Church of Jesus Christ of Latter-day Saints. As a youth, Gordon had a great love for singing and playing the piano. He graduated from the University of Utah with a bachelor's degree in music education. He later received a master's degree in choral conducting. Due to family situations, he was unable to fulfill a mission as a young man.

Gordon and I were married on 27 June 1957 in the Salt Lake Temple. We were blessed with three children, James, Paul, and Cheryl. Gordon taught music in the Salt Lake area public schools for 30 years. He joined the Tabernacle Choir in 1958 and sang with them for 22 years and loved being part of that great organization. Through the years, he conducted many community and church choirs, including a choir of former members of the Tabernacle Choir. He enjoyed composing and arranging music for his choirs. He was known as a quiet, unassuming man who communicated with others through music.

Through the years, Gordon and I talked about serving a mission together when we retired. As the years passed, we felt the need to retire early and did so when we were 62 years of age, on 30 June 1998. Gordon told his sister, "If we don't go on a mission soon, we may never be able to go," as if he had received a spiritual prompting.

We were thrilled to receive a call to serve a Church Education Mission with the Church Institute in Leeds, England, and left on 10 August 1998. In a visit with the director of the Church Education System in Salt Lake City, we learned that Elder Quigley's responsibilities were to organize an Institute choir to encourage more students to attend the institute as well as to teach a Book of Mormon class. We loved the opportunities to visit numerous Church history sites in the country.

Our first year was a challenge, as most of the students had never sung in a choir. Elder Quigley worked with them, meeting once a week for choir practice in preparation for Christmas, Easter and Spring concerts, as well as singing in stake conference. When classes began in September, Elder Quigley was excited to begin a new year with a new choir.

On Wednesday, 20 October 1999, he felt ill and thought he was coming down with the flu. By Thursday evening he was in terrible pain, and we drove to the hospital emergency room. After many tests, they found acute pancreatitis and admitted him as a patient.

He was given oxygen and treated with morphine to relieve the pain and was in a ward with five other men for nine days. He needed more oxygen so was transferred to intensive care. During that time, even though he struggled to breathe, he spent time talking to a visiting chaplain about the Church and what he and his wife were doing in the country. The chaplain was greatly moved and impressed.

Elder Quigley was fitted with a respirator, later required a tracheotomy, and for the next nine days was sedated. I was without family to comfort and help me until our daughter, Cheryl, arrived in England on 9 November. Three days later, we were told there was nothing more that could be done for Elder Quigley. The director of intensive care suggested we give permission to remove his support equipment. Before doing so, we talked with the attending physician, Mike Larvin, who specialized in pancreatitis. With tears in his eyes he said he was so sorry he was not able to save Elder Quigley. Dr. Larvin was a wonderful doctor, and I was pleased with his care of my husband. I gave permission to turn off the support, and within 45 minutes, Elder Quigley returned to his Heavenly Father on 12 November 1999, bringing the 15 months of our mission to an end. He was 63 years old.

Elder Quigley's patriarchal blessing states that he was sealed up to live long on the earth and fill the measure of his creation. It continues, "When you have finished your work here upon the earth it will be said of thee, well done, thou good and faithful servant, enter into the joy of thy Lord."

Through the years, Elder Quigley had regretted not having served a mission when he was a young man, but he loved his mission and talked of serving another after we were released from our calling with the Church Educational System.

The Lord did not forget me at this time. Before we went to the hospital on 21 October, I looked at some newly developed photos of Gordon. I had a strong feeling that I was looking at something that happened long ago, and I felt very nostalgic. I received that feeling twice as I looked over the pictures. I remember thinking, "He is going to be all right—he just has the flu."

At 4:00 a.m. after Gordon was admitted, I returned home to get some rest. As I lay down on our bed, I had a very strong feeling that my beloved husband would not be coming home. I put the feelings out of my mind, because I did not want to believe them. When Elder Quigley was placed on the respirator, I knew the Lord had blessed me with the knowledge that my husband had fulfilled his purpose on this earth, and that was a great blessing to me. I knew that the Lord needed him and I had to let him go. Although I was devastated, I was blessed to know that the Lord called him home and that the Comforter would help me through this ordeal.

The Leeds Mission President sent our names to be added to the First Presidency's prayer list. Our home ward and the Leeds missionaries held a fast for Elder Quigley. I know that the Lord heard these prayers and sent added blessings to me.

A memorial service was held in Leeds on 16 November for Elder Quigley. I was grateful to have my daughter, Cheryl, and my son, Jim, with me at the service. President Spencer W. Condie, Area President; David T. Seamons, Leeds Mission President; David Cook, Church Education Director of the British Isles; and George Yokl, Director of the Leeds Institute, spoke. Alex Drago and Rachael Parrish, two of our institute students, also spoke.

Alex Drago stated, "I want to tell you about your contribution for the Institute choir. . . . You and your husband really did lift people's eyes heavenward. In Britain we are very good at looking at our feet, so to help a whole group of people look to the sky instead of the gutter is a tremendous doing. There was a special spirit present last year, almost indefinable, which gave confidence to the whole Institute [which is now] lacking 'cause you're no longer here. Looking back, it was almost as if the Lord had decreed that we were to have the best Institute choir, and there was a special spirit which you brought which allowed us to grow and develop. For the first time ever, Institute students could say with great pride: 'I'm from Leeds Institute.' Other people would stand around in admiration and envy that they weren't a part of it. Your presence will continue to be felt in my life and the lives of others."

The Institute choir sang, "Go Ye Now in Peace." A line from that song gave me great comfort: "Know that the God who sent His Son to die that you might live will never leave you lost and alone in His beloved world." With the help of the Comforter, I was able to direct the choir as a tribute to Elder Quigley.

I received letters of condolence from Gordon B. Hinckley, Thomas S. Monson, and James E. Faust, members of the First Presidency; Elders Henry B. Eyring and Stanley A. Peterson, of the Church Educational System; as well as Elders Earl C. Tingey, Sheldon C. Child, John B. Dickson, and W. Craig Zwick, of the Missionary Department, who sent letters of sympathy.

We arrived home in Salt Lake City on Friday, 19 November 1999. Elder Quigley's body had been sent home by church administration. His funeral was 23 November 1999, and he is buried in the Wasatch Memorial Park in Salt Lake City, Utah.

Missionary work is very important to our family. Our son Jim served a mission in Sweden, and our son Paul served in Taiwan. Our daughter Cheryl also served in Taiwan. We feel missionary work is a wonderful part of the Church. It is a great experience to bring others to the knowledge of our Heavenly Father and His plan for us. I am grateful for the opportunity to serve with my dear husband in Leeds, England. I have many wonderful memories of that time we spent together. Since returning from England, I have remarried, and my husband and I recently completed an 18-month mission to the Philippines.

Rebecca Ann Reeve (Becky)

Born: 15 May 1940, Salt Lake City, Utah
Parents: Elder Rex C. Reeve and Phyllis N. Reeve
Siblings: Rex, Jr., JoAnn, Roger W., Venice, Barbara, David A.
Mission: Western States Mission, headquarters in Denver, Colorado
Time of service: October 1961 to November 1962
Nature of injury: Dislocated 5th and 6th vertebrae;
paralyzed from the neck down
Date and place of injury: 17 November 1962, Portales, New Mexico
Age at time of injury: 22
Story related by: Self

I did not die. Doctors told me that I would live 15–20 years, but because of the blessings of the Lord, the outstanding care given by my family, supportive friends, and the Sit Tall–Stand Tall Program, I have now lived over 45 years as a quadriplegic.

OUR HOME WAS LITERALLY a heaven on earth, and I had a wonderful childhood as the second child and the oldest girl in the family. I was mature for my age and was tending my brothers and sisters and neighborhood children by the time I was eight years old. I was able to handle the responsibility of running a household and tending children. I loved children, and my goal was to be the greatest mother in the world!

My mother was literally an angel, was motivated completely by love, and was the heart of our home. She loved Dad with all her heart and supported him in all major priesthood leadership callings. In his loving way, he found time to work, attend his many meetings, and support all his children in their basketball, football, wrestling, volleyball matches, and horse shows. Our home was a busy place, always open to family, neighbors, or loved ones.

Our family experienced some difficult trials. My brother Rex required surgery for a BYU football injury, developed colitis, and nearly lost his life. Grandpa Reeve was in the hospital for over three months following a terrible car crash. Dad and Mother cared for him for over 18 months as he recovered. Then, mother suffered a miscarriage, almost lost her life, and was recovering, just before I was injured.

Before my junior year of college I was working with some other girls to prepare the BYU library for dedication. One of the girls, Timsy Weigle, asked, "Becky, how old are you?" When I answered that I was 21, she asked why I was not serving a mission. I had never thought of a mission but could not get her question out of my mind. That night, I asked my dad what he thought; he told me he would support my decision. I visited my bishop and told him I wanted to be the greatest mother and to finish my education. He told me that he would fast and pray and that he would get back to me. As I left his office and walked to my car, tears ran down my face. I knew—yes, I knew—that I was going on a mission. I said to myself, I will put aside my desire to be a mother, and although I don't know how to be a missionary, I will learn how, and I will be the greatest sister missionary in the Church. I received my call to the Western States Mission. Printed on the farewell program was 1 Nephi 3:7, my favorite scripture.

I loved my mission, both the good and hard experiences. I wanted to be a credit to the Reeve name. I was the first missionary to serve from our family, and I had "big" shoes to fill. All 16 lines of my ancestors came across the plains before the railroad, many of them paying the ultimate price. The Lord blessed my efforts and my companions, and I brought several people and families into The Church of Jesus Christ of Latter-day Saints.

My companion, Sister Persis Brown, and I were to drive to Roswell, New Mexico, for Zone Conference on 17 November 1962. It snowed the night before. We couldn't sleep, so we got up early, prayed, and prepared for the day's travel. I was driving and stopped to fill the gas tank. We decided to leave a Book of Mormon with our contact who worked at the station.

I noticed frost on the snow, and tested the brakes to see if the road was slick. It was, and I told my companion that even if we were late, I was not taking any chances, and drove 35 miles an hour rather that the posted 70. All of a sudden, the car began to slide sideways. There were no other cars in sight, so I let the car slide off the road and onto the sand. I was sure we had stopped, but it felt like someone was trying to push the car over. The car rocked to my side, again and again. I thought, This car is trying to roll on its side, although it didn't seem there was enough momentum for the car to roll, but it did, rolling 2 ½ times from a dead stop. There were no seatbelts, and my door flew open. I was thrown nearly 100 feet from the car. I landed so hard on the back of my head that I became unconscious, and my 5th and 6th vertebrae were dislocated, pinching my spinal cord. Sister Brown received only minor bruises.

When I awoke, my chest felt as if it had turned to stone, and I could hardly breathe. My arms, hands, and feet felt as if they were floating up to the sky. I was 800 miles from home, injured, and afraid. I closed my eyes and whispered, "Father, I am in trouble. Please help me." Instantly, a voice came into my head which said, "Your neck is broken; you must not move!" I then knew that God knew my tragic situation, and He told me what to do.

I saw my companion running around me in a circle, she was shaking her hands and screaming, "Oh, Sister Reeve, don't die on me."

I told her I was not going to die and asked her to kneel down by me. I offered a prayer, which the Lord answered, and Sister Brown calmed down. I was able to tell her what to do, and she brought my coat from the car, covered me, flagged down a car, and sent the driver to town to get an ambulance. As we waited, I told her that when I got to the hospital, I wanted her to phone the branch president and ask him to give me a priesthood blessing.

Other drivers stopped to see if they could help, wanting to move me to try to make me more comfortable, even though I kept insisting they were not to move me, as my neck was broken. I asked God to help one man understand that he must not move my head. An idea came to me, and with as much excitement as I could muster, asked him, "How much do you know about the Mormon church?" I will never forget the funny look on his face as he answered, "Anything you want to tell me, Sweetheart, go right ahead." At that point, I didn't want to tell him anything and told him to talk to my companion. He stood up and walked away.

When the ambulance arrived, I heard the driver radio to the hospital saying, "It looks like we have a broken back and a dislocated shoulder." "No," I said, "I have a broken neck. Please treat me like I have a broken neck." They did, and I finally relaxed. I learned later that I shared the first discussion with the ambulance attendant on the way back to the hospital. When you work 90 hours a week teaching the gospel, you can't stop because of a broken neck.

The hospital in Portales, New Mexico, couldn't handle my serious case, so I was transferred to Lubbock, Texas, where a neuro-surgeon was available. My life was threatened many times following the accident, but the Lord was with me; guardian angels were close by. Five days following the accident, I was stable enough to have neck surgery. I was in full-body traction and stayed in intensive care until I was strong enough to be moved home.

Dad and my brothers were building an extra room in our basement when the phone rang. Mission President Horace A. Christiansen told Dad about my accident and that I was in serious condition. Dad flew to Albuquerque, New Mexico, where two elders met him and drove him to Portales. Doctors told Dad there was no hope for me, my internal organs were paralyzed, my temperature was rising, and I would die. But, I did not die, and arrangements were made for my flight home. Since I was unable to sit up, there was no place for me on a train, bus, or airplane. Finally, the Utah Air National Guard agreed to pick me up in a cargo plane, accompanied by a doctor, a nurse, and several crew members. My bed was lifted 17 feet into the air so it could be loaded into the plane. An ambulance awaited my arrival in Salt Lake, and I was taken to LDS Hospital.

A special fast was held for me in January 1963, and I received a blessing from Patriarch George M. Williams, who promised, "The day will come when you will stand on your feet and bear witness of the goodness of God in your life." The next morning, my left index finger wiggled. I had visits from so many wonderful and supportive friends–Bishop Victor L. Brown, President Thomas S. Monson, and many others. I was told in one blessing that I knew before I came to earth that I was prepared for this experience.

Every day for nearly 45 years has been filled with spiritual experiences. I have learned to trust the Lord, and like the Prophet Joseph, in D&C, Section 122, I feel the Lord spoke to me as well: *". . . . know thou, my son, that all these things shall give thee experience, and shall be for thy good."* One of my earnest desires while serving in the mission field was to come to know the Savior so well that when I knocked on a door and even had the chance to speak His Holy Name . . . they would be able to feel a special spirit before they slammed the door. I feel these past years have been an answer to my heartfelt prayers as a missionary. I have come to know and love the Savior in such a precious and sacred way. My love for God the Father, His Son Jesus Christ, and the Holy Ghost penetrates every cell in my body. My desire is to live in such a way that I can bring souls to them wherever I am.

When I left for the mission, I put aside my desire to be the greatest mother in the world and went out to be the greatest sister missionary for the Church. After my accident, I lay in traction wondering what can I be? I won't be the greatest mother in the world, and I can't be the greatest missionary. What can I be? My answer came—I can be the greatest cripple in the world!

James L. Ricks

Born: 18 September 1944, El Paso, Texas
Parents: Artel Ricks and Focha Ricks
Siblings: David, Richard, Douglas, Marie, Donald,
Raymond, Ronald, Rosanne
Mission: Andes Peru
Time of service: Set to begin 14 October 1963
Cause of death: Motorcycle/auto accident
Date and place of death: 13 October 1963
Age at time of death: 19
Place of burial: East Lawn Memorial Gardens, Provo, Utah
Story related by: Artel Ricks, father

JAMES L. RICKS WAS THE THIRD CHILD of Artel and Focha Ricks. Six more children were eventually added to our family, and James became one of nine siblings: seven boys and two girls. James loved them all and was loved in return. James enjoyed life, growing physically, socially, intellectually, and spiritually along with members of his family. James loved scouting, which was very important to our family, and to me and my brothers, starting in the 1920s. Five of my brothers reached the rank of Eagle, as did James and his brothers. After becoming an Eagle Scout, James earned 10 more merit badges and was awarded the Bronze and Gold Palm awards. In addition, he was elected to the prestigious Order of the Arrow.

In 1962, James left our home in Falls Church, Virginia, to attend Brigham Young University (BYU) to become a mechanical engineer. With his brothers, James had designed many rockets, including a 10-foot tall, two-stage rocket equipped with a mercury switch for the second stage ignition. He won many prizes for his designs and had considered becoming a rocket designer. James enjoyed his freshman year at the "Y."

He attended general conference in Salt Lake City in April 1963. He wrote in his journal: "Apr 7. I went to Conference. Saw President McKay from about two feet away. I got a nice seat in the balcony."

James received his mission call from The Church of Jesus Christ of Latter-day Saints to the Andes Mission, headquartered in Lima, Peru. He was to report at the mission home on 14 October 1963. We were especially delighted he had been called to Peru and had always hoped one of our children would have the opportunity to teach the gospel to the Lamanites. We encouraged our children to include Spanish in their high school studies in preparation for such an opportunity, and James had followed our counsel.

He studied the scriptures before receiving his call and doubled his efforts after, participating with the full-time missionaries in their studies and proselyting activities. He seemed happy and could hardly wait to begin his mission.

Our exuberance was tempered a little by a strange feeling I experienced and described in a letter to my brother dated 14 October: "Since the day James had his mission call, I have had an uneasy feeling that he would not go to Peru. I thought he might be switched to another mission. I wondered if perhaps he might fail to do well enough in his Spanish, but this seemed unlikely."

I tried to put such ideas out of my mind, attributing them to normal parental concerns about sending our son so far away for such a long time. We did the only thing we could—put our trust in the Lord.

A month after he received his call, James was ordained an elder. His farewell testimonial was scheduled for sacrament meeting on 6 October. His favorite scripture was Alma 29:9, which was a perfect reflection of how James viewed his mission: *"I know that which the Lord hath commanded me, and I glory in it. I do not glory of myself, but I glory in that which the Lord hath commanded me; yea, and this is my glory, that perhaps I may be an instrument in the hands of God to bring some soul to repentance; and this is my joy."* A close friend, Roseanne Tueller, was invited to sing James's favorite song for the meeting, "How Beautiful upon the Mountains." She was called out of town, so a different musical number was performed.

On his way to Salt Lake City to report to the mission home for three months of intensive language training, James stopped along the way to say goodbye to as many friends and relatives as possible. He went to Utah by way of El Paso, Texas, and Albuquerque, New Mexico, meeting with loved ones who traveled to be with him at his various stops. He bid farewell to his grandparents, Donald and Olive Black, and when he arrived in Provo, visited with his Grandma Ricks and other aunts, uncles, cousins, and a host of friends who lived in Utah. James wanted very much to visit with his friend Roy Kohler, who lived in Heber City, Utah, and tried to borrow a car. After not finding one, James rented a motorcycle and invited his friend Robert (Bob) Grossnickle to accompany him, and they headed up Provo Canyon to Heber on 12 October.

At the entrance to the canyon, the road curves sharply, creating an optical illusion that is misleading to drivers, often causing serious accidents. The motorcycle veered into the path of an oncoming truck. Robert was killed instantly; James never regained consciousness and died the following day. The watch he wore at the time of the accident stopped at exactly 10:00 a.m. Two good Samaritans at the scene knelt and gave our son a priesthood blessing as he lay on the road. We never learned the names of those brethren, but will always be grateful for their courage, kindness, and concern.

I was in Virginia attending a seminar, and that morning I awoke with a shaky feeling that stayed with me until noon, and then I felt calm and peaceful. I was overcome with the beauty of the day and my surroundings and burst into singing, "How beautiful upon the mountains are the feet of him that bringeth good tidings. . . ." Minutes later I received a phone call from my wife that James had been in a serious accident and the doctor thought we should get to Provo immediately. Focha and I flew out that night to Salt Lake City, taking our baby, Rosanne, with us. We met my brother Clyde there and drove to Provo. Minutes after arriving, we learned that James had just passed away of serious brain damage.

We had many decisions to make in a short time, including where the funeral should be and where he should be buried. Our son David had just completed his mission in New Zealand and was on his way home, stopping in several countries in an effort to fulfill his dream of traveling around the globe. We weren't sure how to reach him.

Richard was serving as a missionary in England, Rosanne was with us, and there were five children in Falls Church, being watched over by friends and loved ones. We didn't plan to continue living in Virginia and felt we should have the funeral and burial in Provo at the East Lawn Memorial Gardens. That cemetery is located in the foothills of the mountains overlooking Utah Valley. After the burial, many lingered for some time, absorbing the magnificent view and enjoying the sweet spirit there.

At the same time as the funeral in Provo, a memorial service was held in our chapel in Falls Church, which was attended by our family members and a large group of our friends. A highlight was having Sister Leila Horne sing, "How Beautiful upon the Mountains," taken from Mosiah 12:21, *"How beautiful upon the mountains are the feet of him that bringeth good tidings; that publisheth peace; that bringeth good tidings of good; that publisheth salvation; that saith unto Zion, Thy God reigneth."*

Since there were no temples east of Salt Lake City, the practice at that time was for missionaries who lived far away to be endowed when they arrived in Salt Lake. James had not been endowed, but we were given permission for me to stand as proxy for James, and that ordinance was performed on 17 October 1963. My brother, Marc, an MD, came to Provo to help and comfort us, accompanying us to the temple.

Marc related that around noon on the day of James's accident, he was with some brethren, looking at the beautiful mountains in Northern California. He suddenly found himself singing the song "How Beautiful upon the Mountains." He had not heard it for some time and had no reason to sing it then, except that he was moved by the beautiful sight before him.

Following James's death, a close friend, Reed Haroldson, wrote a letter of comfort to us. He related that during their teenage years, he and James did everything together, and he fashioned his life after James. James reminded Reed that he should never forget to pray, and that he should never be afraid to take the initiative to kneel and pray with friends or roommates. Reed stated, "I get a warm feeling every time I think of this and when I think of James, that is the first thing that comes to mind."

He continued, "When I heard of James's death, the first thing I did was pray. I wanted to know why, and I wanted assurance of his worthiness. I now know that James will go to the celestial kingdom. . . . He was chosen to do a great mission in heaven. Were I in your position, I would thank Heavenly Father that you were worthy and lucky enough to be parents of such a fine boy. I'm going to miss James, but . . . I will know he is on a mission and that very soon we will all be together again. It takes only people who are ready to do the big jobs. James was better prepared than anyone I know, and he can thank you both for this. . . . I always considered myself as James's adopted brother."

We have a box of mementos we have collected from James's life. One of our most prized possessions is his missionary journal in which he had written only a few words. Since we have an absolute assurance that he continues his mission on the other side of the veil, we hope sometime to read the rest of his missionary diary. Perhaps he is assigned to labor among spirits of Lamanite descent who lived in the area served by the Andes Mission.

Bradly Alan Savage

Born: 8 January 1980, Coalville, Summit, Utah
Parents: Conrad (Pete) A. Savage and Keri J. Savage
Siblings: Kelly, Jennifer, Katie, Jeffrey
Mission: Iowa Des Moines
Time of service: January 1999 to 28 January 2000
Cause of death: Auto accident
Date and place of death: 28 January 2000, Murry, Iowa
Age at time of death: 20
Place of burial: Lehi, Utah
Story related by: Parents

BRAD CARED ABOUT THE PEOPLE around him. His smile was contagious and drew people in. He cared for us, so we cared for him. He was careful not to offend others and quick to apologize or admit when he was at fault. He was athletic and talented, worked hard to achieve his goals, but never bragged. It seemed that since he was very handsome, he wasn't taken seriously and had to prove he could work hard for what he wanted. He took state in diving four years in a row during high school. When he was 13, he worked on obtaining a pilot's license and flew a Cessna aircraft. He was crazy about flying and was promised a diving scholarship to the Air Force Academy, where he wanted to fly jet fighters.

One of his best friends, Brennon, died in a car accident, and Brad had to deal with the loss of his dear friend, but he continued with his mission plans and preparations. Brad wanted to serve and was excited to be a missionary for The Church of Jesus Christ of Latter-day Saints. He wasn't afraid of hard work and was confident his service would help make him a better person. He chose Alma 37:6 as his favorite scripture: *"Now ye may see this as foolishness in me; but. . . that by small and simple things are great things brought to pass."*

Although Brad loved and missed his family, he loved being a missionary in the Iowa Des Moines Mission. His journal reflects his personal growth and happiness in the work. He wrote he had never been happier in his life.

We had no concerns when he left, but a couple of months before Brad's accident, we sensed something was going to happen. Keri states, "The morning of January 28, I was taking out the garbage and ran into members of our stake presidency in front of our home. I joked that we must have been 'really bad or really good' to have them come to our home. They did not smile, and I knew it was not good news. When we went inside the house, President A. Roger Merrill told us there had been an accident that afternoon and that Brad had been killed. Everything started to move in slow motion. I looked at President Merrill as I tried to wrap my brain around it, and he just shook his head 'yes.' In the background I heard my husband moan. Pete said, 'Forty thousand missionaries out there and Brad gets killed.' He had thought Iowa would be safer than many places. As time went on, we felt a protective bubble around us—the Comforter was with us.

Brad and three other missionaries were returning home from a Zone Conference. Their car crossed the median and hit a pickup truck head on. All the missionaries and the driver of the truck were killed. An article in the *Church News* reporting the deaths of Brad and his three companions said that this was the first time that four missionaries had been killed at the same time. Coincidentally, the road they were traveling on is known as The Mormon Trail in Murry, Iowa.

"I always said I couldn't lose a child," relates Keri, "but the Lord showed me that I could. After I heard about the accident, I prayed to the Lord not to let him be burned because I thought he was so beautiful. He was not burned at all. I guess the Lord knows what we can handle."

We both felt an urgency to get him home. We later learned that Sister Chatterly, the second counselor's wife in Iowa, went to the funeral home to clean up the boys' bodies and remove the soot before they came home. "I later asked her why," continues Keri, "and she said, 'As one mother to another, I would hope that someone would take care of my son.' I thought that was very kind of her."

We had never planned a funeral, but people around us stepped in and helped fill in the blanks, each one doing whatever he or she could. President Thomas S. Monson, who was then First Counselor in the First Presidency, kept checking on Pete, giving him words of comfort.

People began visiting our home immediately. Brother Draney, a counselor in the bishopric of our ward, came in such a hurry that he had put on his suit, but no socks. We were touched by this, because he was more concerned about being with us than about his appearance.

"It was the little things that touched me," writes Keri. "Children from one of the wards in Des Moines, where Brad served, sent a few quarters taped to their letters, saying that was all they had to send and hoped it would help. Those little things buoyed us up." Bishop Newman of that ward wrote, "I have been so deeply touched by the number of children in our ward who were influenced by Elder Savage. The notes you will find enclosed will confirm to you the great love that he gave to us in our ward. The donations came from the hearts of the children. They asked that I forward them on to you to do as you see fit." We used all the donations to purchase Brad's headstone, which was a collaboration of many donations and the reason we included "Elder" Savage on the lettering.

We received letters of condolence from as far away as Australia. In the Iowa Des Moines Fourth Ward, a Brother Anderson that Brad had worked with was baptized the day after the accident. He wrote to us these tender words: "We are confident that his offering to the Lord has been accepted. We love you and thank you so very much for sending him to be with us on his mission. His cheerful spirit and wonderful missionary smile spoke volumes about his love for the Lord and his testimony of Him whom he represented, even Jesus Christ. His work ethic and dedication to the people within our ward confirmed his great conviction to the truth, which made him so very happy."

Brad's mission president and area president called to offer their condolences, President Robert Rowley saying the missionaries were four "perfect sons." Elder Hugh Pinnock of the Quorum of the Seventy traveled to Iowa to follow up on the tragedy, and the First Presidency sent a letter of condolence. President Monson phoned several times. Elder Dennis B. Neuenschwander, of the First Quorum of the Seventy, also called to offer words of comfort, and both he and President Monson spoke at Brad's funeral. President Monson has kept in touch with us periodically to see how we are doing.

Keri shares the following: "Two weeks before the accident, Brad called home to get some dental information. His companion was sick, so we ended up talking for four hours. He kept repeating the words, 'I love you with all my heart,' and I responded, 'I love you with all my heart too.' No regrets. We knew where we stood, and that has been a huge comfort. After Brad's accident I realized he wasn't perfect, but he was good enough for the Lord, and I realized I am too—it didn't seem attainable before the accident.

"One day at lunch two months before the accident, I told my friend I didn't think Brad was coming home. She said, 'You just miss him. I missed my son when he was gone. Write him a letter and tell him you love him.' The night of the accident my friend reminded me, 'You said this would happen.' I feel the Lord was preparing me so I would look back and realize this wasn't just an accident. As Brad's missionary scripture reminds us: 'The Lord doth work by means to bring about His great and eternal purposes; and by very small means the Lord doth confound the wise and bringeth about the salvation of many souls.' I realize this now more than ever."

Knowing that Brad was on the Lord's errand has made a hard thing a little easier. We know it was not happenstance; he is still on the Lord's errand. Pete thought that I would curl up in a ball and die, and I thought Pete would be angry. But because Brad was on his mission doing the Lord's work, we both felt that other members of the Church were watching and that we had to be strong and pull through. Those expectations actually helped us to be stronger. We are good friends with the families of the other three missionaries who died with Brad, and we all realize the Lord is in charge.

We are sure that everyone who loses a loved one in the mission field has had similar experiences, but each person's pain is very real to him or her. As I presented Brad's life sketch at the funeral, I became too emotional to speak at one point. President Monson later related that although he felt a desire to get up and comfort me, the Spirit prompted him to wait. My husband is not very comfortable on the stand, but he was moved by the Spirit to come up to console me and hold my hand. These kinds of experiences have brought us closer together as husband and wife.

Since Brad's death, we have sent two other missionaries to serve, and although we were nervous, we have felt direct help from the Comforter. We would rather have our children on a mission than home if something were to happen to injure or kill them. Three years after Brad's death, another of his friends, Ashton, died in a scuba accident. It had been easier to deal with Brad's death because he was serving the Lord on a mission.

Others who relate to our experience truly care, and we realize how much we are loved. We recognize that such an experience can make or break a person, but this has brought our family closer and strengthened our testimonies. Although we would not choose to go through this experience again, we would not want to give up the knowledge we gained. We tell those sending missionaries that we would do it again. We have learned that the Iowa Des Moines Mission has grown four times larger as a direct result of this experience, and people open their doors to the missionaries out of curiosity. As a result of Brad's passing, a tradition of memorial firesides, horseback rides and a monument have been developed. Also, The Brad Savage Award for Excellence and Performance has been established at his high school.

We see things from an eternal perspective now, and although we miss him terribly some days, we would not change anything for the blessings and sure knowledge that we have received.

Jennifer Schulz

Born: 25 November 1972, Salt Lake City, Utah
Parents: Helmut Schulz and Elfriede Schulz
Siblings: Carola Michel, Kerstin, Ramona, Melinda, Roy, Daniel
Mission: Japan Fukuoka
Time of service: 12 January 1994 to 4 May 1995
Cause of death: Serious fall
Date and place of death: 4 May 1995, Fukuoka, Japan
Age at time of death: 22
Place of burial: Mountain View Memorial Estates, Salt Lake City, Utah
Story related by: Elfriede Schulz, mother

JENNIFER SCHULZ IS THE SIXTH of seven children in the Schulz Family. An older sister served a successful mission in Ireland, and a brother blessed many people's lives while serving a mission in Austria.

Jennifer loved her sisters and brothers, nieces and nephews. Her youngest sister, Melinda, was her best friend. She loved children and loved helping others. Jennifer was known to give her last penny if someone was in need. The gospel of Jesus Christ was very important to Jennifer, and she was busy performing missionary work before she served a mission to Japan for The Church of Jesus Christ of Latter-day Saints.

Jennifer had met a young man in high school whom she encouraged to read the Book of Mormon. He told her he spoke Spanish and could not read English well. She bought a copy of the Book of Mormon in Spanish, waiting to give it to Richard when he was ready to read it.

211

One day, Jennifer wrote from her mission: "Dear Mom, I have a Book of Mormon in Spanish in my closet at home. Will you please go to the place where Richard works and give the book to him. He promised me that he will read it." I did what she asked. Several months later, she wrote that Richard had sent her a program for his baptism. She was worried he was being baptized to please her and she didn't want that. When we met Richard later and asked how he was doing, he told us he had received the priesthood, was passing the sacrament, and would be ordained a teacher soon.

Sister Schulz spent two months at the Provo Utah Missionary Training Center (MTC), where she learned Japanese. Learning the language and being away from her family were very hard for her, but she made friends wherever she went. One elder who knew Sister Schulz in the MTC wrote the following: "I had the privilege of serving with your daughter . . . in the MTC. I knew her pretty good and had the chance to talk to her quite a bit. She was a good friend, not as a person I knew every day, but just like my sister. I was always singing, and she would sing along with me and make fun of my voice, just like my sister."

From a letter to a friend who was thinking about serving a mission, Sister Schulz wrote: "My heart is so full with so many feelings that I would love to share with you about how I feel about missions. But the only thing I can tell you is JUST DO IT! Please. There are so many of our brothers and sisters who are lost who need your [testimony] and mine to help [them] find their way back. It is true that a mission has its ups and downs, but in the eternal look at it, it is worth it. I know that the Lord truly carried me. He was by my side all the time. I know you will see blessings from going on a mission. Please help to bring our brothers and sisters to the knowledge of this wonderful gospel.

Mosiah 16:9—I really like this scripture. Please read [it.]. *"He is the light and the life of the world; yea, a light that is endless, that can never be darkened; yea, and also a life which is endless, that there can be no more death."*

In her first area lived a woman who was not a member but had come to church for years. She had gone on vacation, and Sister Schulz phoned to see if the woman had returned from her trip and how she was doing. When Sister Schulz invited her to a baptism meeting, the woman paused, then replied, "Yes, I am coming." When she arrived, she had brought her towel, thinking she would be baptized at that meeting. The bishop interviewed the woman for baptism, and she was baptized the following week.

Jennifer had the talent and ability to talk to anyone, which made it possible for her to teach the daughter of a Buddhist priest, who later wrote to us, stating, "Because of Jennifer and her love, I have joined the Church, and now I am preparing to go on a mission." Her father was not excited about the prospect, but did not stop her. When the daughter returned from her mission, we heard from other missionaries that her father requested she teach her sister the gospel. He seemed to be very impressed with what he saw in his daughter.

In another incident in a different area, Jennifer's companion had advised her not to try to talk to a woman they met who worked in a nearby shop, saying that nobody was able to communicate with her. Jennifer was not convinced and spoke with the woman anyway. She had no problem talking to the woman and built a friendship with her.

After teaching a young lady for some time, Sister Schulz and her companion spoke of baptism. The custom was for the mother of the young lady to give permission for the baptism. However, the mother told her daughter she could not be baptized and was not to talk to the missionaries any more. The next time the sisters went for an appointment with the girl, she wasn't home. They waited for her and learned she was not allowed to be baptized. Sister Schulz's companion was upset by the news, but Jennifer said: "It's ok. We will still love you, be your friends, and teach you English."

Jennifer loved her assignments to teach English to kindergarten children or to help in homes for the elderly. Her life was about service, about loving and giving. She wanted to be a good missionary to the end of her mission, and she wanted to work hard for the Lord, which is exactly what she did until she passed away 4 May 1995, her appointment book still filled with many scheduled visits. Our beloved daughter, Jennifer, was transferred home to Heavenly Father to continue her mission.

Sister Nakahara Shimai (sister) served as a companion to Sister Schulz at various times during the mission. Sister Nakahara loved Jennifer dearly, and they sang together a song entitled "Lisa Marie" for a program at one time. Sister Nakahara wrote to us and came to visit us twice before Jennifer's passing. She wrote to us that she named her first child "Lisa Marie." Many other Japanese people wrote and visited us after Jennifer's passing to tell us how much they loved Jennifer.

Elder Taylor, acquainted with Sister Schulz in the MTC, wrote, "I am a zone leader in your daughter's mission. The reason I say she is still in our mission is that she left a legacy of love and joy that will remain forever. . . . I've heard a lot of really wonderful things about your daughter, and

I want you to know she served very well and worked very hard and touched many people's lives like no one else could. I'm very privileged to have had a chance to proselyte with her. . . . I'm thankful for the love and support I received from her. You should be very proud of her, as I'm sure you are. Please hang in there and know that you are loved by your Father in Heaven. He knows your pain and is there to assist you always. There is always a reason for everything. I thank you for the role you play as a great parent and for raising such a great kid. I love the Church, I know it's true. Your daughter is with Heavenly Father."

A memorial service was held for Jennifer by the members of Isahaia Japan Branch, Jennifer's last area where she died in a serious fall. They hung her picture in their chapel and said of Sister Schulz, "She was one of our people."

From the memorial service come the following words spoken by the mission president. "In a recent interview with [Sister Schulz], she shared with me some very personal and sacred things. She bore a strong testimony to me that she loved her Heavenly Father and knew that she had been sent here to accomplish a special work for the Lord. I can bear you my solemn testimony that she was ready to be called home. She stood blameless before the Lord, for Sister Schulz had prepared herself in such a way as to ensure that her calling and election was made sure. . . . Those who have lived a good life do not taste the bitterness of death, for the scriptures tell us it is sweet to them. . . . Her new mission is Heaven's Paradise Mission, Japanese speaking, and I am certain that she and her new companion, since this transfer, have many teaching appointments every day. And as those people accept the gospel in its fullness, they too will commit to baptism. The problem with that is, they may have to wait 'til their temple baptism work is done by faithful brothers and sisters, which may be many years. Still, the work must be done, for this is the Lord's plan."

Funeral services were held 12 May 1995 in Salt Lake City, and Sister Jennifer Schulz is buried in Mountain View Memorial Estates, Salt Lake City, Utah.

Nicholas Martin Silcock

Born: 2 December 1981, Burley, Idaho
Parents: Robert Silcock and Leah Silcock
Siblings: Stephanie, Christopher, Megan, Skyler
Mission: Jamaica Kingston
Time of service: 11 April 2001 to 10 June 2001
Cause of death: Suspected heart attack
Date and place of death: 10 June 2001, Kingston, Jamaica
Age at time of death: 19
Place of burial: View Cemetery, Burley, Idaho
Story related by: Leah Silcock, mother

ELDER NICHOLAS MARTIN SILCOCK was the third of our five children. When Nick was one month old, he spent two weeks in a neo-natal intensive care unit in a Twin Falls, Idaho, hospital, diagnosed with a rapid heartbeat. Physicians worked to keep his heart beating normally, and he was sent home with two separate medications to control the problem. Over the next two years, he continued taking medications until doctors were satisfied he would not have additional episodes with his heart.

During the next 17 years, there were only a couple of short-term episodes, but these incidents corrected themselves. Nick was able to participate in state, regional, and national tumbling and trampoline championships, bringing home many gold, silver, and bronze medals. Nick set a good example by his obedience and helpfulness. He was a friend to everyone, and he had a great sense of humor, a happy nature, as well as a winning smile.

After graduating from Burley High School in May, 2000, Nick worked full time in order to earn money and prepare to serve a mission for The Church of Jesus Christ of Latter-day Saints. On 29 November 2000, Nick's call came to the Jamaica Kingston Mission. He was thrilled to be going to a warm and beautiful place, and he spent the next five months making preparations.

The first time he told us he wasn't coming home from his mission we didn't take him seriously. We assumed he meant that he would never want to come home from such a beautiful island. He brought up the subject a few more times, the last being two weeks before he was to leave. The look on his face and the tone of his voice told me he was serious, and fear clutched my heart. With tears in my eyes, I looked at him and said, "Nick, you are coming home, even if we have to go get you!" He never brought up the subject again, and I forgot the incident until later.

Nick reported to the Missionary Training Center (MTC) in Provo, Utah, on 11 April 2001. We expected to have the same bittersweet experience we had with our oldest son, Chris, two years earlier. But this time it was different; not a tear was shed by anyone. The blessing of peace as a constant companion in our lives had already started.

Nick was more than ready to head to Jamaica and left after a short three weeks in the MTC. Upon his arrival in Kingston, Nick was assigned to Elder John Mallya, who became his companion and trainer. Nick wrote home about his admiration and respect for Elder Mallya, who was the most humble person he had ever met.

On 9 June 2001, Nick performed his first and only baptism. Dwayne McPherson was a young man recruited off the street by a ward member. He was willing to listen to the discussions and committed to baptism. Nick's journal entry stated: "Today we baptized Dwayne McPherson, and it was glorious!"

The next day, a Sunday, began much like any other sabbath in Jamaica. The elders attended church and then joined other missionaries in the area for dinner before returning to their assigned areas. Mission assistants to the president offered Nick and Elder Mallya a ride home. They had gone only a short distance when Nick admitted he was not feeling well; his heart was racing and he needed to lie down. He and his companion were dropped off at their apartment, where Nick promptly changed clothes and lay down on his bunk. Elder Mallya climbed up to his own bunk to take a nap. He reported that he had just closed his eyes when he felt the bed shaking and looked down to see that Nick was convulsing. He quickly called for help and then gave Nick a priesthood blessing. A doctor happened to be close by and worked on Nick until the ambulance arrived and transported him to the hospital, but by then it was too late. Nick was gone and couldn't be revived. Word traveled quickly around the Kingston District. Back in Idaho, that same afternoon following our church meetings, we received a phone call from Bishop Alan Gerratt asking if he and his uncle, Stake President Larry Gerratt, could come to our home and visit. They arrived a short time later, and I will never forget what transpired. President Gerratt sat across the kitchen table from us and said, "Bob and Leah, I don't even know how to tell you this." Then with tears in his eyes he said, "Elder Silcock passed away today" and shared the details as he knew them.

Bob phoned his family members and expressed an urgent need for them come to our house. I was shocked by the news, but not surprised since the Lord had been preparing me for many years. Many times I experienced thoughts concerning Nick and his early departure from this world, but I had pushed them aside, not wanting to become overly protective. I knew it was his time to go.

We began the difficult task of sharing the news with our children and other family members. News travels quickly in a small town, and within an hour we began receiving the first of hundreds of visitors. Food arrived, and offers of help were extended again and again. A bishop's fireside had been scheduled for that night, but instead of delivering his planned message to the youth of our ward, Bishop Gerratt shared the news of Nick's death and sent everyone home. Instead of returning to their own homes, they came to ours. We were encircled about by so much love.

The Jamaican government would not release the body until an autopsy was performed to determine the cause of death. Those procedures were performed only once a week, on Thursdays. Nothing conclusive was found, which meant waiting until the next Thursday for additional tests. We were devastated. Nick's mission president, Norman Angus, did what he could to get Nick's body released sooner, but nothing could be done. So, we sought help in other ways. Bob and I received blessings. The Spirit confirmed that Heavenly Father was mindful of us. We asked for ward members to join us in a fast, and we began contacting local and state politicians to request their help. We were ready to fly to Jamaica, but very soon our prayers were answered, and the government agreed to release Nick's body. A second autopsy was still required but could be done from tissue samples. Nick was finally coming home. On 20 June, Nick's body arrived, and we learned there had been definite signs of stress to his heart. Unfortunately, the second set of samples had been contaminated, so a final diagnosis has never been pronounced.

President Angus held a memorial service in Jamaica, where Nick's death had a strong impact on ward members. So many attended that there was standing room only. We began preparations for a funeral service at home on 23 June. We were overwhelmed at the love and support from the more than 500 people we estimated attended, including Elder F. Melvin Hammond, of the Quorum of the Seventy, who spoke at the service, giving us a comforting promise that we would see Nick kneel at the altar to be sealed to his eternal companion, and that they would have children. The trip to the cemetery was also a surprise. When we arrived, there was a line of cars behind us that stretched for almost two miles. It was an incredible sight, and we truly felt loved.

Photographer Sheri Peterson donated a beautiful framed picture of Nick, with a plaque stating, "Returned with Honor," and five hundred wallet-sized pictures of Nick which we gave to those who attended the funeral. Nick had collected John Deere tractor models, and we went to his favorite store to buy one for the top of the casket. The manager would not take any money for our purchase, saying it was an honor to pay tribute to Nick in that way. We received numerous cards and letters, including notes from the First Presidency of the Church, Quorum of the Twelve, and Area Authorities.

One young man we had not met before expressed his admiration for Nick. He told us that Nick had always been kind to him when others were not. Nick often gave him rides home from school or walked with him to class—so typical of Nick. He had a compassionate side, always willing to help others in need. We felt blessed in so many ways by the kindnesses shown to us.

Although we don't know yet just why Nick received his transfer to the spirit world, we do know that since his death, we have felt the tender mercies of our Father again and again, and the blessings just keep coming. The mother of another missionary who died shared these words: "You will receive the greatest blessings you would not wish on anyone." We know this is true, and we also know we have received blessings that could not have come any other way. We have felt Nick near us, in numerous and sacred ways, and we have felt peace. He helped his nephew Cole find his way home after getting off the bus at the wrong place, confirming to me, "I was [with Nick], Mom, every step of the way!" He was there to assist a family friend,

Trent Vorwaller, following a job-related electrical accident. Nick prevented our youngest son, Skyler, from stepping out in front of a speeding car while he served his mission.

Skyler expressed his personal desire to follow Nick's great example. He wrote, "If Nick can go on a mission with the knowledge that he would not return home and still go forth and preach the gospel, then apparently it's very important and worth dying over. So, who am I that I would not go on a mission. If Nick was willing to sacrifice his remaining time on this earth for the gospel, then I, too, must go and share the Lord's message with others."

Not a day goes by that we don't think of Nick or how much we miss him, and that we don't express our deep gratitude to a loving Heavenly Father, who is aware of us and our needs. Because of our Father's great plan of happiness, we know that Nick is not far away. He is always here when we need him most. We have been blessed with the sealing power of the holy priesthood of God and will be with Nick again one day. We know that Nick is still going about the Lord's work as a missionary in the spirit world, and one day he will report his mission to us. We will learn why Nick was called home early, and when we do, we will be filled with joy and gladness. This knowledge helps us find peace in this life and hope for our future.

So, Nick, it is with love that we pay this tribute to you and thank you for all you are doing for us. We look forward to that day when we will be united once more as a "forever family."

Benjamin Doxey Snow

Born: 25 July 1974, Salt Lake City, Utah
Parents: Susan D. Snow and Wayne S. Snow
Siblings: Emily, Mary, Brian, Wesley, Katie
Mission: Brazil Recife South
Time of Service: 22 September 1993 to 3 February 1995
Cause of death: Truck–bus accident
Age at time of death: 20
Date and place of death: 3 February 1995
near Arapiraca, Maceio, Brazil
Place of burial: Salt Lake City Cemetery, Salt Lake City, Utah
Story related by: Susan D. Snow, mother

BEN DOXEY SNOW WAS THE PERFECT SON—so obedient. People asked, "What are you doing to raise such a great young man?" We answered, "He just came that way." He was a secure, grateful person. Ben was the oldest of six children, and all his siblings looked up to him. He figured out incentives so Saturday work would be productive and fun.

One morning when Ben was nine years old, he told me of an incredible experience he had the night before. While saying his prayers, he had expressed his love for Heavenly Father and said, "Heavenly Father told me He loved me and missed me."

We were amazed at his remarkable unselfishness. He once asked if he could use his birthday money to support a Church-sponsored fund to assist African people who were affected by a severe drought. His willingness to give was a consistent pattern throughout his life. He kept life in perspective. He calmed the fighting over fairness at neighborhood games, and our stake president, President Charles Norton, referred to Ben as "a promoter of harmony."

Always a conscientious student, Ben was named to the honor roll even though he took Advanced Placement (university level) classes in high school. He was a talented athlete, lettering in tennis. He refused to compete on Sunday and won the respect of his coaches and teammates. As a student at Ricks College, he was an environmental economics major during the 1992–1993 academic school year. While there he was an enthusiastic missionary and was instrumental in the baptism of a fellow student.

When a member of the stake presidency set Ben apart for his mission for The Church of Jesus Christ of Latter-day Saints, he said, "I bless you to come home in glory." What I heard of that phrase, with relief, was that Ben was coming home in safety.

Ben chose 1 Nephi 1:20 as his mission scripture, *". . .But behold, I Nephi, will show unto you that the tender mercies of the Lord are over all those whom he hath chosen, because of their faith, to make them mighty even unto the power of deliverance."*

His letters home focused on his love for investigators, new converts, and the work of a missionary. In spite of difficult situations, he kept a positive attitude. He spent his life protecting and developing self-esteem in others and helped many missionaries feel of worth and important.

Ben became ill and was in the hospital for 15 days. Ana, wife of the branch president in Pão de Acúcar, cared for him as if he were a member of her family, making hydrating teas, and wrote us of her love and concern for our son. We would not have known about his illness if she hadn't written, as he didn't want us to worry.

Ben's journal reflected his happiness as a missionary in the last journal entry he made: "I know the missionaries love and support me. That's good because I sure do need it. I love this mission. I love this country. I love our Zone and everyone in it. I love our investigators. I love my family. The gospel of Jesus Christ is true. He is our Savior and I'm coming to know Him. I love Him with all my heart. I still don't live all the commandments perfectly which makes me sad. I know, however, that one day I'll be made perfect through my faith, repentance, and the Atonement of Jesus Christ, having been baptized and having received the Holy Ghost."

In January of 1995, before President Gordon B. Hinckley, acting for President Howard W. Hunter, dedicated the Bountiful Temple, he referred to the Saints in Brazil, stating they are as deserving of a temple as we are. It seemed he was speaking directly to us, and Wayne and I spoke of what action we should take as a result. Just days later, Ben was killed; we had our answer.

President Charles Norton, our stake president, phoned my husband Wayne at his office on 3 February 1995. At the time, Wayne was bishop of the 21st Ward. President Norton related: "I asked if I could meet with the family. Bishop Snow sensed there was something wrong with Ben. I confirmed the fact and stated that I would really like to meet with the family. Bishop Snow said, 'President, you can tell me on the phone,' and I said, I would like to be with both you and Sue, but because you are the bishop of the ward, I will tell you.' I then proceeded to tell him what had happened to Ben. I sensed that the bishop had thoughts even prior to Ben's departure that something like this may happen to Ben because he was truly a pure spirit. We made arrangements to meet at his home in 30 minutes. I then received another call from the mission president giving more details."

A bus loaded with steel rebar had crashed with a Mercedes Benz truck leaving 6 people dead and 18 injured. The accident occurred at 4:30 in the morning, about 2/3 of a mile from Arapiraca. The impact was so violent it destroyed the front left side of the bus. Both drivers were killed instantly, a woman died, and our son, Elder Benjamin Doxey Snow died. The bodies were taken to the Arapiraca Medical Institute by the police at 8:00 a.m.

The night before the accident which claimed Ben's life, Wayne and I attended the temple in Bountiful. Late into the night we talked of eternity and God's merciful Plan of Salvation. We said that we are not afraid of death; in fact, it is certainly a sweet experience for those who are prepared, one of the Lord's "tender mercies" in our lives.

We received a letter dated Saturday, 4 February 1995, 10:24 p.m., from Elder Hickey, who had lived in the same apartment with two other missionaries and with Ben for a month. Our family is intensely grateful to Elder Hickey for his caring sacrifice while attending Ben's body. His words answered many questions about Ben's death and increased our testimony that the Lord is intimately involved in our lives.

"Dear Snow family, I thought I should write you to express my condolences in this trying experience and to try to share with you how the body of your beloved son was cared for after the accident. During that entire ordeal I was there—for some odd reason which I could not explain until now I felt the entire day yesterday that I should be completely involved in every moment of the time that his body spent here in Arapiraca until it went to Recife to be sent to the U.S."

Elder Hickey explained that he woke at 5:30 a.m. in anticipation of the arrival of Elder Trigo and Elder Snow from Recife. The missionaries didn't arrive at their scheduled time, but it was assumed they had missed the 10:30 p.m. bus and would arrive later that afternoon. As Elder Hickey and his companion left their house for the day, the next door neighbor informed them that a news bulletin reported a bus accident had happened, a Mormon was killed, and the body was at the city morgue. A member of the ward happened to be passing by, and Elder Hickey asked him for directions to the morgue. The member, Elder Hickey, and his companion speed-walked to a nearby supermarket owned by a member and reported what they had heard.

Elder Hickey wrote: "[The market owner] phoned District President Antonio [who] had already been informed of the accident by the mission president, President Moreira. He confirmed that Elder Snow had been killed. I cried when I heard that—cried tears of sorrow because I would not see my good friend again. I did not cry because I felt sorry for him, because I felt then as I feel now—Elder Snow was the purest Elder I have ever met and if anyone was spiritually prepared to go to the other side, it was him.

We got in the car and went to the morgue to identify the body. As we approached the morgue entrance there were several dozen people outside the gate waiting to see the bodies. . . . I was permitted to enter, as was my companion and the men with us because we were recognized as Mormons.

"I entered the room where lay five bodies, including that of Elder Snow. Not to try and horrify in any way, but the other bodies, that of the two drivers and another passenger, were grossly mangled. Only the body of Elder Snow lay on the table in perfect form. . . . [He] looked to be asleep and at total peace. To see him among that group was a shock and I cried some more. I felt he did not belong there. I got hold of myself quickly as this was no time for tears. We went through his clothes to try to find his ID card, but it was not there. So we took his garment top (which had been ripped off by the EMTs) and found a sheet to cover him. . . . He was left in dignity—just as he always conducted himself."

Around 10:00 a.m., President Antonio arrived and they found Elder Trigo in good condition in spite of a fractured nose, cuts and bruises. After President Antonio confirmed Elder Snow's death to Elder Trigo, he asked if he had Elder Snow's ID.

Elder Hickey continued: "[Elder Snow's ID] was at the police station in Igaci, 10 minutes from the scene. We gave a blessing of health to [Elder Trigo] and the other elders stayed to give him assistance. We went to the police station. . . . We saw the bus and truck up close. . . . Elder Snow simply flew forward, but his flight was stopped abruptly by a steel rod that

223

was directly in front of him. He was killed instantly, and painlessly. He was, as Elder Trigo noted, in a deep sleep, and he simply closed his eyes and never woke up. This is a sign to me that the Lord wanted Elder Snow on the other side and this was the best way to get him there. He did not wish Ben or his companion to suffer. The accident also happened close enough to Arapiraca that he could be taken care of and sent to the states as quickly as possible. In a trip that takes eight hours by bus [from Recife] the Lord let it happen 20 minutes from Arapiraca. This was truly planned by the Lord. We must recognize his divine hand in this."

Elder Hickey and Elder Dias returned to their house to get a fresh set of clothes for Elder Snow to be buried in. President Moriera had told them to dress Ben as if he was "going out to work," that is, missionary attire. However, since he was an American, under church responsibility the mortician demanded an unreasonable sum of $5,000 Real, or about $6,000 American dollars, to embalm the body. After phoning the mission president, and learning that morticians normally charge R$500 in Recife, the price was lowered to R$1000, to which President Antonio agreed.

Following the embalming, Elders Hickey, Linford, and Germaro and two other brethren asked the morticians to allow them a few minutes to dress Elder Snow in his "sacred religious clothing."

"I must tell you what an experience it was," explained Elder Hickey, "what a privilege it was to dress Elder Snow . . . in his missionary clothes. I truly felt the Holy Ghost there with us as we placed the holy garment on him, put his missionary attire on him, and finally placed his name tag on him for the last time. I felt truly blessed to play a part in his departure like that. I don't feel worthy really to have been there for this—I felt as if Ben deserved angels dressing him. It was an experience which I will never forget."

Several dozen members of the Church had waited the entire day in the morgue to see Elder Snow's body off to Recife. The coffin was then sealed and the branch president from Pãq de Acúcar, where Elder Snow had spent a good portion of his time in Brazil, gave a beautiful prayer to our Father in Heaven, thanking him for Elder Snow, and for the example of purity and righteousness he had been to everyone. He asked that the body might arrive safely in Recife, and that we, as well as those in the States, might be comforted. A special prayer was said for Elder Snow's family, the coffin was loaded into the station wagon, his luggage and personal things, and with the bodies of the drivers of the vehicles. About 9:30 p.m., Elder Snow left Arapiraca for the last time. The next day a simple memorial service was held for Elder Snow in Arapiraca, many eulogies being delivered by those who loved him.

I kept thinking we would get a phone call telling us that Ben had not been killed. Reality set in at the mortuary as I dressed him with the mortician, one of the last services I could do for our son. Then I stroked his hair, held his shoulders in my hands and ran my fingers along the folds of his clothing. I told him what an exemplary man he is and how much we love him. "I know you can hear me, Ben," I said. In my mind I heard his humorous response, and I laughed and cried at the same time.

After the initial tears had subsided, I admitted that several times during Ben's life I had the feeling he would be taken at a young age. Reading Ben's patriarchal blessing, which he received when he was 14 years old, changed my feelings, and I had the impression that he would need to live a long mortal life to accomplish all he was promised.

Funeral services were held Wednesday, 8 February 1995, at 12 noon at the Farmington North Stake Center. In the obituary we requested that in lieu of flowers, contributions be sent to the General Temple Fund for the Brazil Recife Temple.

Our stake president, Charles Norton, spoke at the funeral. He quoted Orson F. Whitney, of the Quorum of the Twelve, "No pain that we suffer, no trial that we experience is wasted. It ministers to our education, to the development of such qualities as patience, faith, fortitude and humility. All that we suffer and all that we endure, especially when we endure it patiently, builds up our characters, purifies our hearts, expands our souls, and makes us more tender and charitable, more worthy to be called the children of God ... and it is through sorrow and suffering, toil and tribulation, that we gain the education that we come here to acquire."

Soon after Ben's funeral, I questioned the member of the stake presidency who had set Ben apart, "Do you remember saying, 'I bless you to come home in safety' when you set Ben apart? I want you to know it has been a source of comfort to me while Ben was on his mission. He did come home in safety in the sense that his physical body was miraculously preserved during the accident and his worthiness assures us that his spirit body returned home in safety also." He answered, "I remember it well, except, as I was about to use the word *safety*, the Spirit stopped me, telling me to say, 'I bless you to come home in *glory*' instead."

I made a great effort to endure everything patiently but found myself screaming in my head, "I just want to see my son!" That night as I slept, Ben came to me dressed completely in white with his beautiful smile. He approached me and we embraced for a wonderfully long time. I thank God for his many kindnesses to us.

225

I wanted very much to know what he was doing after he passed from mortal life. I assumed he was a missionary but needed a definite answer. One day while attending the Bountiful Temple, I was granted the absolute knowledge that Ben continues to serve as a missionary as outlined in Doctrine and Covenants Section 138, verse 57.

We received many letters of comfort from people we did not know Ben personally; some were sent anonymously. Each one expressed sorrow at hearing of Elder Snow's passing and shared words of comfort: "I rejoice that another one of our Father's children has proven himself sufficiently to return to his Father's arms and receive an everlasting salvation in God's kingdom, worlds without end. . . . I believe in your goodness and pray that you will be faithful and soon find your Ben back in your arms again."

Another, mailed three years after Ben's passing, stated that the writer had cut the obituary from the paper, having been touched by the kind of person Ben was, even though he did not know him personally. He felt that he was truly inspired to be a more Christlike person because of the way Ben was and that he would try to be the kind of missionary he imagined Ben to be.

Time moved on, and in every prayer I expressed gratitude to our kind Heavenly Father for the blessing it was to have raised Ben, who had such an extraordinary spirit. I pled for patience, courage and understanding. I was concerned that I was wearying the Lord with my prayers and was directed to read my patriarchal blessing. A sentence stood out as if in bold print: "The Lord is mindful of your wants but he requires that you turn to him for help and guidance, both morning and night." The Lord taught me I was not wearying Him with my prayers; not only does He want me to ask for that which I need, He requires it.

One afternoon as I prayed, I was prompted to open Ben's scriptures. He had bookmarked and highlighted John 16:33, which reads: *"These things I have spoken unto you, that in me ye might have peace. In the world ye have tribulation: but be of good cheer; I have overcome the world."* Joy for the Atonement filled my heart; I could be patient because eternity did not seem so far away any more. My courage was renewed, and my understanding had more depth.

Seven months to the day after Ben's death, on 3 September 1995, I was feeling really low. I went into my bedroom to pray. All I said was, "Let heaven give comfort once again," quoting lyrics from the music of Kenneth Cope's "My Servant Joseph," which we listened to repeatedly.

The phone rang, and it was Ben's mission president, President Moreira, calling from Brazil. With great excitement he exclaimed, "Sister Snow, we have a stake in Arapiraca! Since Elder Snow's passing the missionaries are on fire! Sister Snow, it was Elder Snow's last assignment to help prepare Arapiraca to become a stake. We want to invite you and your husband, Brother Snow, to Brazil to be part of the formation of this stake."

The night before we left for Brazil, our stake president, Glen Leonard, gave each of us a blessing. He blessed me that I would travel in peace and comfort and that the Brazilian women would bathe me in their tears of gratitude for Elder Snow's service to them. He also said we would return safely and tell of Ben's life and our experiences, which would strengthen the testimonies of family and Church members. After the blessing, he told us we might be called on to speak during the stake conference in Arapiraca.

We were asked to speak at that conference. As I stood, the Spirit prompted me to bear testimony of conversion, preparing to enter the temple, and making our homes places where we can feel the Spirit of God. At the conclusion of the meeting, Wayne and I had the privilege of greeting members of the newly formed stake in Arapiraca. And yes, the women bathed me in their tears of gratitude for the service of our son. We learned of his sacrifices for them, through stories we had not heard before.

Elder Daniel Trigo, a native Brazilian, who had been our son's last companion was currently serving as an assistant to the mission president. Elder Trigo drove us to the mission home in Recife and pointed out the crash site, where we stopped for a few minutes. Several Brazilian people came from their homes and bowed their heads in reverence and respect. Elder Trigo explained, "They know who you are because they know who I am."

Elder Trigo explained the events of the night before the bus accident. He and Ben were zone leaders and had interviewed the missionaries at the conclusion of the zone conference. Prior to their boarding the bus, Ben embraced the elders, who told him they felt they were saying goodbye for the last time. When Elder Trigo and Elder Snow boarded a later bus, Elder Trigo said, "I want to go home [to São Paulo]; something bad is going to happen." Ben answered, "I know, but it's going to be ok."

"There was such peace in his voice," related Elder Trigo, "I know that he really was fine with what was about to happen. I also was certain that Ben knew something was about to happen." Ben sat directly behind the bus driver, motioning for Elder Trigo to sit by the window. Ben fell asleep immediately while Elder Trigo stayed awake the entire journey. He told us that each time he looked at his companion, he was struck by Elder Snow's purity.

About 10 minutes before the accident, the bus driver approached Ben, grabbed his shoulders, shook him violently, and asked in a loud voice, "Do you want to get off here?" Elder Trigo told the bus driver to leave him alone and was surprised that Ben made no response, either verbally or physically. Perhaps Ben was taken even before the accident.

Elder Trigo was thrown from the side window and landed 100 feet in front of the bus, standing up and facing the bus! His first thought was, "I must be dead, I can't just be standing here," but then he became aware of the pain in his face, which was covered with broken glass from the window. He continued, "I knew Ben was dead, but I had to see him for myself. I looked inside the bus and there sat Elder Snow as though nothing had happened. He still appeared to be in a peaceful sleep."

We were blessed with an abundance of spiritual experiences while visiting Ben's mission. It was apparent from our experiences that the Lord orchestrated our time there.

Our youngest son, Wesley, entered the mission field nearly 10 years after Ben's passing. He too was called to serve the people of Recife, Brazil. When Wesley opened his mission call and learned where he was to serve, we all cried, but our emotions were not of fear or anxiety. Many people have asked how I could be willing to allow our other two sons to serve missions and how the Lord could allow Ben to be taken from us. My answer is, "You send them because you have a testimony that God's church is on the earth. The truth is, you never go through these challenges alone. The Lord sustains you through experiences which you think you cannot endure."

Ben was truly protected while serving his mission. His body came home intact, a miracle when one considers the force of the crash which took his life. Ben was protected spiritually in that he was prepared to leave this earth. Quoting from a funeral memorial given by the Prophet Joseph Smith, "He has had revelations concerning his departure, and has gone to a more important work. When men are prepared, they are better off to go hence."

My husband, Wayne, said, "I wouldn't trade this for anything, except for it not to have happened," and I feel the same. Our testimonies of the reality of the Savior, Jesus Christ, have been strengthened. We have felt the Savior near, and His Spirit is in our hearts. We know that angels have lifted us.

The gospel of Jesus Christ is true. He is our Savior, and I am coming to know Him. I love Him with all my heart. I still don't live all the command-ments perfectly, which makes me sad. I know, however, that one day I'll be made perfect through my faith, repentance, and the Atonement of Jesus Christ, having been baptized and having received the Holy Ghost.

Lindsey Spjute

Born: 21 February 1985, Salt Lake City, Utah
Parents: Mark Spjute and LuAnn Spjute
Siblings: Laura, Melanie, April, Alicia, Greg
Mission: England Birmingham
Time of service: 25 October 2007 to 10 May 2008
Cause of death: Physically collapsed while running
Date and place of death: 10 May 2008, Coventry, England
Age at time of death: 23
Place of burial: Centerville City Cemetery, Centerville, Utah
Story related by: LuAnn and Mark Spjute, parents

LINDSEY SPJUTE BEGAN HER ADVENTURE in life on 21 February 1985. She was the fifth daughter born to Mark and LuAnn Spjute. With her bright blue eyes and sunny blonde hair, Lindsey quickly showed she was no ordinary girl. In her early years she raced her trike up and down the street, sometimes pausing to collect rocks or sticks to later be used for an invention. Lindsey had an unlimited imagination, and when wearing her Batman cape, she could do anything!

Most of her growing up years were in Farmington, Utah, surrounded by beautiful mountains to explore. This setting nurtured her love for the great outdoors, where she spent much of her time climbing trees, hiking, or sitting by a stream to read a book. Lindsey was very artistic, like her mother and Grandma Jensen. She spent many afternoons painting side by side with Grandma as they developed a special relationship.

Lindsey was very athletic, unlike the rest of her sisters. Her mother relates that when she visited Rexburg for the annual Mother's Week at BYU Idaho, she and Lindsey attended a breakfast for mothers and daughters. Lindsey walked ahead, and her mom heard one of the college students whisper, "That's the girl; she has a championship t-shirt in every sport!"

She played on the Farmington Junior High basketball team in 9th grade. In her journal she recorded, "I'm not the best player on the team, but I've befriended everyone and tried to make every practice fun." When she began dating, Lindsey quickly realized she often had to hold back when competing against boys so she wouldn't embarrass them on the field. If she wasn't on the field, she was on the sidelines cheering her friends on. She and her friends hauled a huge blue couch named "Baloo" to the school soccer games to sit on while they cheered for the team.

Lindsey loved music. Like her siblings, she practiced the piano for hours. Her favorite high school activities involved her participation in choir and school musicals. She learned to play the guitar, and it accompanied her on many adventures. She taught herself to play the mandolin. In the weeks before her mission, Lindsey spent a lot of time brushing up on her piano skills so she could share the gift of music in England.

She graduated from Viewmont High with honors and went right on to college at BYU Idaho and then Utah State, where she majored in special education. Lindsey had a gift for working with children and hoped to increase her education to further that talent.

She was reluctant to leave her schooling because she was so anxious to receive a teaching certificate and work full time with special-needs children. She was a favorite teacher's aide at the elementary school and worked one-on-one with autistic children, helping many of them to make great progress. She took great joy in telling her friends about each of them.

Lindsey is extraordinary. She had many friends who tell similar stories about this person of light who brought happiness, fun, and faith into their lives. Lindsey widened her ever-growing circle of friends at college, and her antics grew to the task. She jumped off bridges, went rock climbing, arranged gold fish races, spent one night in a snow cave and another in a water slide at the local park. She loved to go dancing and basically had more fun than any 10 people.

Lindsey never had a boring day in her entire life. Her friends included the popular and unpopular, each thinking he or she was Lindsey's special friend, and each one was! She found good in everyone and recorded in her journal characteristics she learned from the people she met. Her nieces and nephews quickly learned that Aunt Linz was more fun than a barrel of monkeys, and she was all too happy to teach them to play hard.

Lindsey paid her way through college, working at a bakery and with the grounds crew on Temple Square. She enjoyed working with the arborist crew at BYU Idaho and loved roping up into a big tree with a chain saw strapped to her belt to trim the large trees on campus. Most recently she worked as a member of the Centerville Cemetery grounds crew, caring for the grounds and digging graves. She loved to tell people she was a grave digger!

Despite her school and workload, she was active in her student wards, serving as Relief Society president at one time. She had always wanted to serve a mission for The Church of Jesus Christ of Latter-day Saints but struggled to discover when the Lord wanted her to serve. When she was 22, after much prayer and fasting, she knew the time was right and submitted the paperwork to become a missionary. Her copy of the missionary manual *Preach My Gospel* was worn out before her mission began.

Though Lindsey will always be known for her fun-loving ways, her spiritual depth was her most amazing feature. People were attracted to Lindsey, both for her outward beauty and her inner beauty. She had a strong love and interest in everyone. Her journal is full of her experiences with people, her worry for them, and the good times she had with people she dearly loved.

Lindsey wasn't satisfied with having a testimony. She wanted to understand and know and live the gospel to the best of her ability. She had a maturity beyond her years, causing many to think she had already served a mission. She left notebooks full of scriptural topics she had studied and researched and applied to her everyday life. It all became a part of her. Nothing about her was insincere or thoughtless; she was genuine in every trait she had. When she concluded her talk in church before leaving for her mission, she bore a sincere and fervent testimony of Heavenly Father and His Son, Jesus Christ and then said firmly, "I am sure of it."

In a letter to her mission president before arriving in England, she wrote, "I feel greatly blessed to serve the people of England and invite them to come unto Christ through the restored gospel. I am humbled to walk in the footsteps of so many great missionaries and have been eagerly learning of their history in Birmingham."

Then Lindsey left to serve in the England Birmingham Mission on 25 October 2007. She never worked harder in her life, nor loved her work more than when she was preaching the gospel of Jesus Christ. She loved learning and teaching and helping the people she served.

For one of her weekly service projects, she and her companion helped an elderly woman with some yardwork, and she told us how great it was to get her hands back in the dirt. She loved the diverse cultures and people, and she learned to say "thank-you" in 12 different languages. In one of her last letters home she wrote, "We knelt in prayer with someone yesterday who had never offered a prayer in their entire life—I never get tired of that."

Lindsey's approach to life and her mission is evident from this quote in a letter home: "We had . . . interviews last week and I was really troubled as I asked President Moffat, 'I'm enjoying this and having so much fun. . . . Is that wrong?' He explained that as long as I'm working hard, I am allowed to enjoy the work too. I felt relieved. Even after our most devastating of days last week as we walked through the busy streets of Coventry, I had such an over-whelming feeling of peace and joy inside which is indescribable. This is the greatest work to be engaged in. I know that it is the Lord's and that as we serve others we receive so much more in return than we ever actually give."

Lindsey's mortal mission ended much sooner than anyone could have imagined. On 10 May 2008 in the early hours of a Saturday morning, in Coventry, England, Sister Spjute and her companion, Sister Bannister, were scheduled to do their morning workout at a nearby park, but Lindsey asked if they couldn't please, please run in the forest, and they did. Not far into their run, Lindsey collapsed, unconscious and not breathing. Sister Bannister administered CPR and called for help. A nearby police officer came running into the woods, called for an ambulance, and took over the CPR. However, Sister Bannister reported that as she held Lindsey, she became aware that Lindsey's spirit had slipped away and she was gone. Despite heroic measures by the ambulance crew and the doctors at the hospital, Lindsey could not be revived.

That Lindsey would collapse while running was a shock to us. She was an avid athlete and had run the Ogden marathon just a year before. An autopsy was performed in Coventry and no cause of death was found. Lindsey was healthy in every way; she was simply called home.

"Have you ever imagined life beyond today? I have, and you know some-thing? It's a wonderful image. Believe in the greater cause that is this life, and remember God will always take care of you, as I have seen Him take care of me, regardless of my many inadequacies."

—Sister Lindsey Spjute

232

Carl Ludwig Ferdinand Stelter

Born: 13 March 1870, Piepstock, Regenwalde, Pommern, Prussia
Parents: Freidrich Wilhelm Ferdinand Stelter
and Johanna Louise Helke Stelter
Siblings: Herman, Wilhelmina, Bertha, Albert,
Augusta, Emelie, Emmanuel
Spouse: Elizabeth Seidletz Stelter
Children: Martha, Arthur, Carl, Eric, Anna, Bill,
Elizabeth, Clarence and Clara (twins), Ellen
Mission: Swiss German
Time of service: 1922 to 1923
Cause of death: Heart failure
Date and place of death: 12 April 1923, Berlin, Brandenburg, Germany
Age at time of death: 53
Place of burial: Salt Lake City Cemetery, Salt Lake City, Utah
Story related by: JoAnn Isaac Ball, granddaughter

MY GRANDMOTHER, ELIZABETH ROSALIA SEIDLITZ, was working with some other girls as a housekeeper in Berlin. Their employer
allowed the girls to have some nights off to go to dances for the soldiers
stationed in Berlin. At one of these dances, Elizabeth chose to dance with
a polite, clean-cut, handsome young man who didn't use bad language like
some of the soldiers. His name was Carl Ludwig Ferdinand Stelter, and he
was serving the mandatory two years in the German military.

They had to wait to marry until Elizabeth was 21 years old, and they married on 7 July 1893 in Spandau, Germany, near Berlin. They lived in Stettin, which was part of Germany at that time, but is now Poland. Carl worked on the railroad for the government, which provided living quarters for their workers. Carl and Elizabeth lived in an apartment house where some of the other family members lived.

When missionaries from The Church of Jesus Christ of Latter-day Saints first came to their home, Carl would not let them in and refused to listen to their message. However, his brother Herman and a friend, August Lange, went to a missionary meeting. They liked what they heard and convinced Carl to go with them to the next meeting. Carl also liked what he heard and felt, so he studied the gospel for some time before he was baptized.

In about 1898, Carl Stelter was baptized by Elder Cola Robinson. Some of the other missionaries who taught Carl were Bruce Brown, brothers Alma and Elijah Larkin, William Guild, and a Brother Budge.

After Carl and Elizabeth had been members of the Church for about three years, they wanted to go to America but didn't have the money to do so. Brother William Guild, whose father owned a hotel in Piedmont, Wyoming, loaned them $500, and they were able to sail to Boston and then travel overland to Piedmont. Brother Guild let them stay in his hotel until they found a log house to live in. At that time, the Oregon Shortline Railroad trains stopped in Piedmont, and Carl got a job there. Today, however, Piedmont is a ghost town; the railroad no longer stops there.

The family later moved to Salt Lake City, where Carl worked for the railroad and Elizabeth took in washing, living by the Jordan River. She said she often knelt by the washtub and prayed to Heavenly Father to protect her children while she worked. Carl joined the prayer circle in the Salt Lake Temple on Sunday mornings and walked to the Tabernacle for Sunday afternoon meetings. The older children read the scriptures on Sunday afternoons.

About this time, President Joseph F. Smith called Carl to serve a mission. Carl felt he couldn't leave his wife and children with no means of support, so he didn't serve then. In 1909 they moved to Rexburg, Idaho, to farm. While there, the family had a very spiritual experience. The children became ill with scarlet fever. The oldest, Martha, was so sick her eyes became glassy and set. Two of the boys went to get their father, who gave Martha a blessing, and she got a little better.

One Sunday morning as Martha lay in bed, someone appeared in the doorway. He was a nice, big young man with a pleasant look about him. Martha asked him to sit down, and as he pulled up a chair and sat, two other men stood behind him. As the first man leaned over and got close to Martha, she could see he was the devil. She had a horrible feeling come over her, and she screamed. The men promptly disappeared. One of Martha's brothers, Bill, the youngest, had a similar experience. He jumped out of bed and started running around the house crying, "The devil is after me. Don't let him catch me." Carl caught Bill and held him while he offered a prayer commanding the evil spirit to leave. Carl had great faith and believed in prayer.

A man living nearby said a good woman had lived in the house before Carl and his family moved in. After she went to the temple, she was bothered by evil spirits. The house had a root cellar outside and some people saw strange men suddenly appear and go into the cellar, then move into the house. After my grandfather offered his prayer, the cellar caved in and no more strange spirits came.

The family moved back to Salt Lake when the children grew older. Two of the girls had married, and the older boys had jobs, so Carl decided in 1922 to go on the mission he had been called to so many years before. He returned to his homeland to serve the people of Germany. A "farewell testimonial" meeting was held in his honor on 13 June 1922 in the 24th Ward Hall, at 8:00 p.m. There was to be a program and dancing, and voluntary contributions would be accepted, prior to his departure for the Swiss German Mission.

From Elder Carl Stelter's mission journal we read: "Sunday, 8 April 1923, Berlin. Prayer/Breakfast. Dressed for Sunday School. From there to family Huhndorfs. Evening, my last opportunity to be in the meeting. I had the desire to thank the good people for what they had done to me. Every missionary speaks at his farewell. [Carl, however, was not allowed to speak at his farewell.] It was bad behavior from Brother Norton to be so cruel. Thursday, 12 April 1923, Berlin. Awoke 6:40 a.m. Prayer. Had a very bad chest pain. I laid again in bed with strong faith."

While in Berlin, Carl began having stomach problems, which he received treatment for, but in those days, doctors didn't know that heart problems can cause stomach problems. On the evening of 12 April 1923, as Carl prepared for bed, he began removing his shoes, fell off the chair, and was dead. Carl's companion, Elder Hermann Strauch, wrote the last part in Carl's diary and said that all the missionaries and members were shocked and saddened by his sudden death. They donated money for a casket and flowers and held a funeral for Elder Stelter in Berlin. A large crowd attended the funeral, including Carl's sister Augusta and a niece, Margarete, who were still living in Germany.

Elder Stauch wrote: "April 12, 1923, Berlin. . . . The members told me that he had a strong testimony and when he left he said: *Auf Weidersehen* in Zion or in the other world.' These were his last words. Then he left that place and . . . came home 10:45 p.m. . . . Brother Stelter took off his clothing and sat on a chair, took off his shoes, when suddenly he fell backwards. After three minutes, he was gone. Brother Franks who was also in the room went out for a doctor.

"Friday, 13 April 1923, Brother Wolf went out to Brother Norton and gave the News to him. Brother Stelter was lying on the bed. I closed his eyes, laid a white handkerchief over his face, and stayed by him. Sister Wolf came. . . . Other members came; the news went fast around. All wept bitterly. Then he was brought to the August Hospital for embalmment. So the days went on. Sunday the 15 Apr. in the meeting place the members were so excited over the news and hardly could believe it. Then they were all very quiet or calm, and everyone thought about him. They all loved him.

"Berlin, 20 April 1923. . . . Last Sunday I established a fund for Brother Stelter. The members gave with love so much. . . . The amount was 55,000 Mark. I bought a wreath, artificial flowers, and a nice ribbon. Brought it to the hospital in a special hall where he was lying for the viewing. Most all members came from all the wards or branches from Berlin and also all the missionaries were present. Burning candles were around the coffin, and . . . through a glass window all members and missionaries could say again, *'Auf Wiedersehen.'*"

President Hansen spoke about Elder Stelter's work and said that the Lord would give him his reward. The glass window was covered and a beautiful wreath laid on the coffin.

Elder Stauch packed Elder Stelter's missionary belongings into two suitcases, and Brother Dietz accompanied the body and personal belongings to America.

Elder Stauch concluded, "So I did my duty and wrote down what you in Zion should know. I give you my condolence. Never in my life will I forget him. I lived with him for two months, and he was like a father to me. He was a gospel fighter, worked hard for the Lord. . . . If I should ever come to Zion I can tell you more. Many greetings and deeply depressed, your brother in the gospel, Hermann Strauch, Missionary."

A booklet was sent to Anna Stelter from President Heber J. Grant, dated 11 May 1923, with the words, "With heartfelt sympathy." The booklet, entitled "When Great Sorrows Are Our Portion," contains personal reminiscences and comforting stories and poems. When Carl's body arrived home, a graveside service was held in the Salt Lake City Cemetery on 27 May 1923.

2 June 2007. After reading my grandfather's diary, my mother's history, my Aunt Martha's history, and my grandmother's history, I have a greater outlook on my grandfather's life and found he was a very spiritual man. I wish I could have known him and my grandmother. Actually I know him only from the written word. His missionary experiences were better than I had been told.

Ransom Marion Stevens

Born: 1 May 1864, Fairview, Utah
Parents: Raymond Absalom Stevens and Tranquilla Ann Stevens Brady
Siblings: Mary Ellen, Kaziah Frances, Arnold, Lois Ann,
Lindsey Absalom, Warren Abraham (Abram), Elizabeth Tabitha,
Justus Perry, Tranquilla Ann, Rhoda Matilda, Sophia Beatrice
Spouse: Annie Dorothea Christensen Stevens
Children: Stella Sophronia, Ray, Marion Christensen
Mission: Mission president, Fagalli, Samoa
Time of service: 17 March 1892 to 28 April 1894
Cause of death: Typhoid fever
Date and place of death: 28 April 1894
Fagalli, Upolu, Samoa
Place of burial: Fagalli, Upolu, Samoa
Age at time of death: 30
Story related by: Ruby Cox Smith, niece of Annie D. C. Stevens;
and Robert Foss Hansen

RANSOM MARION STEVENS WAS FROM Fairview, Utah, and was called "a fine young man" by his future wife, Annie Dorothea Christensen, whom Ransom married on 14 April 1886, both aged 22. Ransom was the eldest son in a family of 12 children. Annie was the eldest daughter in a family of 11 children.

Their first child, Stella, was born 11 September 1888, but died less than a month later. Second child, Ray, was born 9 November 1889 and died 18 November 1891. Soon after, Ransom received a mission call from The Church of Jesus Christ of Latter-day Saints to the Samoan Mission, and Annie decided to accompany her husband. She then received a call also, and they worked together to prepare for the journey.

Goodbyes were said at their home and also at the Fairview train depot, where some 200 friends and relatives gathered to see them off. They boarded their train for Salt Lake City, where they met some former Samoan missionaries who gave them some advice. Ransom and Annie were told what to expect in Samoa and what to take with them. They also received instructions from LDS church authorities and were set apart as missionaries.

Another couple, Brother and Sister Thomas H. Hilton, were to accompany the Stevens and would be traveling companions as well as missionary companions during their mission. The Hiltons brought with them a son and had two daughters, who all died in the mission field.

The two couples traveled to San Francisco by train and from there sailed to Samoa, leaving 17 March 1892 and arriving at the mission home in Fagalii, Upolu, Western Samoa, on 17 April, three days after the Stevens's sixth wedding anniversary.

Annie kept a journal of special events and some of her feelings while serving in Samoa with her husband. The journal consists of 32 poems in her handwriting. All except the first and last two were written in Fagalii, between 9 May 1892 and May 1894.

Annie and Sister Hilton spent much of their time at the mission home, where conferences and meetings were frequently held. The elders spent their time proselyting in various villages on the island or on other islands in the same mission, returning to the mission home every two weeks or so, as needed.

The Samoans called Annie "Anei" and Ransom was called "Setafano." They with the Hiltons comprised the presidency of the Samoan Mission. After the Hilton's children were buried in Samoa, Thomas Hilton and his wife returned home childless to the United States.

At the age of 29, after serving two years, Elder Stevens, president of the Samoan Mission, died of typhoid fever, complicated by a heart problem, on 28 April 1894. He was buried in the newly vacated grave of Sister Kate Merrill, whose body had recently been exhumed and sent to the United States. Elder Merrill had completed his mission and returned to the States, taking his wife's body, and that of their baby daughter who had been buried with her. Ransom's remains are still on the island of Samoa in his burial place in

Fagalii Cemetery. The small cemetery at Fagalii was neatly maintained for many years, and President David O. McKay visited there in 1921.

Annie's last poem is entitled, "Farewell." She bids goodbye to her eternal companion and husband, Ransom, to Sister Hilton, her friends, and to the people of Samoa she loved so dearly.

> My hopes, my joys are buried there
> With him I loved so well.
> To them and thee, thou mound of earth,
> I bid adieu, farewell:
> And yet, I would not if I could
> Forget the sacred spot,
> Nor would I of thy noble trust
> Erase one single thought.
>
> May grasses grow and flowers bloom
> Around and on thy mound,
> May holy angels hover near
> To keep and guard thee well,
> A resting place for his remains,
> Grave of my dead, farewell!

Elder Stevens's widow, Sister Annie D. Stevens, sailed home by steamer on 23 May 1894. She reached Ogden on Sunday, 10 June, where she was met by President Joseph F. Smith and Elder Franklin D. Richards of the Quorum of the Twelve. On 11 June she had an interview with the First Presidency (President Wilford Woodruff) in Salt Lake City and then went on to her home in Fairview, Sanpete County, with her father, arriving in Fairview at 6:00 p.m.

At the time of her husband's death, Annie was pregnant with a son, who was born at 11:00 p.m., five hours after her arrival home, 12 June 1894. He was named Marion Christensen Stevens after his father's middle name. He lived only a short time and died 1 July 1894.

Fourteen years later, Annie Stevens married Andrew Warren Palmer and raised his child, Lewis Dean Palmer, born 1897. Annie died in 1932 and is buried in the Salt Lake City Cemetery.

The following information is related by Ruby Cox Smith, niece of Annie Dorthea Christensen Stevens:

"Before my Aunt May Christensen Hammond's death, she entrusted to me a book of poems that her sister Annie had written in Western Samoa.

Annie and her husband, Ransom Stevens, were there on a mission for the LDS church from 1892–94. It was not until after I retired that I took the time to really read each of the thirty-two poems. They told a great deal about Annie's and Ransom's experiences in that Pacific Isle. I did other research, including obtaining information regarding the Church account of the Samoan mission at the time Annie and Ransom were serving there.

"Finally, in February of 1986, I flew to Hawaii and then on to the Samoan Islands to see first hand some of the places Annie had written about. I wanted to see Uncle Ransom's grave and, also, the graves of little Jennie and Harold Hilton, located as Annie describes, "on the mount under the palm trees." I longed to see for myself the island circled with the coral reef, the verdant land with its graceful palms, the native huts, the harbor at Apia, the port city where the steamer brought mail from loved ones; the beautiful blossoming trees, the dainty ferns, the profuse flowers, the brilliant sunshine, the murmuring ocean. I had to taste the native food, especially the *palusami* Annie had written about.

"My stay was short, but delightful. I was able to tour some of the island, to feel the sun, see the graceful palms, the lovely flowers and the various greens. The 'Early Mormon Missionary Graves' are well noted by a sign at the roadside in Fagalii. One can follow a neat little path to some stone steps and climb them up the hillside to the 'hallowed spot' Annie wrote about. I attended a Samoan LDS Sunday meeting. The Samoans were interested in why I had come to their island and voiced their love and appreciation for the early missionaries who sacrificed so much on their behalf. I thought how pleased Aunt Annie and Uncle Ransom must be, that the seed they and others had planted had flourished so well. I wondered if they ever dreamed there would be a temple there."

Trenton Blaine Thompson

Born: 18 July 1984, Orange, Orange, California
Parents: Curtis and Kathi Thompson
Sibling: Trevor
Mission: Directly into the spirit world
Cause of death: Automobile accident four days
after final mission interview with stake president
Date and place of death: 24 April 2003, Fresno, California
Age at time of death: 18
Place of burial: Fresno, California
Story related by: Kathi Thompson, mother

CURTIS AND I WERE UNABLE to have children of our own, and after seven years of humble prayers, our first son, Trevor, was born in 1980. We experienced true joy as we held our first child in our arms. Three and a half years later, another valiant spirit was sent to us. Trenton Blaine Thompson blessed our home on 18 July 1984, and we expressed our gratitude to the Lord for sending us two sons. We were a close family, and our boys blessed our lives in many ways. They were both involved in sports and we supported them in all their activities. We loved being parents!

Trevor was called to serve in the Taichung Taiwan Mission for The Church of Jesus Christ of Latter-day Saints in 1999. His testimony grew as he served his mission, and our family was blessed during his time of service.

Trent graduated from Clovis West High School in Fresno, California. He had excelled in basketball, participating on three championship teams. During his senior year, he served as captain of the basketball team and was the only member of the Church on his team. He was selected as the Clovis Independent Athlete of the Year. He was well liked and respected through the San Joaquin Valley.

He had his last name embroidered on the back of his letterman jacket, along with the words, "The Saint." Trent's membership in the Church was a well-known fact, and he was respected for living his religion. Everyone also knew he was planning to serve a mission after his high school graduation.

Trent anticipated his mission with great excitement. His best friend, Tyson Parker, was a month older than Trent, and together they filled out mission papers. Trent's mission papers were ready by February 2003, and he planned to send them three months before his 19th birthday. He would graduate in June and hoped to leave immediately on a mission. Tyson received his "big white envelope" containing his mission call on 18 April 2003 and invited our family to come over when he opened his call. Our family and Tyson's were all gathered around while Trent videotaped the event. Tyson was to serve in the Moscow Russia Mission. Trent was excited for Tyson and wondered aloud where he would be called to serve.

Trent's final mission interview with Stake President Craig Mortensen was on Easter Sunday, 20 April 2003. Trent excitedly told us that President Mortensen had found him prepared to serve a mission!

Four days later, on 24 April, Trent was killed instantly in an automobile accident. He was returning from lunch just two blocks from his high school. A friend was driving and turned into the path of an oncoming truck, which hit the passenger side, where Trent sat.

The feelings of pain and loss we felt are indescribable. Numbness came over us, and feelings of horror and disbelief ran through our minds. At the same time, I felt an unseen presence surrounding me with a feeling of love and warmth. I felt Trent's presence and the comfort he offered me.

I met Curtis at the high school, and together we learned the details of the accident from school administrators and the police. Our bishop, Craig Cleveland, gave us each a blessing later in our home, and friends and family gathered to offer love and support. The Lord sent the Holy Ghost, which completely filled our home. Everyone who left our home felt the love, peace, and comfort that come from the Spirit.

As we finished up the details for the funeral service, Bishop Cleveland told us he had been contacted by the president of the Fresno Temple,

President Dredge, who told our bishop he had a very strong feeling that Trent's temple ordinances needed to be performed before the funeral. He felt that since Trent had been found worthy to serve a mission and had completed his final interview four days earlier, it was very important to do his work. President Dredge had contacted Church administrators in Salt Lake and was given permission to perform the ordinances so Trent could immediately begin his work in the spirit world.

Tyson was in Provo, Utah, at his sister's graduation from BYU the day Trent died. He was devastated by the tragedy and sought comfort. Tyson's uncle, Steve Cleveland, BYU men's basketball coach, contacted President Thomas S. Monson and BYU President Merrill Bateman to meet with Tyson. They agreed, and President Monson listened intently as Tyson poured out his heart. He then told Tyson that his dear friend, Trent, had been called to the other side to perform a great mission. He gave Tyson a blessing and quoted the promise the Lord made to missionaries in D&C 84:87–88: *"Behold, I send you out to reprove the world of all their unrighteous deeds, and to teach them of a judgment which is to come. And whoso receiveth you, there I will be also, for I will go before your face. I will be on your right hand and on your left, and my Spirit shall be in your hearts, and mine angels round about you, to bear you up."*

President Monson told Tyson that Trent would be one of the angels who would bear him up while he served his mission. He advised Tyson that there would be times while working with his companion that there would be an unseen third companion: Trent. He encouraged Tyson to serve a "mission for two." Tyson shared his experience with us, which brought much comfort to our broken hearts.

Trevor was proxy for Trent at the Fresno Temple two days after the accident. Curtis was given permission to ordain Trent to the Melchizedek Priesthood. The spirit was very strong, and Trevor and Curtis felt Trent's presence during the ordination. As we gathered in the session to perform ordinances for eight of my family members, we were unable to hold back tears.

There are no words to express what we felt when we said our last goodbyes to our dear Trent the night before his funeral. He looked angelic, and tears filled our eyes as the spirit bore witness to our hearts that we were gazing upon a majestic being. Dressed in the robes of the Melchizedek Priesthood, Trent was now ready to begin his great work in the spirit world. Our hearts were moved by the strong spiritual presence we felt in the room. We bid him farewell and had our last prayer with him in this life. Love and gratitude filled our hearts for the loving and kind son Trent had been. We were honored to be his parents, and we would miss him so much. Our hearts were tender with emotion as the words, "God be with you 'till we meet again" filled our minds and hearts. We look forward to a joyful reunion with Trent.

Trent's funeral was very well attended. The Clovis *Independent* newspaper reported that hundreds of students, teachers, and athletes poured into the chapel to say goodbye to Trent, who was often called the "angel of Clovis West." Teammates and competitors wore basketball jerseys over their shirts and ties. Bumper stickers depicted crosses and halos over Trent's jersey number, and messages like "Bros forever" clung to car windows.

Curtis told of an interview he had with Trent when he was eight years old. Curtis gave Trent a card with a picture of the Salt Lake Temple on the front, and the words "Begin the Journey." Trent and his parents had signed the card as witnesses of Trent's commitment to uphold the Word of Wisdom at all times, keep himself morally clean and chaste, be honest with others and himself, provide service to those in need, willingly obey the law of tithing, and attend church meetings and activities. Curtis found the card in Trent's wallet.

The day after Trent's funeral was especially difficult as we felt the reality of his loss. As Curtis and I read the many cards we had received, I suddenly felt Trent's presence and felt his arms around me. The spirit of love was so powerful I didn't want to move, and soon, Curtis also felt Trent near. Later, we found an envelope in our safe, labeled "Trent's good-bye letter." Several years before, in a Family Home Evening lesson, we had each written a good-bye letter to the family. Tears came to our eyes and our aching hearts were filled with peace as we read Trent's expressions of love to each of us.

Following Trent's death, many people shared personal stories of their friendships with Trent. He had reached out to those who were different, comforted those facing challenges, and gave a smile and encouraging word to everyone he met. He stood up for what he believed, showing you don't have to give in to peer pressure to be respected. He was a joy to be around and was loved by so many. He touched many lives by his Christlike love and example. His life stands as an example of how our lives can be a positive influence on others when we follow the example of Jesus Christ.

We are grateful for the plan of salvation and our knowledge that families are forever. My mind flashed back to the day in the Los Angeles Temple so many years ago when our family knelt around the altar and were sealed for time and eternity. How grateful we are for that wonderful day. Losing Trent makes each one of us more determined to live worthy to become an eternal family.

Judson Bliss Tomlinson

Born: 26 June 1878, Camp Point, Adams County, Illinois
Parents: James Berry and Mary Carrie Rood Tomlinson
Siblings: Mary Alice, James Weller Addison, Sarah Leolia,
Joseph Elisha, John Enoch, Carrie Edith, Jessie Faith,
Eva Lallula, Judson Bliss, Pearl Ethel
Mission: Samoa Apia
Time of service: 19 June 1900 to 18 May 1902
Date and cause of death: Bells Disease or Acute Delirium
Date and place of death: 18 May 1902
Fagalii, Upolii, Sama
Age at time of death: 23
Place of burial: A vineyard in Samoa
Story related by: Dorothy Saley, niece

JUDSON BLISS TOMLINSON WAS THE NINTH of ten children born to James Berry and Mary Carrie Rood Tomlinson. When he was one year old, his parents moved to Kansas. Although his mother, Mary, was not a member of The Church of Jesus Christ of Latter-day Saints at that time, his father, James, taught him the gospel. When Judson was 13 years old, the missionaries arrived in that area and baptized him.

Six of the children had moved to Utah, and Judson was anxious to follow them. In 1892 his mother was convinced to travel to Utah to attend the wedding of one of her daughters. It wasn't long before Mary gained a testimony of the gospel of Jesus Christ and sent for the rest of her family to join her in Utah for a happy reunion.

As time went by, Judson fell in love with a beautiful young woman named Mary Holladay, who had moved into the ward Judson and his family attended. However, Judson was called to serve a mission in Samoa. Although it was difficult to leave Mary, he had received a vision that the call came from God, and he would let nothing allow him to falter or fail that call. His mother wrote: "Dear Judson, our youngest son and the only son we had at home, was called on a mission to Samoa. . . . As we believed it was a call from God, we cheerfully resigned our will to his, and in the beautiful month of June, 1900, we bid him a fond and lingering farewell bathed in tears because the parting was so painful."

From Judson's journal we read: "My daily record started Friday, 8th of June, 1900 for my mission to Samoa Islands. I left from home at 6:30 A.M. to receive a blessing from Dear Bishop Sperry. He blessed me that I would be prosperous on my mission and would bring many souls unto Christ. The language would be difficult but I would learn it with great rapidity and I would have a safe journey there and return."

Judson went to Mary's home, and she and her mother walked him to the depot. Mary boarded the train and traveled with Judson to Ogden. He gave her a bracelet, kissed her, and they parted for what they thought would be three long years. Judson wrote: "The last kiss is given and the train so cruelly parts us as we wave as long as we can see one another. I content myself as I know it is a call from Almighty God."

Judson visited his two sisters in San Francisco, and they made his stay as happy as possible, but he was very sad, since it was his first trip away from home, his family, and his sweetheart, Mary. Elder Tomlinson bid his sisters a fond adieu and sailed away on the large ship *Mariposa*, with four other elders going to Samoa.

The tone of Elder Tomlinson's letters home was warm and loving. In a letter to his younger sister by five years, Pearl, 4 Nov 1901, he wrote: "I am glad if my letters are appreciated by you, and also pleased you pray for me. I feel the efficacy of your Prayers. I also pray for you all. . . . You seem at a loss to understand, '*oi 'oi, 'oi! On te alofa ia te ro tele lava.*' It is equivalent to saying in English: 'It is astonishing! How greatly I love you.' Well Pearly, you say your heart rejoices on receiving letters from me. I will assure you, I am always cheered by your loving messages. . . . I am well and enjoying my labors as a Servant of our Saviour."

The last four days of entries in Elder Tomlinson's journal, entered before his death on 18 May 1902, tell of his progressing illness which began with a bad cold, and stomach and kidney trouble. Wednesday morning, May 7, he wrote from Laulii, "I held morning worship and returned to bed, having been in bed both Monday and Tuesday with sickness. I did nothing but nursed myself."

From the Samoa Apia Mission History, 1888–1983 by R. Carl Harris, President, Samoa Apia Mission, we read the following: "Elder Judson B. Tomlinson, who arrived in Samoa on 27 June 1900 was overtaken by a sickness . . . Bell's Disease, or acute delirium, for which they had, at that time, no cure. He was nursed by loving hands over quite a period of time. He would have seizures which necessitated . . . four or five Elders to hold him down. . . . He could not recognize people around him. . . . He seemed to have no consciousness of his surroundings or of his own internal state. Elder Tomlinson died on May 18, 1902. . . . This, no doubt, is the saddest event that has occurred to the Samoa Mission since the death of Brother Stevens. Brother Judson Bliss Tomlinson died this morning at 8:00 at Fagalii. He passed away peacefully. He went to sleep last night at about 7:30 under the influence of drugs and awoke again about 11:00. He fell asleep again at 11:50 and never awoke again in this world. . . . Nothing could prevent the hand of death. Preparations were made as soon as possible for his burial as . . . the corpse would not remain long in good condition. He was laid away in the best form possible under the circumstances. . . . The Pesega boys . . . dug the grave. There were but a few present at the services, which were held after 5:00 p.m. Brother Little presided. He, and Brother Molander and Brother Iverson each spoke a short time. It was after 6:00 when the little procession left the house, and the internment was made by moonlight which was most excellent. Brother Tomlinson spent a year and ten months in most active labor in the vineyard of Samoa. A letter was sent to President Merrill in Pago Pago informing him of conditions described above; he will send the sad news to the deceased Brother's parents as he sees fit."

After learning of their son's death in Samoa, Judson's mother, Mary Carrie Rood Tomlinson, wrote the following: "He labored faithfully, was a noble and beloved Missionary for one year and eleven months, when he was taken down with a tropical fever, and the Lord called our dear boy to himself." When she and her family learned that their son was very sick, she asked her family to pray, but knew he had passed away. She wrote, "Judson was buried two weeks before we knew of his death; we were advised to leave his remains there, which grieved us all greatly."

A memorial service was held at the Fourth Ward. The president and missionaries who had returned from Samoa spoke about Elder Tomlinson, saying he had been called on a higher mission. Mary wrote, "All the words comforted our hearts, but God alone can heal the void."

President Merrill returned Elder Tomlinson's belongings at his family's request but told them it was impossible for his remains to be sent home. He advised them to put a nice fence around his grave for the time being, adding it would cost between $400–$500 to send his body home. He wrote the following: "Your son is buried on the brow of a lovely hill about 200 yards east of the mission house. . . . Jos. H. Merrill, President of Samoan Mission." Later, President Merrill wrote to the family that there was a balance of $20.97 for the doctor bill that needed to be paid. He proposed a plank headboard be placed at the head of Elder Tomlinson's grave, discouraging the family from sending a stone marker.

Judson's mother wrote: "His Sweetheart, Mary Holladay, did not marry for eight years after his death, then she married a Mr. Richins from Idaho. When she left on the train, the platform was crowded with her friends, and in nine months they were gathered there again to receive her body. She had lost her life, in giving birth to their son, Orthello."

On 22 October 1903, President Martin F. Sanders, who had replaced President Merrill of the Samoan Mission, wrote to Sister Tomlinson with an update as to the final resting place of Elder Tomlinson. He reported that he took a group of elders to the grave where they cleaned and hilled up the graves, repaired and extended the fence, and planted flowers and shrubbery.

Years later, I received the following information about the others buried near Elder Tomlinson: "Ella Adelia Moody of Thatcher, Arizona, born Oct. 31, 1874, 68th missionary to go to Samoa; arrived Nov. 2, 1894; died May 24, 1895. Ransom M. Stevens of Fairview, Utah, born May 1, 1864, 35th missionary to arrive in Samoa, April 7, 1892; 'Setefano,' Samoan name; died April 28, 1894. Judson B. Tomlinson of Salt Lake City; born June 26, 1878; 132nd missionary to Samoa; a seventy; arrived in Samoa June 27, 1900; 'Pelese,' Samoan name; died May 18, 1902. Loi Roberta; age, 1 year 7 months; born Aug. 18, 1898; died March 3, 1900."

An unknown author wrote: "Elder Tomlinson was taken in his youth, when life seemed full of promise. . . . Elder Tomlinson has won a Victor's Crown. By the sacrifice of all he held dear, to engage in the service of the Lord, and the proof he offered of his great love for his fellows in being willing to lay down his life if necessary for them.

"We feel assured that our brother is none the less a 'Missionary,' now he has passed from mortality."

Jonathan Guy Twitchell

Born: 6 June 1960, Payson, Utah
Parents: Charley Dee and Virginia Mathena Twitchell
Siblings: Keith Leon, Del Rulon, Veloy Dee, Edwin Ray, Brenda Lee, Calvin
Neal, Anita Kay, Alison Eliotte, Lyle Greg
Mission: South Africa Johannesburg
Time of service: June 1978 to October 1980
Date and place of death: 24 October 1980, Durban, South Africa
Cause of death: Auto accident
Age at time of death: 20
Place of burial: Payson, Utah City Cemetery
Story related by: Parents

JONATHAN GUY TWITCHELL WAS BORN 6 June 1960, to Charley Dee
and Virginia Mathena Twitchell. Jonathan was child number 6 in a family
that would grow to 10 children.

Jonathan was a very happy and determined young man. He was self-
driven, never asking for or requiring help with his many activities. He loved
his schoolwork, his teachers, friends, and everything the world had to offer.
He was active in Scouting, and over the course of his youth he earned some
90 merit badges, was a member of the Order of the Arrow, and after receiving his Eagle Scout Award, he earned four Palms. He received many ordinances at the hand of his father, including his baptism and ordination to the
office of elder.

He actively participated in LDS Seminary, receiving a number of awards, including "Upholding the Honor Code" in 1976 from the Payson Senior Seminary. He participated in the Utah Valley District scripture chase contest, Old Testament Division, and received certificates of merit for that and numerous other Seminary Bowl contests. He had numerous perfect attendance awards and earned "The Great Reader Certificate of Merit" for reading 3,090 pages.

When Jonathan was 14 years old, his family received word that their missionary son, Veloy Dee Twitchell, who was serving in Australia, was seriously injured in a car accident and was in a coma. When he woke, he required major surgery to repair his femur, which had been pushed up into his body, narrowly missing his brain. Doctors were uncertain he would be able to complete his mission, but he was soon up and walking, determined to complete his work, which he did, returning home safely.

Following his high school graduation, Jonathan worked as a carpet layer and attended Utah Valley State College, where he studied and excelled at technical drawing. Jonathan's patriarchal blessing stated words of promise and comfort that would bless him and his family as the years went by.

Jonathan had always planned to serve as a missionary for The Church of Jesus Christ of Latter-day Saints and was excited when the call came to serve in the South Africa Johannesburg Mission, Lowell D. Wood, president. He was to report to the Provo Missionary Training Center in June 1978. Soon after the call had been opened, Jonathan won $396 from a "Dialing for Dollars" T.V. show, which he put toward his mission.

The tone of his letters home was positive and full of optimism and excitement. He met a number of wonderful people who accepted the gospel and became members of the Church. As with everything Jonathan did, he moved forward with love, zeal, and dedication. He loved his companions, his mission president, and the people of South Africa. The work was difficult, but Jonathan kept going, in spite of knee problems he began having.

After approximately one year into his mission, President Wood determined Jonathan should return home for knee surgery. He was home for two weeks, the cartilage repaired, and he was pronounced well enough to return to his mission. He was walking well and physically fine, but he was troubled at the prospect of returning to the field. He didn't want to go back. He was unsettled and worried, sensing that something wouldn't go right when he returned. His bishop and stake president met with Jonathan, prayed with him, and encouraged him to return. After much prayer and concern, Jonathan did return to complete the remaining year of his mission.

An excerpt from a letter Jonathan sent home three days following his 20th birthday, reads: "As usual, this is from your long-lost son in the wilds of Africa among the wild pygmies and man-eating tigers. . . . We will be baptizing two people on the 18th and 21st of this month. One is completely Afrikaans, so that is a real challenge to teach someone in another language. . . . I can't ask for anything else than to be able to see someone join the Church."

At that time, Elder Twitchell and Elder DeWaal from the South Africa Pretoria Ward were companions and were given a car to drive, as they both suffered with knee problems. They expressed their desires to be companions and had been transferred together to Durban. They drove the back roads, eager to reach their destination and complete their assignment, but they never arrived.

Some time during their journey there was a fatal accident, the cause of which is still under speculation. It is thought the elders were driving into the sun, which blinded them, and they ran into the side of a bridge. Five to six hours later, someone finally came upon the scene and found both elders were dead.

Back at home on that day, Jonathan's mother knew something was wrong. She related that the day was gloomy and overcast, she didn't feel well, and she knew something had happened to her son. At 5:00 p.m. when the stake president phoned, Sister Twitchell already knew Jon was gone. His father had gone deer hunting and returned a few hours later to learn of his son's death.

Church officials covered all the arrangements to have Jonathan's body returned home, but it was a difficult process, and his unembalmed body finally arrived in a body bag, 12 days following his death. The mortician picked up the body at the Salt Lake City, Utah, airport, and his father and brothers assisted with his temple clothing to make certain everything was in order, even though the casket was closed during the funeral.

President Lowell D. Wood of the South Africa Johannesburg Mission sent the following letter:

"As you know, Elder Twitchell worked in the office and was often in our home. I feel that I became his very close friend and associate. We were able to talk freely and openly, and I know that he loved both of you very much. . . . Please be assured that he was loved by the missionaries and members of the Church in the areas where he worked. He truly had a very bright mind and was familiar with many subjects. I am sure that you will be comforted by the letters and phone calls from former missionaries and members from South Africa. Brother and Sister Twitchell, I have a very calm and peaceful feeling, the witness of the Holy Ghost, that Elder Twitchell and Elder DeWaal, were transferred to the next world to continue their missionary labors."

Elder G. Homer Durham, of the Quorum of the Seventy, and our son Edwin spoke at the funeral in Payson. Letters from missionary companions and members came to our home, along with cards and condolences from people we didn't know.

In spite of all the words of comfort and gestures of love, the shock and grief were unbearable. His mother was angry and bitter about the loss of her son, and grieved for a very long time. Several months after his passing, Jonathan appeared to his mother as she visited his grave in the cemetery. He clearly told her that she had to stop grieving, saying that he couldn't progress unless she changed. After three years of inactivity, she sought advice from the stake president, who suggested that she read Jonathan's patriarchal blessing and that she continue reading until she understood a statement from it:

"When thou art prepared, thou shall be called from this mortal existence. Thou shalt not approach this transformation with fear, but shall look forward with anticipation to the new work and opportunities that await thee. ... When you have perfected yourself, you will be taken from this earth, and it will be sweet unto you."

Jonathan's death didn't deter other family members from serving missions; three more of his siblings served. When the time had come for Calvin to serve a mission, his mother admitted being afraid to send him after the injury to Veloy and the death of Jonathan. She point-blank said, "You can't go," to which Calvin replied, "Well, I'm going anyway," and the process began. Jonathan's parents later served a couple mission to the Sioux Indians in South Dakota and later as stake missionaries, eventually seeing half of their 21 temple-class attendees sealed in the temple.

Jonathan's father stated, "Jonathan had a testimony of the gospel even before he served a mission. He was the sixth son of a sixth son born on the sixth of the sixth month (June). Two of Jonathan's great-uncles served missions in the late 1800s, and his great-grandfather, Ansel Twitchell, served as a member of the Mormon Battalion."

Charley Twitchell continued, "Nobody wants to lose a child, but if you have to, the Lord will compensate for that. Even if there is a chance a missionary will not come back, the family will be blessed eternally."

Sione Laulota Veamatahau

Born: Nuku a'lofa, Tonga
Parents: Uateson Tu'ipulotu Veamatahau, father, and
Salote 'Ahovala Laulotu Veamatahau, mother
Brothers: Tevita Lilo, Setelo, Heamasi 'Ahokava, and Sioeli Fakapulia
Sisters: Susana 'Auhangamea V. Tavake, Sala, Soana, and Mele Nanasi
Mission: North Carolina Charlotte Mission
Time of service: unknown to 9 March 2002
Date and place of death: 9 March 2002, North Carolina
Place of burial: Family Cemetery
Tafengalolo, Matahau Tonga Island
Story related by: Susana Veamatahau Tavake, sister

I COME FROM A FAMILY of four sisters and five brothers, of which I am the oldest and Sione was the oldest son. Our mom was very active in the Church, and my dad was not. Sione was a good brother and son. If you needed help, he was there for you. As a young man he was not very active in the Church, but Mom kept preaching to him about the Church and encouraged him to show a good example to his younger brothers, saying, "Whatever you do in life, your brothers will follow your footsteps."

Sione always had a great smile, and it didn't matter if he had a bad day or a good day, he was smiling and made sure everybody at home was smiling. He was always willing to do his share of the work and never complained about the difficulty of it.

One Sunday, Mom dressed all the younger kids for Church, and the younger sister said, "Hey Sione, you want to come to Church with us today?" Sione replied, "Yes, but not today." The next Sunday, Mom went to wake him up, and Sione was already dressed, and Mom said, "Sione are you going somewhere?" "Yes, Mom," he replied, "today I'm going to Church and I want to be a missionary someday."

When he received his calling to the North Carolina Charlotte Mission, we all made fun of him by telling him how he cannot speak English, but he said, "It doesn't matter if I don't speak English, because I have faith that Heavenly Father is going to help me. The most important thing is my faith, because if I have faith, then everything in life is easy."

Before he left for the mission, he told my dad to go back to Church because "There is nothing in life that will make you any happier than being a good member of the Church." Dad said, "I'm going to wait for you to return home to take me to Church." But Sione warned, "Dad, someday I'm not going to be here to take you to Church; you don't need me; I know you can make it by yourself."

A few months went by, and then I got a call from my Mom saying that Sione was dead. At first I cried, but later I remembered one of his letters to me where he said, "I know you are a good sister to me and a good example to us, and if it is time for me to go, you can make sure that our father is going back to the Church. Be strong for him because you know better."

His body was sent back home to Matahau, Tonga Island, and he was buried in the family cemetery of Tafengalolo. After they sent his body and belongings down to the island, my Mom found five letters in his bag: two for her, one for my dad, one for me and my husband, and one for his brothers.

The letters to Mom were a thank-you letter and a Mother's Day letter. The letter for my dad asked him to go back to Church and not to complain about the Lord for what has happened, because it was a blessing for our family for him to go and prepare a place for us. The letter for me and my husband was just a thank-you letter for the things we bought for him while he was on his mission, and he also said to make sure that my sons are preparing to be missionaries to preach the gospel of Jesus Christ. The letter to his brothers tells them that there is nothing in life more important than being servants of the Lord; if you serve with all of your heart and if you die, then everything is all right because you know you did your best in His work.

Our family was poor, but my parents taught us to love one another, share with and help each other. Some days we would look so sad because there was no food, but Sione would always make us laugh, and we would forget that we did not have a meal for that day.

When my oldest son and I visited with Sione in 2000, he would wake early in the morning and cook food for us. Sione said we should always love one another, because that is all we would have if something were to happen to this Earth and there were no food, or anything else.

Three of Sione's brothers served missions. Tevita served in Panama; Setelo served in San Francisco, California; and Heamasi served in the New Zealand Wellington Mission. One of Sione's brothers is not yet 19 but is thinking of following in his brothers' footsteps.

At this time in 2009, Susana is married with children, Tevita is married, and Setelo married and has children but passed away in December 2008. Hemasi, Sala, Soeli, Soana, and Mele are still single and are still in school.

Orin A. Voorheis, and his wife,
Chartina Voorheis

Born: 19 November 1976
Parents: Wayne and Florence Voorheis
Siblings: Lyle, Yovonda, LaDocia, Ladd, Virginia,
Elwin, Jacynthia, and Tyler
Spouse: Chartina Jarrett Voorheis
Mission: Argentina Buenos Aires South
Time of service: 22 May 1996 to 19 November 2002
Nature of injury: Gunshot wound to the head
Date and place of injury: 9 April 1997, 20 miles south of Buenos Aires
Story related by: Wayne L. Voorheis, father

ORIN WAS A NORMAL FUN-LOVING KID. He liked motorcycles, girls, and sports, and he had a great afro hairdo for a while. There was no problem for him when it came time to get his missionary haircut; in fact, he had it cut on prom night to surprise his date and his parents. Orin wanted to serve a mission because he knew it was expected of him, and he had a testimony of the gospel enough to know a mission would change his life.

He received his call to serve in the Argentina Buenos Aires South Mission, and he entered the Missionary Training Center (MTC) in Provo, Utah, on 22 May 1996. While there, the following scripture made a very strong impression on him: Alma 17:11: *"And the Lord said unto them also: Go forth among the Lamanites, thy brethren and establish my word; yet ye shall be patient in long-suffering and afflictions, that ye may show forth good examples unto them in me, and I will make an instrument of thee in my hands unto the salvation of many souls."* This passage is highlighted several times in different colors by Elder Voorheis in his scriptures. A note in the margin indicates that this message, written centuries before, is specifically for him. The words "patient and long-suffering and afflictions" have been very prophetic for Orin. However, many souls have been brought to a knowledge of the truth because of what happened to him.

On a rainy Wednesday Preparation Day, after Orin had served about ten and a half months, he and his companion, Elder Barry (from Ohio), were returning home from picking up their laundry at about 9:20 p.m. Half a block from home, they saw three men standing in the road, talking. As Elders Voorheis and Barry split up to go around the three men, they were grabbed and their money was demanded. When only $3 or $4 Pesos were produced, one man pointed a small caliber pistol to Elder Voorheis's head and demanded the rest of his money. As Elder Voorheis struggled to get his backpack off, the pistol fired, and he collapsed. The bullet entered behind his right ear and passed through his brain, to richochet off the inside of the upper left side of his skull, and back into the brain.

As the robbers were momentarily distracted, Elder Barry broke free and ran for their apartment to call the police, ambulance, and mission president. The lady in the kiosk next door made the calls, and Elder Barry ran back to Orin's side.

Elder Voorheis lay lifeless on the ground, and a crowd of local residents began to gather. Elder Barry cradled Orin in his arms and gave him a priesthood blessing that he would live. In Elder Barry's own words, "I felt the life come back into him." Emergency personnel soon arrived, and Orin was taken to a clinic nearby, then to Hospital Britannica (British Hospital), the best equipped hospital in Argentina. There, a German doctor, trained at Harvard, was called in to operate on Orin, as he had recently studied specific techniques in handling traumatic brain injury.

In Utah, our stake president, Lynn Jarvis, phoned to say he needed to speak with us in person; Orin had been hurt. The very fact that he wouldn't talk to us over the phone meant to us that Orin had died or was very seriously injured. When President Jarvis and our bishop came a few minutes later, we were prepared for the worst.

We were blessed to be sent to Orin's bedside in the Buenos Aires Hospital Britannica. Church administrators cleared the way and made reservations for us. Doctors had not expected Orin to live, but he was still alive. He spent almost three weeks in Hospital Britannica before he was well enough to be flown back to the University of Utah Hospital in Salt Lake City. Near the end of Orin's stay in Hospital Britannica, he showed some signs of awareness and recognition.

Elder Jon Huntsman sent his private jet to Buenos Aires with a crew of medical personnel from LDS Hospital to bring Orin home on 30 April. Orin was prepared for the move, and the medical crew was briefed in his care. He was transported through Argentine military airport security to the plane. Elder Voorheis is 6'5" tall, and when he lay on the stretcher with one person standing at each end, it presented an interesting challenge to get him in the door of the plane and down the narrow hallway to where he would ride home. The stretcher had to be at a steep angle to get around the corner.

Orin's story was on the news regularly. TV stations filmed him coming home from Argentina, as he landed and deplaned from the SL Airport. News reporters followed his progress daily, then later had special updates on his progress.

We received phone calls, postcards, and letters from many people. Among them were parents of four young men who expressed a desire to serve missions because of what happened to Orin, not in spite of what had happened to him.

Orin spent about three weeks in an isolation room of the Neural Intensive Care Unit at the University of Utah Hospital. President Gordon B. Hinckley and some members of the Quorum of the Twelve visited Orin in the hospital at the University of Utah. President James E. Faust came to our home twice to visit us and Orin and to offer his encouragement to him and to us. Orin's mission president, Steve Oveson, has been very supportive and still visits Orin and his family from time to time.

Orin was then moved to Eastlake Care Center in Provo. The next day he was taken to the emergency room at Utah Valley Regional Medical Center with pneumonia. After about three weeks, he was returned to Eastlake Care Center, where he stayed until 31 December 1997. In November and December of 1997, the family took Orin on weekend trips for a change of scenery and for more stimulation. He even went to the open house of the newly completed Vernal Temple. During his stay at Eastlake Care Center, his mom bore the brunt of his watch-care while I went to my office nearby at BYU. I went to the care center early in the morning to be with Orin when he woke and stayed with him until I had to leave for work. Family or friends from the community came to make sure someone was with Orin during the hours he was awake. Orin received many kinds of stimuli, such as lemon juice on the tongue, hot and cold water on his hands and arms, range-of-motion exercises, music, and lots of conversations, hugs, and kisses, all to keep Orin involved and stimulated so he could recover faster. His condition gradually improved, and Orin was able to move his head and perform small tasks on command. We finally decided we could handle Orin's care at home. We were then able to bring him home to care for him. This was made possible by the community building an addition on our home to accommodate his care.

At one point when our faith seemed to be fading, we were reminded during one of our weekly temple visits of the Lord's love for Orin and us. It was a very much-needed source of strength.

We did not see this life-changing event coming, but nonetheless, we were prepared in small ways to accept it without anger or blaming the Lord or the Church for what happened to our son. We turned him over to the Church for the Lord's work, and we knew he was in the Lord's hands. We do not blame, hold in contempt, or have anger toward the persons who were instrumental in Orin's injury. We do wish they had been wiser in their actions, since this will be a heavy burden for them in the hereafter.

We feel we are the same as any other parents of missionaries. We will do what we need to do to support and love our children. In our case, we still have the opportunity to care for, and almost daily show our love for, our son. He in return, lets us know how much he loves us in many ways. It is a great opportunity to send a son or daughter to serve Heavenly Father. We have another son, older than Orin, who decided to serve because of what happened to Orin; he may not have taken the opportunity to serve otherwise. His life has been very blessed for his service.

Following Orin's injury, missionary work in the immediate area increased significantly. The missionaries serving there at the time felt the need to do a little extra to make up for their brother who had been injured, and the work advanced dramatically.

Even when the doctors said there was only a 20% chance that Orin would live, and that he would be as a "vegetable" if he did live, faith has made a wonderful difference. Although Orin cannot feed himself or walk yet, he has a very distinct personality, still intact. He has a great sense of humor, is very compassionate, and loves children. He is a big tease.

In December, 2005, Orin was sealed for time and eternity to Chartina Jarrett. By then, Orin's mission president was a member of the 2nd Quorum of the Seventy, and he performed the sealing in the Manti Temple. Chartina lived near the Voorheis family and helped care for Orin for more than five years before becoming his wife. She has been the angel of his life and has a wonderful eternal perspective, looking past Orin's physical limitations toward the restoration the resurrection will bring.

Even though Orin is sometimes frustrated by his limitations, he longs to serve. On most Thursdays, Orin is in the Mount Timpanogos Temple, performing sealings for people unable to do so for themselves; he loves the opportunity to help.

Orin began painting watercolors and has won several ribbons in the Utah State Fair for his artwork. Orin understands what is said to him, and even though he is unable to speak, he communicates through his eyes and with sign language. Would he do things differently if he were able to live his life over? He says no, and adamantly affirms he would still serve a mission, and would not change places with anyone in the world.

During the 2008 Christmas holiday, Orin finger spelled "H-A-P-P-Y" to his wife, Chartina. With a little questioning, she determined that Orin was saying that he is happy with life. That is a great example we can all learn from.

Todd Larry Walker

Born: 29 May 1968
Parents: Larry Walker and LuJean Walker
Siblings: Jenny, Joni, Kenneth, Scott, Brett, Robyn, Jeff, Amber
Mission: Michigan Lansing
Time of service: August 1987 to 14 January 1988
Cause of death: Auto accident
Age at time of death: 19
Date and place of death: 14 January 1988, Traverse City, Michigan
Place of burial: Pleasant Grove, Utah
Story related by: Larry and LuJean Walker, parents

WE WANTED CHILDREN. We would have children but they would be born about six months along, and in those days they could not be saved as easily as today. We lost three children, one at six months died at birth, the second lived 20 minutes, and the third lived 12 hours. We had wanted to have many children, but after having six miscarriages and three premature babies who died shortly after birth, it seemed adoption was our only hope. Those were hard days.

We decided adoption was the answer, but after months with adoption agencies and many turndowns, because they said we were able to have our own children, we finally got a break.

Our son Todd Larry Walker was a wonderful blessing in our lives. He was an answer to many prayers and pleadings with the Lord. Todd came into our family as a three-day-old beautiful little boy through miraculous circumstances. Our prayers were heard and our lives were changed forever. He was the first of our family of five more children and many foster children. We were very blessed.

As Todd grew older, it became evident he had learning disabilities. He was diagnosed with dyslexia, which answered so many questions. He was very bright, having a high IQ; he just couldn't read or write as others could. We placed him in a resource school where he excelled scholastically. His self-confidence soared.

At age 16 he was diagnosed with brittle diabetes. It was a blow to all of us. But for a 16-year-old who loves living life to the fullest, it was very disheartening. He lived to go hunting and fishing. He was very active in Scouting and camping and worked hard to earn his Eagle. He had great friends who were more like his brothers. They were very close and had amazing experiences together. They proved to be a great support to him, along with all his family. He learned how to eat differently and to take insulin shots, and once he got the feel for that, he did much better. Yet he was so brittle that it was very hard to keep his blood sugar under control. He did well, but struggled throughout his life.

When Todd reached the age to go on a mission for The Church of Jesus Christ of Latter-day Saints, he had no hesitation. He wanted to serve. He was called to the Michigan Lansing Mission and was so excited to go. It wasn't easy for him with his problems, but he had the faith that if you try hard enough all things are possible. While in the Missionary Training Center, he had an experience that tested his faith and proved to him that all things are possible. It was Preparation Day, and he and other missionaries were playing basketball. Todd went up for a shot at the basket when another elder jumped up and pushed him down. He landed on his hand, pushing up on his shoulder and tearing the rotor cuff. We were contacted by the MTC, saying we needed to take him to our family doctor for treatment.

After the confirmation that he had torn his rotor cuff, the doctor said he needed to be seen by a specialist who would be back in his office after the weekend. The doctor bound Todd's arm to immobilize it against his body and then excused himself to call to make an appointment for Todd with the specialist. While the doctor was gone, Todd said to me that he didn't want to have surgery because he wouldn't be able to leave the MTC with the rest of his district. He knew it would be hard to stay behind until he could be released by the doctor. I asked him, "How much faith do you have?" He asked me what I meant by that. I told him of an experience my brother had as a teacher in the MTC. He was approached by an elder who had broken his leg in three places and wouldn't be able to leave the MTC with his district before it was approved by his doctors. My brother asked that missionary how much faith he had; the elder said he thought he had enough. After fasting and prayer, my brother gave that missionary a blessing through the power of the priesthood and the missionary was told his leg was healed. After the blessing, my brother told the elder to come with him to the doctor to have the cast removed. After making the arrangements, they did go to the doctor, whose response was that he would not remove the cast because the leg hadn't had time to heal and there were multiple breaks. My brother asked if he would x-ray the leg to see if there were any changes. The doctor finally agreed to take an x-ray and found that there was no sign of a break or crack in the leg. It was as though it had never been broken. The elder's cast was removed and he was able to leave the MTC with the rest of his district.

I asked Todd how much faith he had. He said he had enough. I told him to go back to the MTC and have a priesthood blessing. We were away for the weekend and as soon as we arrived home the phone was ringing. We answered and it was Todd. He said he had received the blessing and he would not need to go to the doctor again. His shoulder was healed and he had been out playing baseball. He had great faith and was healed through the power of the priesthood.

Todd was on his mission for about three months when his diabetes became very unstable. He had been bleeding from behind his eyes and at times he lost his eyesight for a period of time. It was very frightening for him. He was taken to the hospital, where he had to stay until his blood sugar could be regulated. While there, he called home very discouraged. He was feeling as if he was holding back the work. His companion had to stay with him, yet Todd felt he should be out working and this caused more discouragement. Todd said he wanted to come home in two weeks at transfer time and then after getting his health back he would go back on his mission. We told him that would be fine, but for those two weeks we wanted him to get out there and forget about home, take care of his health, keep praying constantly, and work as the missionary he was called to be. If he still wanted to come home after he did all these things, we would welcome him with open arms. He did as he promised he would do. A week later, he called home again and said he was staying on his mission if it was all right with us. Was it? Yes! We were so proud of him and the rededication he made to the Lord, his mission, and himself.

We still would have given him the same counsel even if we had known he would be killed in a car accident just five months into his mission. It was very hard for us to hear of his death and of the death of three other missionaries who were in the car. They were traveling to a Zone Conference on icy snow-covered roads. It was a tragedy that shook all who were affected by it. The love and support of so many people in his mission, and the leaders of the Church in Salt Lake City, and family and friends was overwhelming. The mission president said that our son had changed so much in the last few months that he was well prepared to meet his Savior. We know it was because of his rededication that he was so prepared for this, his last transfer.

Many lives have been changed for good through respect for Todd. Because of his death, and the example he set for others, many have served missions who had not planned to do so before. He only served a short time, yet the difference he made in this world, and the lives he touched and changed, cannot be numbered. His legacy goes on still. We feel very blessed to have been given the privilege of being his earthly parents. We are looking forward to the day when we can all be reunited as an eternal family.

Doris Dalby White

Born: 3 August 1912, Rexburg, Idaho
Parents: Ezra Christiansen Dalby and Rosella Anderson Dalby
Siblings: Cleon Ezra, Lisle Walter, Allan Byron,
Donnetta, Eugene Frederick, Della
Spouse: Howard Victor White
Children: Howard Dalby, Deloris, Robert Morgan, Rosemary
Mission: Pennsylvania Harrisburg Mission
Time of service: August 1979 to June 1980
Cause of death: Complications from surgery to cure her trigeminal
neuralgia (or tic douloureux).
Date and place of death: 4 June 1980, Harrisburg, Pennsylvania
Age at time of death: 67
Place of burial: Wasatch Lawn Cemetery, Salt Lake City, Utah
Story related by: Deloris White Strong
and Rosemary White, daughters

OUR MOTHER, DORIS DALBY WHITE, was the youngest of seven children born to Ezra Christiansen Dalby and Rosella Anderson. Her life began 3 August 1912 in Rexburg, Idaho. At the time of her birth, her father was serving as principal of Ricks Academy. Her mother, Zella, had a rich pioneer heritage, an abundance of humor, and a talent for handicrafts.

Both parents were dear to her, but she especially adored her father. Because he was a scholar, writer and educator, he filled her life with the love of learning and the love of words. She greatly admired his book *Land and*

Leaders of Israel, about the men and women of the Old Testament and the inspiration that young people could draw from them. After 13 years as head of Ricks, he became a teacher of religion at LDS High School in Salt Lake City. Mother was one of his students. She always strove to please her father, and she wanted him to be proud of her.

After graduating from LDS High, Mother entered a church-wide public speaking contest. The topic for all speakers was: "We stand for physical, mental, and spiritual health through obedience of the Word of Wisdom." While everyone else talked about the Word of Wisdom, she spoke about the importance of standing for something. She won the contest.

Mother had dreams of following her father's footsteps by going to college and becoming a teacher, but the Great Depression of the 1930s changed her plans. She ended up working as a secretary at the Salt Lake branch of the Federal Reserve Bank. It was there she met our father, Howard Victor White, a young man famous in Salt Lake for his whistling ability. They married in 1935, after a two-year courtship, and had four children: two sons and two daughters. During the years of raising a family, Mother was active in The Church of Jesus Christ of Latter-day Saints and in her community. She served as Young Women's president, Relief Society president, and PTA president. She was also known as an expert quilter and a wonderful cook. Dad got a government job, working for the Federal Home Loan Bank Board as a savings and loan examiner. He later became an examination supervisor, and this promotion meant transferring their home from Utah to Oregon and then to Washington state.

They were living in Redmond (near Seattle) when Dad retired after 23 years of federal employment. While they were active members with decades of Church service, the last thing they had in mind for retirement was going on a mission. After long years away from family, they were looking forward to returning to Utah, enjoying their grandchildren, and building a new home on a hillside above Farmington.

One day our parents received a message that their bishop wanted to see them. Mother thought he wanted to talk about the building fund. When they went to the meeting, the bishop asked something they never would have predicted. He asked them to serve a mission. "This is what the Lord wants you to do," he told them.

Our parents were stunned. They wanted to be faithful, but this was asking so much of them. It meant everything they wanted to do with their retirement had to be placed on hold for 18 months. Their eldest grandson had just been called to serve a two-year mission in Oklahoma. For him, at age 19, two years was a small portion of his future. For our parents—in their 60s—the length of a mission seemed a huge sacrifice of precious time.

Something else to be considered was mother's health. She suffered from trigeminal neuralgia, a disorder involving the three-part facial nerve, often described as "the most excruciatingly painful human condition in the world." She had tried numerous treatments to ease her suffering, but nothing had worked. Maybe, she thought, making a sacrifice and losing herself in service would help. Maybe a miracle would take the pain away.

Our parents accepted the call from the bishop, sold their home in Redmond, and moved their belongings to Utah, putting everything they owned into storage. Mother received more medical treatments, including an alcohol block, which was injected into her face. Her doctors hoped this would stop the pain long enough for her to serve.

The assignment letter from Church headquarters arrived, and mother's hands trembled when she saw they would serve in the Pennsylvania Harrisburg Mission. It seemed an answer to prayer, as an estranged, inactive son was living near there. Mother hoped this meant she could see him and share her testimony with him. Our parents drove across the country to Pennsylvania. They were not assigned to an area near their son but were sent to the small coal-mining town of Philipsburg. They loved the area and the hardworking, salt-of-the-earth people they found there. They did some door-to-door tracting, but their true strength was working with the members of the town's tiny struggling branch. Dad was called as counselor to the branch president, a man who had been in the Church only two years.

About halfway through the mission, mother's suffering began again as the temporary alcohol block wore off. Her condition was no better. In fact, the pain was more intense than ever. A member of the mission suggested she see a surgeon in Harrisburg. She did, and the doctor told her about a surgical procedure that could, if successful, cure the neuralgia completely. The operation, which called for her to sit while the surgeon went into her head behind her ear to work on the facial nerve and nearby blood vessels, was terrifying to contemplate. After much thought and prayer, she decided to have it done. The results of the procedure seemed positive at first, but complications soon appeared, and during that week she endured two more major operations. Many prayers were offered for her recovery. Her name was placed in the temple and she was anointed with oil consecrated in Israel. Our father rarely left her bedside. She was in the hospital five weeks, but she never recovered from the original surgery. She was conscious but not able to walk or communicate verbally. Since she was constantly in bed, she developed blood clots and lung problems.

Her children knew her prognosis was not good. We were summoned from our homes all over the country to be with her during her final days. Our dad, three of her children, and the mission president were at her bedside in the early hours of 4 June 1980 when her valiant life came to an end.

The loss was heartbreaking for our family, but it was especially devastating for our father. He lost a cherished companion just a few months before their 45th anniversary. All the dreams he had for building a new home and sharing a long, happy retirement were shattered.

There was also the terrible feeling that our mother did not have the quality medical care that she should have received. Our parents did not get good advice from those who suggested the hospital and the surgeon who operated on her. But there were no lawsuits, no threats, no bitter words. All of that might have been warranted, but it wasn't done because it wouldn't have changed anything or brought our mother back.

Church leaders were very kind to us. The mission president and his wife opened their home to our family. A Church representative helped return our mother's body to Utah. When we arrived in Salt Lake, we were told that the Church office is "rocked" when a missionary dies. The First Presidency sent their condolences.

Mother's funeral was in Salt Lake City on 7 June 1980. Two Church leaders, Joseph B. Wirthlin and Marion D. Hanks, of the First Quorum of the Seventy, were speakers. It was comforting to hear that, because of her service and sacrifice, "her salvation was assured." She was buried in a plot facing her beloved Utah mountains in Wasatch Lawn Memorial Park. On her headstone we placed the words: "I'll go where you want me to go, dear Lord." Two other memorial services were held. One was in her ward in Bellevue, Washington, where she had served as Relief Society president. The third was in Philipsburg. The humble branch, with no building of its own, held a memorial to our mother where they had met together every week—in a room above a hardware store.

When the memorials were over and the tributes stopped, the family was left to carry on. That's the hard part. As the years passed, older family members recalled our mother in loving, private conversations, but it often seemed she had become invisible to everyone else. When a missionary dies in a grim and tragic way, it is not viewed as a faith-promoting experience, and there were no invitations to speak about it. At least not until now.

The family is grateful for this opportunity to tell her story. Our hope is that, despite the sadness of her death, it will be remembered that she was a woman who loved the Church and loved serving the Lord. She did indeed "stand for something." We think her father would be proud.

269

James Almon Wight
Anna Elizabeth Howard-Osborne Wight

Date and place of birth: 24 December 1915, Thatcher, Box Elder, Utah
Parents: Almon Nelson Wight and Anna Elizabeth Young Wight
Siblings: Bessie, Francessa, Mary, Leslie, Helen
Spouse: Anna Elizabeth Howard-Osborne Wight
Children: Irene, James Darrell, Clayton Almon, Lorraine Elizabeth
Missions: First mission: Australia
Second mission: New York Rochester Mission
Third mission: New York Rochester Mission
Time of service: 1930s
July 1982 to January 1984;
early 1985 to April 1986
Cause of death: Complications due to heart surgery
Date and place of death: 17 April 1986, Rochester, New York
Age at time of death: 70
Place of burial: Ogden, Utah
Story related by: Lorraine Cragun, Irene Brewer, daughters

JAMES ALMON WIGHT WAS BORN and raised on a farm in Thatcher, Utah. He later attended Utah State University in Logan, Utah. He served a two-year mission in the 1930s in Australia, where he initially met his future spouse, Anna Elizabeth Howard-Osborne. Anna eventually immigrated to the United States, where she and James were married in 1940. They established their home in Thatcher, Utah. James served as a bishop of the Thatcher Ward for approximately 10 years before he moved with his wife and children to Ogden, Utah, in 1954, where he worked as a custodian for the LDS church until his retirement.

James and Anna talked often about serving a mission together for The Church of Jesus Christ of Latter-day Saints. It was never a question in his mind, and the two of them started the process well before his retirement. James had an unusual love and respect for the Prophet Joseph Smith, and when their mission call came for them to serve at the Smith home in Palmyra, New York, they felt it was a miracle. They were amazed and over-whelmed at the honor, and their service was the highlight of their lives.

It is always hard to leave loved ones for any extended period of time, but the anticipation of their service far outweighed any concern they might have felt. Their letters were upbeat, happy, and full of fun information about their experiences. Dad enjoyed telling his family all the details of their serv-ice. Dad loved missionary work, especially reactivation. He was responsible for reactivating several people who remained active for the rest of their lives.

At the conclusion of their mission in 1984, they decided to serve another mission. They had a deep desire to return to the Smith home but made no specific requests when they turned in their application papers. To their great joy and satisfaction, the second call came to the same place!

About one year into the second mission, Dad suffered a moderate heart attack. He recovered quickly, and the decision was made that they should re-main in the field and complete their missionary service. Several weeks later as he walked up the path to the Sacred Grove, he experienced angina pain. His cardiologist performed an angiogram and discovered a blocked major artery in the heart, and bypass surgery was necessary. Sister Wight and a daughter were with Elder Wight in Rochester, New York, at Strong Memorial Hospital. The surgery went well, but complications began which meant two additional surgeries and extreme stress on his heart. One of the young surgeons attending the procedure was an active member of the Church and knew Elder Wight. As circumstances started to deteriorate, he asked Dr. DeWeese, chief surgeon, if he could give Elder Wight a priesthood bless-ing. All in attendance stood back, and the blessing was administered. The young surgeon later told the family that all was done that could have been done and that the Lord needed Elder Wight, who passed away peacefully on 17 April 1986. Sister Wight, a son, and a daughter had the sad duty of notifying family and friends of the passing of her husband.

Sister Wight and her children had special spiritual experiences in the days following the death of Elder Wight. Time spent together and alone in the Sacred Grove lent a spiritual peace that could be acquired in no other place on Earth. Even those who weren't there physically felt the significance of that place. Great strength was given to all of us at that difficult time. All who knew Elder Wight were saddened, but we rejoiced in the fact that he died doing what he loved and in a place he loved, with his wife and companion at his side.

Elder Wight's body was flown home to Ogden, Utah, and a wonderful funeral was held in the church building that he had lovingly cared for for many years. Exceptional help and comfort came from Church headquarters. At the funeral, Elder Yoshihiko Kikuchi of the Quorum of the Seventy gave a comforting address which lent great hope and peace to all in attendance.

All was right and proper when our father died. We had confidence in the medical staff and that all was done that could be done. We know the Lord called him home at the proper time. We cannot think of a better way or place to be when life on earth ends than in the Lord's service. To pass to the other side while engaged in missionary activity is as noble an effort as anyone could be doing. The closeness to the Lord cannot be matched.

There are many reasons missionaries lose their lives during their time of service. Our experience isn't outstanding or spectacular; it just happened. The event was not violent or earthshaking, but was a peaceful and spiritual time to us, his family. No one should be fearful to send a loved one to serve a mission. We must remember that missionaries are in the Lord's hands and allow His will to be done.

As generations come and go, Elder Wight will always be remembered for his love and dedication to the Lord and to the Church. We see his influence in the lives of his children, grandchildren, great-grandchildren, and on down the line. His legacy will be revered and remembered for generations to come.

Lydia Ann Winward

Born: 10 August 1955, Vernal, Uinta County, Utah
Parents: Lloyd Winward and Alta Rae Weeks Winward
Siblings: Lloyd L., Linda R., Lisa M., Laura Lee, Lynn H.
Mission: Washington D.C.
Time of service: February 1977 to June 1978
Cause of death: Cardiac arrest
Date and place of death: 14 June 1978, Johns Hopkins Hospital,
Baltimore, Maryland
Age at time of death: 22
Place of burial: Vernal Utah City Cemetery, Vernal, Utah
Story related by: Linda R. Skeen, sister

LYDIA ANN WINWARD WAS THE THIRD of six children, born in Vernal, Utah, to Lloyd and Alta Weeks Winward. She never wanted to be left out of anything her siblings participated in and wanted to be right in the middle of whatever was happening.

Lydia was a very active person. She dearly loved her family, and she loved life and lived it to its fullest. She had more energy than anyone else and worked tirelessly to accomplish anything she committed to do. She was active in sports throughout her life, always making sure everyone was included in whatever she was doing. Lydia had many friends and made new friends easily wherever she went. She loved to ski, play softball, basketball, and volleyball.

Prior to serving a mission for The Church of Jesus Christ of Latter-day

Saints, Lydia worked in her father's accounting office and attended LDS Business College in Salt Lake City, Utah, pursuing a business degree. Her decision to serve a mission came from her desire to fulfill the promises made in her patriarchal blessing. She was very excited to receive her call to serve in the Washington D.C. area, and looked forward to meeting and blessing the people she would serve. Lydia was anxious to leave for her mission and be about the Lord's work. She was challenged, as all misionaries are, with thoughts of leaving her loved ones behind and was concerned she would feel homesick, especially during special occasions.

She wrote home regularly, writing of her full life as a missionary, and was always interested in what was happening at home. She had acquired the title of Sister Winward on her mission, but also became Aunt Lydia during that time and expressed her anticipation of meeting the newest family members upon her return.

Her mission president, Glen E. Neilson from Cody, Wyoming, made a great impression upon Lydia. He asked her if she had brought her cowboy boots, because she was going to need them. He recognized her ability to manage and run an office, and kept Sister Winward busy in the mission office. Lydia wrote of her love for President and Sister Neilson, but she wanted to work with the people in her mission. When President Neilson's service came to an end and President Ward became the new mission president, Lydia asked for a transfer to the mission field, which he reluctantly granted.

In the spirit of showing a nonmember what hardworking Mormons can do, Lydia collapsed at a farm in Leesburg, Virginia, on 8 June 1978. She had been working with others to load bales of hay on a long trailer. During a break from the work, she became ill and was given CPR until EMTs arrived. She was transported to the Leesburg Hospital, but never regained consciousness.

There was concern that a copperhead snake had bitten her, which caused her to suffer cardiac arrest. Her hand had puncture marks on it and was severely swollen. Anti-venom was administered and the swelling in her hand lessened, but it was unclear to the doctors whether the heart attack was caused by snake venom. We were hopeful that the improvement of her hand was a good sign and that she would continue to progress. However, within 24 hours the doctors became concerned that a lack of oxygen to her brain during the CPR had caused damage to the brain stem. She was on a ventilator and unable to breathe on her own. Her condition was very grave.

My parents were having dinner with family members when President Ward phoned with the news. Plans were made for the family to fly to Lydia's bedside, but there were no seats available on the planes. After explaining the situation to the reservationists, the airline began making calls to ticket holders to see if anyone were willing to give up a seat. A couple offered to travel on a later date, so the family left immediately to make the three and a half hour drive to Salt Lake to catch a flight.

Lydia's cousin, Janet Salisbury Gress, worked in Maryland at the time and was able to assist Lydia's family in arranging for a heart specialist from Johns Hopkins to assess her situation. Upon his recommendation, she would be moved to Johns Hopkins Hospital in Baltimore for more sophisticated testing, but that could only be done if she could breathe without the ventilator. All the missionaries and members in her stake were asked to fast and pray for her, and Lydia was able to wean herself from the machine for the two-hour drive to the hospital. This little miracle seemed to be a gift to my parents to help them through the worst possible time and allowed them to get her the best medical help available. They would have to make difficult and heart-wrenching choices as time went by. When she arrived at Johns Hopkins, Lydia required the ventilator again.

Doctors at Johns Hopkins were able to determine that Lydia had suffered what is commonly known as Sudden Death Syndrome. She had been born with a defect of the aortic artery that was undetectable and inoperable at that time, and doctors were amazed she had been athletic throughout her life, since most babies with this problem don't survive their birth. Doctors considered Lydia's life to have been a miracle.

It became apparent that Lydia had suffered brain stem damage and would never regain consciousness. My parents had to choose between continued life support for an unknown period of time or removal of the support, allowing her to fight for life or return to her Heavenly Father. I saw my father suffer like Abraham when he was asked to sacrifice Isaac, and when the Father watched his Son, our Savior, sacrificed on the cross. My parents bravely signed the papers and held Lydia's hand as she drew her last breath. Lydia passed away at Johns Hopkins Hospital on 14 June 1978.

It was my impression that Lydia was given a choice to assist in the process of her passing, and my parents were allowed to come to peace with the decisions they made. Lydia received several priesthood blessings, which were helpful and comforting to our family. Following the blessing by two young missionaries who had loved and served with Lydia, I witnessed a change in her; her breathing became more relaxed, and she seemed less agitated and more peaceful. The Saints in Washington D.C. and the Baltimore area supported our family. The mission president and some of the missionaries aided in every way they could. Two fasts were held in her behalf by workers at the Washington D.C. Temple, and her name was added to the prayer rolls in several temples.

I sat in her room after she had gone, and I knew that even in her dying moments, Lydia was teaching about the Savior and His love. Lydia and our family had made a lasting impression on a young nurse who had cared for her in ICU. She told me she had never seen a family who had so much love for each other. She and I had several conversations about the Church and our belief in eternal life and eternal families. This young woman told me that she had contacted her estranged sister and asked for forgiveness, and they hoped to build a loving relationship again. She thanked me, saying her life had been changed forever through her association with our family and with Lydia.

Arrangements were made by the Church to return Lydia's body to Utah on the same flight with my parents and me. President Neilson came to the funeral in Vernal and said he had been impressed more than once that he needed to keep Lydia busy in the mission office and that her energetic spirit needed to be protected. I feel that he had been prompted by Heavenly Father to prolong her mission on this earth by keeping her engaged in a safe and less stressful situation in the mission home. His presence in our home was very comforting, and his insights on Lydia's life were helpful. He explained that she had been loved and had served Heavenly Father with all her heart and soul.

This was a difficult time for our family. Although my parents never expressed their intense feelings, I observed their intense emotion. We are all thankful for the knowledge we have of the Plan of Salvation, which helped deal with our feelings of loss. Our family has been strengthened, knowing that Lydia is completing her mission on the other side. We cannot take life for granted and have to trust in the Lord.

I personally responded with disbelief. I couldn't believe that she would be taken while serving the Lord. As time passed, I sent two children to serve foreign missions, and I knew my children were in the best place they could be if they should be called home. I miss my sister more as the years go by, but I know she is still serving the Lord and is happy. Other people who have lost children have said that the example of our family has helped them endure their losses. People in the Vernal area, even after more than 30 years, still say repeatedly how impressed they are with the strong testimonies of our family.

Lydia's loss created a hole in the fabric of our family. The hole is still there, even though time has patched it. The promise of eternal life gives us the knowledge that the hole will completely disappear when our family becomes complete again upon our reunion in the next life.

Carl Hildt Wollenzien
Eleanor Wollenzein

Born: 16 June 1926, Ogden, Utah
Parents: John Wollenzien and Lottie Hildt Wollenzien
Spouse: Eleanor Wollenzien
Children: Linda, John, Ivan, Jeanie, Kathy, and Barry
Mission: Germany Frankfurt Mission
Time of service: 3 May 1993 to 3 December 1993
Cause of death: Heart attack
Date and place of death: 3 December 1993, Friedricksdorf, Germany
Age at time of death: 68
Place of burial: East Lawn Cemetery, Provo, Utah
Story related by: Eleanor Wollenzien, wife

CARL HILDT WOLLENZIEN WAS BORN 16 June 1926 in Ogden, Utah, to John Wollenzien and Lottie Hildt.

When Carl was 67 years old, he and his wife, Eleanor, were called by The Church of Jesus Christ of Latter-day Saints to serve in the Germany Frankfurt Mission. We left our employment as managers of the Village Green Mobile Home Park in Orem, Utah, to serve. We had received many blessings and desired to be part of the great work rolling forth in the Church. Our only concern about leaving home, family, and friends was that we would miss our grandchildren.

Our favorite missionary scripture spurred us on and became our motivation to serve. *"I will go and do the things which the Lord hath commanded, for I know that the Lord giveth no commandment unto the children of men, save he shall prepare a way for them that they may accomplish the thing which he commandeth them"* (1 Nephi 3:7).

We truly enjoyed our time of service and sent letters home that were upbeat and interesting, but we always wanted to know what was happening with our children and grandchildren.

One evening we were on our way to the home of another missionary couple, Elder and Sister Edmunds, for a meal before attending the temple. Carl was driving and stopped at a stop sign. I saw he was having a problem but did not realize he was having a heart attack, nor did I understand how serious it was. I immediately turned off the ignition and called for help.

Two young couples came to my aid and called for the paramedics and phoned the Edmunds for me. The ambulance came quickly, and I expected to go with my husband to the hospital, but the paramedics placed him in the ambulance and began to work on him there. The Edmunds came to be with me, and soon after, the paramedics pronounced that my husband was dead.

I returned to the United States the next day. Our mission president, President David A. Burton, was very kind and helped at this time. It took one week to complete all the forms and paperwork to have my husband's body returned to Utah.

Everyone was so concerned and kind. My son-in-law, Larry Hall, was my bishop, and he took care of many, many details. I felt the guidance and comfort of the Spirit to help me through that time of trial.

My husband, Carl Hildt Wollenzien, was buried in Provo, Utah.

EPILOGUE

Seven years after his brother was fatally injured in a collision in which the mission vehicle was broadsided in an intersection, Jason Berrett shares some poignant memories on the occasion of Joshua Vaughn Berrett's birthday, 16 June 2002:

Joshua Vaughn Berrett, 20, Arizona Tempe Mission

Josh Vaughn Berrett was born and raised in Salt Lake City. Josh died on May 30, 1995, when his companion went to turn left after stopping at a two-way stop. They were out in the country so the speed was faster than a city road. Josh's companion did not see the truck that hit them, and Josh died instantly. Josh's mission president, President Allen, said if you saw the damaged car it would be a testimony in and of itself. He said the car was smashed only where Josh was, and his companion had very minor injuries.

At Josh's funeral in Tempe, Arizona, President Allen said that shortly before leaving to go on their mission he gave Sister Allen a blessing and in the blessing he told her that tragedy would strike one of their missionaries. President Allen had only one month left as mission president and he thought that maybe this tragedy had bypassed them for some reason, but when they got word that Josh had died, he instantly knew this was the tragedy spoken of.

Josh's last companion told a story of some of his last moments with my brother. They were at a member's house and as they were leaving Josh looked up above the door and pointed to a sign that said RETURN WITH HONOR, and Josh said, "We have got to get one of those and hang it above our door in the apartment so every day when we are leaving the apartment we can see it and be reminded."

Josh had more faith than anyone I know. He never had a problem doing what was right and making good choices. Some thought Josh was slow because he would believe anything like a little child and he just loved everyone. Josh never judged anyone. He was teased sometimes and one time I asked him why he let people tease him and he said, "Jason, people tease because they have low self-esteem and because they do not feel good about themselves. If they feel better after teasing me, I will let people tease me all day long." That is just what he was like. Josh was a sincere and a wonderful young man.

Josh loved studying the gospel and during his senior year he would stay up until one or two in the morning on school days trying to understand the scriptures. Josh loved the General Authorities and he thought the prophet was the man.

When we were growing up there was a new Gatorade commercial that came out that was called "want to be like Mike," you know, Michael Jordan. Well Josh made up his own song and it was called "WANT TO BE LIKE CHRIST," and he would sing it even on the basketball court.

Josh was full of love for anyone and everyone, and he was the first to stick up for anyone that was put down. Josh lived the gospel and everyone knew it. He was so excited about his mission and he let everyone know it for years and years before it even happened. I knew Josh was full of character even more when he was out in the field a year and our father died. He was in Tempe and we were in Salt Lake and President Allen gave Josh the opportunity to come home for his dad's funeral. Josh told the mission president he would pray and have his answer in the morning. When Josh woke up he said he knew that my dad and Heavenly Father wanted him to stay on his mission. I disagreed because I was then the oldest since he was not there, but I understand more now that I have also served a mission.

Sometimes I feel bad because I do not always think about him and Dad, but when I do, I cry and get sad because I miss them so much. I struggle with the fact that my brother died at such an early age, but I am glad he died doing what was right. I often think of so many good times we had and that makes me feel better. Today is Josh's birthday and I have cried talking about him so much.

Many years following the death of her brother, Colleen Pierce shared the following reminiscences about him, including an unusual but comforting experience that occurred just two years ago.

Garth Vinton Pierce, 20, Central England Mission

My brother Garth Vinton Pierce was born in Salt Lake City, 10 June 1954. He was the middle child in a family of five. He had a great sense of humor. He liked to tease his brothers and sisters. I was two years younger than Garth. He especially liked to tease me. He was able to find humor in many things. But with most people he was very quiet and shy.

An interesting thing happened with Garth when he was deciding whether to serve a mission. He was having a very difficult time making this decision. He was very unsure if he had a testimony of the gospel. He asked our grandmother if he could go and stay in her home for a week (she was visiting her sister at the time). So Garth went there by himself and spent the time reading the Book of Mormon and praying. When he came home he went straight to the bishop and told him that he wanted to go on a mission. Garth never told us what happened during that week. But I feel he truly knew that it was the right thing to do.

His mission president wrote and told us that Garth put away his quiet ways as a missionary. He learned to love the people in England and Wales and was an extremely effective missionary. He served almost a year in Chester, England, where certain members got to know him so well that some of them started to call him Brother Pierce instead of Elder Pierce. Later after Garth's death a family that he baptized had a baby boy. They named him Garth Vinton Bradley, after my brother.

The last time I saw my brother alive was at the airport as he was leaving for his mission, which was 29 years ago. But I had an interesting experience a couple of years ago. My nephew had returned from his mission to Brazil. He was giving his homecoming talk and started to give his testimony in Portuguese. As he was talking, his face kind of blurred and for a few seconds I saw Garth's face superimposed over his face. It was a very special experience to me.

We have had several sacred experiences about Garth after his death. After we were informed of his death, which occurred on 15 October 1974, a great comforting spirit entered our home. It was like a blanket which covered our house, and we felt it for a long time. Many people could feel it when they came to our home.

I remember that for a while after my brother died, my father kept clippings from the newspaper of other missionaries killed in the mission field. So I will mail copies of these to you.

Editor's Note: Thanks to the clippings his father saved, we have been able to identify a number of missionaries previously not included on our Honor List.

The following account of a missionary son by his father, Don Martin, captures the unique characteristics of a missionary prepared for his transfer years in advance, demonstrating abilities and commitment to excellence at a very young age.

Kenton Leigh Martin, 20, Florida Tallahassee

Kenton Leigh Martin was born in Rexburg, Idaho, 23 February 1978. He spent the first six years of his life living in Sugar City. He is the third of five children born to Don and Linda Lawrence Martin.

Very early in life we became aware of Kenton's unique talents. When Kenton was five years old the family purchased an Intellivision video game that included a game called "Lock and Chase." This game is much like Pac Man. You are the robber and the ghosts are the cops. As you proceed through the maze you collect $20 gold pieces. Kenton would always insist on being player #1 and thus would finish first. He would end with a score of 52,320 (for example) and you would finish with a score of 28,860. He would immediately tell you that he beat you by 23,460! He could add and subtract five digit numbers in his head at age five, and keep a running tally!

When Kenton was nine years old he repeatedly asked me (his dad) to throw the baseball with him. At the time I was very busy writing my dissertation, and I put him off several times. One day, the light clicked on in my head as to what was really most important, and we began throwing the ball. I became the little league coach for his team, and Kenton was the relief pitcher. He had great control. He was a natural! Kenton could stand on one end of the gym and throw a ball into the basket on the opposite end (we have this on video tape filmed during his mission). He always threw a perfect spiral, right on target—hitting the runner in stride. He also had a dead eye 3-point shot and could stuff the basketball backwards and forwards. Basketball was his favorite game and he strictly shot 200 shots every day, concentrating on improving with each shot.

Kenton was always thinking, and during high school he kept statistics of the pro football teams in his head and could quote them on cue. His favorite team was the Pittsburgh Steelers. He kept running totals of the NFL stats in a spiral notebook and committed them to memory. He knew the rankings of all the players in their respective positions, their strengths and weaknesses. For example, he knew who had the most passing yards, which quarterback and team was most and least effective inside the "red zone," etc. Each football season, Kenton would purchase the NFL satellite program and switch back and forth between games, committing each to memory. He could rehearse the entire game back to you at a later date: "Dallas scored first, as 12 yard pass from White to Jacobs, but they missed the extra point via a blocked kick. San Francisco scored next, a 42 yard field goal by Jones." He kept several games in his head at the same time.

Kenton attended Bingham High School until his senior year, when he transferred to the new Copper Hills High School, graduating with the first class of CHHS in 1996. He maintained nearly a 4.0 grade point average throughout high school and received two scholarships and a grant to attend Ricks College. He was a pre-med undergraduate, intending on becoming a medical doctor. If this didn't work out, he wanted to become a statistician for the NFL!

Kenton was VERY shy and you had to be around him for a while to discover his mental and physical abilities. He had a great sense of humor and found humor in things that most people missed. We greatly miss his funny little laugh and his beautiful singing voice.

On the beautiful, calm spring morning of 27 March 1998, Kenton crossed to the other side of the veil. He had been in the Tallahassee Florida Mission for 10 months, and in the small town of Blountstown for only eight days. He was a successful missionary who loved the Lord and the work. Fortunately, he wrote voraciously, keeping a personal journal and a Book of Mormon journal, and corresponded with several friends and family members.

On that morning, he had been reading from Alma 34. Approximately an hour prior to his passing he wrote in his Book of Mormon journal "Christ was so perfect, everyone loved him so much. If I could only remember how much I loved him, and I do with the Spirit. To pray always is so important, always being humble so we can be taught. It is when we are humble that we can overcome anything. I am preparing every instant by my thoughts and actions." In an hour, he would again experience the great love of the Savior.

A letter from Kenton arrived at our home that same day. In it, he encourages us to read Moroni 7. We encourage all to read it and abide by the teachings contained therein, as well as Kenton's missionary scripture, 2 Nephi 31:20.

Losing our missionary son has been a very difficult cross to bear. We know through gospel teachings that all is well with him, that we have successfully returned one of our children to a loving Heavenly Father; yet, we still sorely miss him. We think of him every day, wondering what he is doing, what he would be doing now had he lived. Through this experience we learned how many good people there are in the world and how many of them are our friends, neighbors, and members of our ward and stake, and members living in Florida.

Some of us have been blessed to experience visiting with Kenton in dreams. These have brought great comfort and reassurance, and we have a strict rule that all dreams are shared within the family, no matter how insignificant they may seem.

Kenton, we love you. We miss you. We are proud of you. Until we meet again, take care.

Love, Dad, Mom, Kari Ann, Kelby, Kami, Shane and Rachelle, Kolton and Preston Leigh.

APPENDIX 1
MISSIONS

Alabama Florida, Olson, Dale Lynn, 1975
Andes, Ricks, James L., 1963
Arizona Tempe, Berrett, Joshua Vaughn, 1995
Argentina Rosario, Ellsworth, Benjamin Robert, 2005
Argentina Trelew, Durrant, Royce Harold, 1991
Australia, Ockey, Gerald Lee, 1957

Brazil João Pessoa, Harding, Tyler, 2005
Brazil Recife South, Snow, Benjamin Doxey, 1995
Brazil Salvador, Knoop, Matthew Lawrence, 2008

Central Atlantic States, Black, Norman, 1949
Central States, Kunzler, Arnold Joseph, 1917
Chile Area, Archibald, Dallas Nielsen, 1998
Chile Santiago North, Dewey, Hal David, 1980

Denmark, Peterson, Jasper, 1887
Dominican Republic East, Bennion, Constance Ethel Green, 1998

Eastern States, Burnham, James L., 1843
Eastern States, Esplin, Edgar Cox, 1925
England, Call, Anson, Vasco, Sr., 1867
England Birmingham, Spjute, Lindsey, 2008
England Bristol, Chipping, William Osborn, 1978
England Central, Pierce, Garth Vinton, 1974
England Leeds CES, Quigley, Gordon Myrl, 1999
England London, Hyde, Joseph Edward, 1878

Fiji Suva, Maiwiriwiri, Mosese Kotoisuva, 1984
Florida Alabama, Olson, Dale Lynn, 1975
Florida Tallahassee, Brand, Mark W., 1979
Florida Tallahassee, Martin, Kenton Leigh, 1998

Germany Frankfurt, Wollenzien, Carl Hildt, 1993
Germany Hamburg, Johnson, Wesley Brian, 1976
Germany/Switzerland, Alder, Gottfried, 1899
Germany/Switzerland, Stelter, Carl Ludwig Ferdinand, 1923

Hawaii Honolulu, Nielson, Gary Lane, 1977

Iowa Des Moines, Savage, Bradly Alan, 2000

Jamaica Kingston, Silcock, Nicholas Martin, 2001
Japan Fukuoka, Boivie, David Richard, 1989
Japan Fukuoka, Schulz, Jennifer, 1995

Mexico, Gibbons, Edward Richard, 1918
Mexico Hermosillo, Kinghorn, Robert Wayne, 1965
Michigan Lansing, Walker, Todd Larry, 1988
Missouri Independence, Hess, Venna Tolman, 1980
Missouri Independence, Crowther, Laura May Emery, 2000

New Hampshire Manchester, Owens, William Seldon, 1992
New York Rochester, Wight, James Almon, 1986
New Zealand Wellington, Isle, Bradley Jay, 2006
North Carolina Charlotte, Veamatahau, Sione Laulota, 2002

Oklahoma Tulsa, Anderson, Bryan Keith, 1979

Pennsylvania Harrisburg, White, Doris Dalby, 1980
Portugal Lisbon, Hunt, Roger Todd, 1987
Portugal, Lisban, Potter, Coltan Duke, 2007
Portugal Porto, Jack, Ronald Brent, 1988

Salt Lake City Welfare Square, Packer, Christian Glenn, 1999
Samoa, Stevens, Ransom Marion, 1894
Samoa, Moody, Ella Adelia Williams, 1895
Samoa, Tomlinson, Judson Bliss, 1902
South Africa Johannesburg, Twitchell, Jonathan Guy, 1980
South America, Burt, Keith Wynder, 1928
South Australia, Johnson, Bryan Thomas, 1962
Southern States, Bushman, Lewis Jacob, 1897

Southern States, Peck, Bryan Ward, 1900
Southwestern States, Adair, Thomas Jefferson, 1906
Spirit World, Thompson, Trenton Blaine, 2003
Springville Stake Family History Center, Clement, Barry Grant, 2003
Switzerland/Germany, Alder, Gottfried, 1899
Switzerland/Germany, Stelter, Carl Ludwig Ferdinand, 1923

Texas San Antonio, Murdock, Lorin Lee, 1975
Thailand Bangkok, Bookstaber, Joseph Israel, 1997

Utah Salt Lake City, Hendrickson, Mark William, 1978

Washington D.C.,Winward, Lydia Ann, 1978
Western States, Reeve, Rebecca Ann, 1962

APPENDIX 2
PARLEY P. PRATT MISSIONARY MEMORIAL PROJECT

Honor List

Through the Parley P. Pratt Missionary Memorial Project, we want to honor and recognize the work of all missionaries, but unfortunately we do not have a complete list of those who have given their lives in the service of the Master. Nor do we have a complete roster of all missionaries who now face physical, emotional, or intellectual challenges as a result of accident or illness suffered on their missions. Further, we do not have all the names of those missionaries whose lives were taken before being able to enter the mission field. Finally, we want to include those who died shortly after being released from their mission. Your help in compiling a more complete account of those we would honor will be greatly appreciated.

To share names of missionaries missing from this list or to provide additional information on those who may be honored on this memorial, please call David Tuttle 801-318-1888 or e-mail: tuttledm@gmail.com or direct regular mail to 1593 N. 1400 E. Lehi, UT 84043. Alternately, you may send updates and stories to Susan Woods, compiler and editor at 801-377-1966 or e-mail: s1947w@gmail.com or direct regular mail to 1947 W. 1550 N. Provo, UT 84604.

Memorial Design—Monument and Wall

Dennis Smith, internationally acclaimed artist and sculptor and principal at the Alpine Art Center, has completed a larger wax model of a preliminary design for the Parley P. Pratt Missionary Memorial Monument and Wall. After the executive committee approved the initial design, it was decided to render a more complete maquette of the memorial, incorporating additional elements of the monument for further review. "The gesture is the key," says Dennis Smith, "and this larger model helps us see greater detail associated with that essential element of the design."

Now, architectural drawings will be created to provide a more comprehensive view of the monument and wall in its proposed setting in the Sculpture Park at the Alpine Art Center in Alpine, Utah. Certain to become a destination point for visitors within and without the state, the monument may well become the centerpiece of the park. A showplace and international center for sculpture works from a broad range of artists, the Sculpture Park has recently acquired the services of a landscape architect firm to design the 20 plus acre site to accommodate single works of art as well as groupings of bronze pieces for those who come to enjoy this unique collection.

Dr. David Tuttle, Executive Director of the NextLevel Family Foundation, also invites individuals and corporations to donate funds and in-kind contributions to help support the needs of families of missionaries affected by catastrophic illness or injury suffered in the mission field.

You may mail your contribution to the address below or deposit it in the NextLevel Family Foundation at any ZIONS Bank, specifying account No. 563 000 991 and indicating the Memorial Fund. We will provide a receipt for your tax-deductible contribution.

The Parley P. Pratt Missionary Memorial is a project of the NextLevel Family Foundation, a charitable organization incorporated in the state of Utah as a 501(c)(3) entity. Adonis Bronze and the Alpine Art Center & Sculpture Park are both private businesses. Neither the Missionary Memorial nor the NextLevel Family Foundation is associated with or sanctioned by The Church of Jesus Christ of Latter-day Saints.

Publication Services

Many families have expressed an interest in publishing a more extensive record of their loved one's life and personal story, including family members' experiences too large to fit the constraints of this present publication. Special arrangements have been made with the publisher Digital Legend Press to provide such printing services at a discount to any families of missionaries who suffer trauma or death related to their mission experience. Digital Legend Press also has editing and typesetting resources for hire and will provide a quote for your consideration.

One of the services this publisher provides is to maintain a copy of the manuscript in perpetuity so that books can be ordered any time in the future for just the cost of printing, handling and shipping.

For further information, please contact the offices of Digital Legend Press at 585-703-8760 or via e-mail: info@digitalegend.com or by regular mail to P.O. Box 133, Honeoye Falls, NY 14472.

ABOUT THE COMPILER

For the first time in the history of The Church of Jesus Christ of Latter-day Saints, a book containing the monumental effort of collecting stories from families of missionaries who were seriously injured or who lost their lives during their time of service is available. Few readers can fully appreciate the challenges of a project of this magnitude, but readers will appreciate the results of that work.

Susan Evans Woods was equal to the task perhaps because of her family's experience in losing a missionary loved one in the mission field and because of her desire to provide an enduring archive to honor the memory of those who made the ultimate sacrifice. Susan's testimony and energy allowed her to do the work required to enable people to tell the stories of their loved ones—to identify names, solicit stories from families, obtain permissions, check story accuracy, request photographs, etc., and then to do it all over again when the computer hard drive was compromised with a virus. Through it all, she has maintained a cheerful attitude and has consistently chosen faith over fear to accomplish an otherwise overwhelming endeavor.

In her experience, Susan discovered that many families had never recorded their stories until this opportunity became available. They didn't know how to begin, but with Susan's assistance, they were able to organize their thoughts and emotions into a concise story. One man said that he didn't think anyone would be interested, that his family really didn't care; but when he put the story on paper, they were thrilled and are clamoring for more information about their loved one who died in the mission field.

In the process of compiling stories for this book, additional accounts continue to pour into Susan's archive. These too will be shared in subsequent volumes.

—David M. Tuttle, PhD
Founder, Parley P. Pratt Missionary Memorial Project